SHADOWS
OF
HEAVEN

SHADOWS
OF
HEAVEN

Paul Beekman Taylor

SAMUEL WEISER, INC.

York Beach, Maine

First published in 1998 by
Samuel Weiser, Inc.
P.O. Box 612
York Beach, ME 03910-0612

Library of Congress Cataloging-in-Publication Data

Taylor, Paul Beekman.
    Shadows of heaven : Gurdjieff and Toomer / Paul Beekman Taylor.
        p.   cm.
    Includes bibliographical references and index.
    ISBN 1-57863-034-7 (pbk.: alk. paper)
    1. Toomer, Jean, 1894–1967—Friends and associates.   2. Gurdjieff, Georges Ivanovitch, 1872–1949—Friends and associates.   3. Orage, A. R. (Alfred Richard), 1873–1934—Friends and associates.   4. Taylor, Paul Beekman, 1930–   —Childhood and youth.   5. Authors, American—20th century—Biography.   6. Philosophers—Soviet Union—Biography. 7. Mystics—Soviet Union—Biography.   8. Critics—Great Britain—Biography.   I. Title.
PS3539. 0478Z89   1998
197—dc21   97-52600
[B]   CIP

MV

Typeset in 10 pt. Aldine401 BT

Printed in U.S.A.

05 04 03 02 01 00 99 98
10 9 8 7 6 5 4 3 2 1

The paper used in this publication meets all the minimum requirements of the American National Standard for Permanence of Paper for Printed Library Materials Z39.48.1984.

This book is dedicated to Jean Toomer's daughter
Margot, who has her own story yet to tell,
and to her children Michelle and Philip,
who deserve to have this one.

Table of Contents

Acknowledgments

I thank the Collection of American Literature, Beinecke Rare Book and Manuscript Library, Yale University, for permission to publish material from the Toomer papers. Susan Sandberg, representing the estate of Marjorie Content, has permitted me to publish excerpts from her mother's letters, and has offered photographs for reproduction. Anne B. Orage has given me permission to cite the diaries of Jessie Dwight, the correspondence of A. R. Orage, and to reproduce a late photo of Orage. Rudolph Byrd, Henry Louis Gates, Jr., and Michael Harper have read the first three chapters from an early draft with sympathy and encouragement. Nikolai de Stjernvall has freely offered his recollections of the Prieuré. Luba Gurdjieff was patient with my constant questioning over the past thirty years. I cannot remember all of those who have spoken to me of Gurdjieff in the 1940s and 50s, but among these are Jessie, Richard and Ann Orage, Tatiana Savitsky Nagro, Nick Putnam, Phillip Lasell, Fritz Peters, Patty Welch, Marian Sutta, Iovanna Lloyd-Wright, Dushka [Sophie] Howarth, Bernard Metz, Rita Romilly, Solita Solano, Margaret Anderson, Stanley and Rosemary Nott, Daly King, Sherman Manchester, Roger Manchester, and, most of all, my mother Edith Annesley Taylor and my sister Eve Taylor Chevalier.

I am also in debt to the scholars who have carefully outlined the lives of Toomer and Gurdjieff, particularly to Rudolph Byrd for his fine study, *Toomer's Years with Gurdjieff,* which incited the undertaking of this work by challenging me to review my own.

Quoted material at the chapter openings comes from the following sources: chapter 1, page 1, Jean Toomer, "The Blue Meridian," in *The Collected Poems,* Robert Jones and Margot Toomer, eds. (Chapel Hill, NC: University of North Carolina Press, 1988), p. 65, and Jean Toomer, *Essentials,* Rudolph Byrd, ed. (Athens, GA: University of Georgia Press, 1993), xxxiv; chapter 2, page 15, Jean Toomer, *Essentials,* p. xxi, and Jean Toomer, "The Blue Meridian," in *The Collected Poems,* p. 66; chapter 3, page 39, Jean Toomer, *Essentials,* xxiv and, "People" in *The Collected Poems,* p. 80; chapter 4, page 63, A. R. Orage, cited by C. Daly King, *The Oragean Version* (New York: Privately published, 1951), p. 257, and Jean Toomer, "The Blue Meridian," in *The Collected Poems,* p. 67, and Jean Toomer, *Cane* (New York:

Boni and Liveright, 1922), p. 150; chapter 5, page 119, Jean Toomer, *Essentials,* xxii, and G. I. Gurdjieff, cited by Solita Solano in personal communication to Edith Taylor; chapter 6, page 165, Louis Pauwels, "Du détachement," *Les dossiers H.: Georges Ivanovitch Gurdjieff,* Bruno de Panafieu, ed. (Paris: l'Age d'homme, 1992), p. 60, and James Webb, *The Harmonious Circle: The Lives and Works of G. I. Gurdjieff, P. D. Ouspensky and Their Followers* (London: Thames and Hudson, 1980), p. 15; chapter 7, page 185, A. R. Orage, cited by C. Daly King, *The Oragean Version*, p. 266, and Frank Lloyd Wright, cited by Anne Fremantle, "Travels with a Searcher," *New York Times Book Review,* 8 September 1963, p. 6; chapter 8, page 199, Jean Toomer, *The Wayward and The Seeking*, Darwin T. Turner, ed. (Washington, DC: Howard University Press, 1980), p. 438, and Jean Toomer, "The Blue Meridian," in *The Collected Poems,* p. 53; chapter 9, page 221, Jean Toomer, "The Blue Meridian," in *The Collected Poems,* p. 68, and John Milton, *Paradise Lost*, Merritt Y. Hughes, ed. (New York: Odyssey Press, 1957), Book 5, 574–576.

Chapter One

Memory and Design

Expand the fields, the specializations,
The limitations of occupation,
The definition of what we are
That gain fractions and lose wholes—
I am of the field of being,
We are beings.
              —"The Blue Meridian"

According to what a man is called, so will people respond to him.
                    —*Essentials*

The subtitle for this book, *Gurdjieff and Toomer*, suggests that I am scanning the direct relations between two men. Yet Nathan Jean Toomer spent little time in the physical company of Georgii Ivanovich Gurdjieff between 1924, when he saw him for the first time, and 1935, when he saw him last. Nonetheless, during that period, Toomer spent the greater part of his energies in the service of Gurdjieff, teaching, raising funds, and organizing study groups. In fact, he considered himself attached to Gurdjieff until 1939, when he finally turned away from his master, and in 1953, only three years after Gurdjieff's death, he re-engaged himself in the Gurdjieff work in New York City. Toomer's life with Gurdjieff is, indeed, a major topic of this book, but my title alludes as well to intricate connective relationships that the association between the two men engendered. One strand is Toomer's relationship with my mother, Edith Taylor, and another is his relationship with me, both of which grew out of his participation in the Gurdjieff work. Other strands in the fabric of this story include those experiences of my mother with Gurdjieff, which Jean Toomer influenced directly as well as indirectly, and my own brief participation in Gurdjieff's world, which my mother encouraged. Therefore, although I have assembled the text of this book, I am more reporter than author, for the pages that follow record many voices, among which the most telling are those of Toomer, Gurdjieff, and Edith Taylor. Behind the scenes, the intertwining relationships of these three people were orchestrated and mediated by the

English critic and editor, A[lfred] R[ichard] Orage, and his second wife, Jessie Dwight Orage. They are part of Toomer's story, while my voice is but a narrative frame.

My own intent in writing this book is to understand how Toomer has shaped the lives and thoughts of people. This effort, as I discovered quite young, is necessarily shaped in turn by the ways in which Gurdjieff shaped Toomer's and my own life and thought, both directly and indirectly. My own written recollections of Toomer were begun long ago, with a brief record of my life with him. I found then that I could appreciate much of Toomer's teaching through the filter of my experience with Gurdjieff in my late teens, when the moral aspects of Gurdjieff's teaching were already as familiar to me as Toomer's. I hesitate to qualify either man in any banal sense as guru, thinker, writer, or "teacher," because my views of both men are stubbornly bound to my own experience with each of them. It is enough for me to say at the outset that both Toomer and Gurdjieff were concerned with the fate of humanity, and both dedicated their talents to the task of making others aware of their own capacities to change things for the better.

As I pursued my quest to understand the bonds of feeling and thought between these men, and between them and myself, I discovered my mother's relations with Gurdjieff in France between 1923 and 1935, and with Toomer between 1923 and his death. Alfred Richard Orage was an important advocate for Toomer and my mother to mitigate their unstable stances in the Gurdjieff work. I retain only a vague image of Orage, who died just before my 4th birthday, but his name and his ideas became known to me through his family and his New York friends, who populated my youthful environment. Jessie Orage was my mother's best friend and provided moral support during her turbulent involvement with Gurdjieff. The two remained close friends for their entire lives. My own relationships with Toomer and Gurdjieff were prepared by my mother, and the intensity of her earlier involvement with both men shaped their relations with me, as well as with my sister. This book, then, explores the complex inter-relations between Edith Taylor, Jean Toomer, A. R. Orage, Jessie Dwight Orage, and Georgii Ivanovich Gurdjieff. I am what, in French, would be called an *insérend*: witness, narrator, and occasional participant in their stories.

Toomer, Gurdjieff, and Orage were three of the most extraordinary personalities of the 20th century. Toomer, born in Washington, DC on the day after Christmas in 1894, made his mark on American literature in 1923 with the publication of *Cane*, a lyrical celebration of the moral and artistic energy of the black in the American South of the early '20s. Georgii

Ivanovich Gurdjieff,[1] born sometime between 1866 and 1874 in Alexandropol, Armenia, lived and was educated in Kars, and made his mark in Moscow and St. Petersburg in the second decade of the 20th century as a master of dances and a mystic in possession of secret Asian lore. In 1912, he founded the Institute for the Harmonious Development of Man, which attracted Western notoriety in 1922, when it was transplanted to a château south of Paris, not far from Fontainebleau. Orage, born in 1873 in the north of England, joined Gurdjieff in France in October 1922, after resigning his post as editor and publisher of *The New Age*.

In the mid-1920s, all three men became intricately bound to each other in what they called "The Work," consisting of mastering, living, and teaching a psychological and philosophical system of self-development to which each had committed, for different lengths of time, their full intellectual and moral energies. My mother, born in Providence, Rhode Island in 1896, met all three men within a short span of time between February 1922 and the beginning of 1924. She visited Gurdjieff at his château, the Prieuré, sometime in the winter of 1922–1923, though she had seen and heard him in London on the eve of Saint Valentine's Day, 1922. She probably saw Orage on the same occasion, but she recalled talking with him for the first time after he spoke in New York City on January 2, 1924, and she saw him continually over the next eleven years in France, England, and the United States. Her bond with him was tightened by a growing friendship with his second wife, Jessie Dwight Orage, who died in 1983 at the age of 82.

When we were very young, my sister and I heard from our mother that she had met Jean Toomer with Waldo Frank on a train, traveling along the Hudson River sometime late in 1923. She saw him at a distance at Orage's lectures in January 1924, and both Orage and Toomer were with Jessie Dwight at Gurdjieff's Institute in the summer of 1924, when Gurdjieff suffered an automobile accident that almost cost him his life. In the spring of 1926, Edith and Jean began a love affair that originated in New York, continued in France, and returned to New York, ending in the late winter of 1927. They remained close friends for the rest of their lives. In late 1928, Edith bore Gurdjieff a daughter. Seven years later, she moved to the United States, where she placed her daughter and a later-born son with friends. I was sent to live with Toomer, his 3-year old daughter, and his second wife, Marjorie Content, first in New York City and later in Bucks

---

[1]   In the *Encyclopedia of Religion* entry "Gurdjieff," Michel de Salzmann uses the form Georgii Ivanovich Gurdzhiev. Most writers now use the form Georges Ivanovitch Gurdjieff, and "Gurdjieff" is the way he spelled his own name in documents in my possession. For his patronymic, I prefer the form "Ivanovich." Most of my mother's friends called him either G, the Old Man, or Georgivanich.

County, PA. Edith depended upon Jean as a moral support and counselor for the next thirty years. Though she told me more than once that Jean was the only man she had "really" loved, she had said this of other men at different times.

As infants, my sister Eve and I lived for irregular periods of time at Le Prieuré des Basses Loges at Avon, near Fontainebleau, where Gurdjieff operated his Institute. We visited him frequently in Paris, where he continued his teaching after the sale of the château in 1934, and we were with him often during the last year of his life, from December 1948 through September 1949. Orage had died in 1934, but he was alive in conversations through his wife, children, and former pupils, whom we saw continually during World War II. By the time I finished my university studies, I had read whatever of his writings were available in local libraries.

Toomer and Gurdjieff were the most imposing male figures in my life and the two most influential among the many men in my mother's life. She loved the first and bore a child to the second, but, curiously, though she claimed to have loved many men, she never admitted even token affection for Gurdjieff, for whom she repeatedly expressed, according to the occasion, scorn, amused detachment, or distant respect. "He was not a *nice* man," intoned slowly and gravely, seems to sum up her considered judgment. Both men shaped my moral and intellectual growth, though they touched me, as they had my mother, in very different ways. Jean Toomer had a direct, central, and major role in my education. I knew and loved him as my own father. His image and voice loom and boom large in my memory. Throughout the almost thirty years since his death, I have probed the depth of his impression upon me, while I have both wondered about and questioned the inextricable bond between his teaching and the character and thought of Gurdjieff. My personal experience with Gurdjieff and Toomer often belied the stories others told about them, particularly those of my mother, who had been intimate with both. When I was in my early teens during the war years, I listened as many visitors to our house delighted in shocking, amusing, and amazing a credulous and impressionable boy with their anecdotes about Gurdjieff, "G," Georgivanich, the "Old Man." At the time, I had no reason to wonder why so little was ever said about Toomer in the same company, because I did not know then that Toomer had anything to do with Gurdjieff. My mother was reserved in her conversations about him, even to my sister and myself. Only many years later did she situate herself and Jean together at the Institute.

Over the years since then, I have read, more often out of curiosity than intellectual purpose, many personal accounts of Gurdjieff and Orage, methodical expositions of their teaching, and some of the many critical biographical and literary studies of Jean Toomer. None of these has significantly altered my personal appreciation of their combined influence on my own thought, though I have often regretted some of the things written and said about both that appear to me misinformed and unjustly demeaning. Toomer and Gurdjieff have been particular targets of scandal-mongers and sensationalists, but none of that has eroded my personal image of either of them, though it has incited me to express publicly my own feelings here. Concerning Toomer, there are three aspects I have struggled to reconcile: the man I lived with, the one others saw and spoke of, and the one he envisioned himself to be in his writings and conversation. Perhaps I should add a fourth—the Toomer I now see retrospectively—but I cannot dislodge this figure from the one who impressed me as a young boy.

There are numerous recollections of Gurdjieff, Orage, and Toomer in circulation today. Many of Gurdjieff's early followers and Orage's New York group have written personal accounts of them, though I know of none from Toomer's Chicago group except in a book which Fritz Peters wrote of his experiences with Gurdjieff, in which he does not even mention Toomer's name. More recently, critical biographies and studies of Toomer and Gurdjieff have appeared by scholars who did not know either man personally. Many of these are based on careful and sound research, but the frequent unreliability of sources and the apparent necessity to accept dubious reports are unfortunate and inevitable failings common to them all. In *Feet of Clay*, Anthony Storr has denounced Gurdjieff as a dangerous charlatan, and Frank Kermode, an otherwise cautious critic, in a recent review of Norman Mailer's gospel of Christ, says that some gurus are wrong and others are dangerous; Gurdjieff is both wrong and dangerous. Earlier, James Webb reviewed Gurdjieff's relations with a number of his illustrious followers, including Orage and Toomer; Peter Washington traced Gurdjieff's part in the shaping of the "New Age"; James Moore has scanned Gurdjieff's career with scrupulous detail. The Kerman and Eldridge biography of Toomer documents a gap between his racial identity as an Afro-American and the many roles he played in his public and private life. Toomer's daughter and I are both saddened by the suggestion in that book that he failed in his role as husband, father, and teacher. Arnold Rampersad's review of the book in the *New York Times* assumes from the portrait that Toomer was a negligent husband to Marjorie Content, who apparently "never took on . . . domestic chores in recompense; instead, he indulged himself with self-serving beliefs about the natural inferiority of women, and took their money. He seems to have demoralized his only child."[2] If this is the impression given by what is considered Toomer's definitive biography, the truth of Jean Toomer is grotesquely distorted. Though his daughter, Margot [Toomer] Latimer, prefers to keep her own memories from public view, my recollections and research would temper this impression and restore the image of Jean Toomer to just proportions.

Rudolph Byrd has written a rich, sympathetic, and impressive study of Toomer's writing in the context of Gurdjieffian ideas, as Robert Jones had done before him in his introduction to Toomer's collected poems. Both show that Gurdjieff did not so much introduce Toomer to a new view of himself in the world as he nurtured and strengthened seeds of thought already present in Toomer's childhood. There is perhaps more to be written by those who knew both Gurdjieff and Toomer personally at the end of their productive lives. I am one of these. Though I was an indifferent student of Gurdjieff's system, I was and remain attentive to Toomer's ideas and to the part Orage and Gurdjieff had in shaping them. The image of the man and the echo of his words have worked deep into the grain of my being. I will be richly rewarded if I can balance some of the weight of unflattering portraits of Toomer, while complementing and correcting something of the public record of Gurdjieff. In a sense, then, this book is an adjunct to Moore's and Kerman and Eldridge's excellent biographies.

Though I have lived on the periphery of Gurdjieff's circle and within Toomer's, my own story is ancillary to the fuller and richer experience of my mother with both men. Her scant record sheds light on Toomer's life as a "pupil" of Gurdjieff's and her own as a sadly abused member of Gurdjieff's clan. Important to both stories are Orage's relations with both men and Jessie Orage's detailed observations of these three and her husband between 1926 and 1931, when Orage saw Gurdjieff for the last time. For those concerned with the reasons for the break between Gurdjieff and Orage, Jessie's and Orage's notes are an invaluable testimony to a tense competition for Orage's commitment and affection between family and Gurdjieff. Orage's communications with Toomer and my mother make quite clear the character of Toomer's collaboration with Orage, both for and against Gurdjieff's declared interests. These convergent views of Toomer and Gurdjieff together reveal much that has not been known and expose much which has been misrepresented in published accounts.

---

[2] Until his kidney removal in 1940, Toomer worked hard on the Mill House grounds, tended livestock, repaired machinery, etc. After his operation he continued to run errands for the house, particularly the food shopping, which he enjoyed doing. Neither I nor his daughter ever thought of him as indolent, though he enjoyed an afternoon nap whenever the occasion was offered.

I owe my reader a word of caution. As both observer and actor in the merger of recollection, my own point of view is slanted. Despite what I may think of Gurdjieff's ideas now, I had little conscious use for them almost fifty years ago, and Gurdjieff remains a mystery to me. I supposed then that he had little use for me. If he befriended me out of deference to his connection with my mother and sister, he had little if any obvious reason to tolerate me, though he was known to encourage children's potential. He accused me more than once of being an unhealthy element among his pupils, not so much because I appeared to him, perhaps, as a skeptic who rarely accorded him the respect he must have thought his due, but because I distracted other young people from the "work." Nonetheless, he was extraordinarily patient and generous with me. The case was different with Toomer, because I was from the first moment alert to his every gesture. Every moment with him strengthened the emotional bond between us. I loved him as a father; his home was my haven. Whatever his motives for taking me into his care and confidence, I responded to his person and to his teaching because I found myself in a domestic context in which I was led to exult in the kinds of human contact he nurtured. Because of the space we shared and the intense magnetic power of the man at its center, even if the sense of his words often slipped by me, it was inevitable that I should absorb his ideas.

It was Toomer's speech in personal contexts that left a most distinctive mark on me. He had a large musical voice, so generous of tone and so firm and direct that I felt I had to respond to it whether or not my responses could satisfy him. His voice seemed to emanate from the sure knowledge he offered me, insisting that I must know the thing "up close" in order to know it at all. He disdained knowing people or ideas by their social, political, religious, or genetic identities, or by what he called their "public mechanisms." "You must experience things yourself in order to know them," he said, "and when you know the thing, it will know you and let you know how it is to be called and how it is to be used. There is no knowledge worth the knowledge that you have made your own, and which has become a part of your being. There is a you inside of yourself and one outside that looks at you. They should work together." From guidance like this I learned much, but I should have learned more.

There are telling similarities in the careers of Toomer and Gurdjieff. Both were exiles from their native worlds, mingling in and mastering alien cultures. Both have been charged with being "out of place" because of their respective life styles and public conduct. Toomer has been accused of renouncing his racial background as an Afro-American by ignoring an implicit cultural responsibility to his native blood (one-sixteenth or one thirty-second black, by best calculations), and Gurdjieff has been accused of being a charlatan who claimed that he possessed extraordinary powers which he had brought to the mechanized West from his early life in the spiritual East. No one seems sure of the truth of his stories of himself,[3] but it seems he was born in Alexandropol between 1866 and 1874.[4] Some have claimed that Stalin was a boarder in his father's house when Gurdjieff began his cathedral schooling, before he embarked on the search for knowledge about which Peter Brook made a film in the 1980s, *Meetings with Remarkable Men*.[5] Arriving in Russia after his travels, he established study groups in Moscow and St. Petersburg, where he attracted the attention of the philosopher P. D. Ouspensky, already well known in the Western world for his philosophical treatise, *Tertium Organum*, translated into English in 1913. Ouspensky later wrote a detailed account of his meetings in Russia with Gurdjieff in *Search for the Miraculous*, which remains, as far as I know, the most influential and convincing analysis of Gurdjieff's "system." Events during World War I forced Gurdjieff into exile in the Republic of Georgia, from where he began a migratory exile in search of a new home. His first stop was Constantinople, then Berlin, London, Paris, and finally, in the autumn of 1922, Avon near Fontainebleau, where he leased and later bought the Prieuré, once a monastery, later the property of Dreyfus's lawyer.

Quite simply, Gurdjieff taught a harmonious development of our physical, emotional, and rational faculties. He wanted people to regain control over their relations with both their inner selves and their environment, control he felt had been progressively lost and which was in particular peril in the mechanistic structure of life in the 20th century. The immediate goal of his teaching is to restore a primal coordination of our threefold being—sense, emotion, and thought—and thereby to increase efficiency, satisfaction, and pleasure in daily tasks. The long-range goal of his teaching is to guide people toward a spiritual reunion with the essential forces of the universe. His method, which combines physical, emotional, and mental labor in programmed exercises, attracted to him a large num-

---

[3] I assume this from his autobiographical account of his search for hidden truth, *Meetings with Remarkable Men* (London: Penguin Books, 1963). James Moore, *Anatomy of a Myth* (Rockport, MA: Element, 1991), is by far the most reliable authority concerning the facts of Gurdjieff's life

[4] The only passport I saw of his, in 1949, listed his date of birth 1874, but most of the members of his family I have talked with think that 1869 or 1870 is closer to the truth. Moore assembles convincing evidence that he was born in 1866. For a recent review of the question, see William Patrick Patterson, *Struggle of the Magicians* (Fairfax, CA: Arete, 1996), p. 32n.

[5] Luba Gurdjieff, *A Memoir* (Berkeley: Ten Speed Press, 1993), p. 3, recalls her mother saying she was born in the same house as Stalin and played with him there.

ber of people: scientists, writers, teachers, actors and actresses, the rich, the bored, the ill, and sincere seekers after sacred truth.[6] Within a matter of months in Fontainebleau, Gurdjieff had gained a reputation as both charlatan and magician. He became notorious from reports circulated about Katherine Mansfield's last days under his care at the château.[7] For a time, an excursion from Paris to see the Institute became a sort of tourist attraction, though few made it inside the gates. He had a reputation for being insensitive and even sadistic to pupils, but my own experience with him during his last days revealed little antagonistic fire of character. As for Gurdjieff's teaching, I lack the psychological, philosophical, and religious expertise to evaluate it; but I offer in the pages below a brief summary of what I understand of his essential but enigmatic work, *All and Everything*, for those unfamiliar with Gurdjieff's thought.

Orage presents a different and puzzling case to many who knew him. He was born in January 1873 in Yorkshire, studied in Leeds, and came down to London in 1893, where, in a very short period, he became an influential editor and leader in the Fabian Society and an advocate of the Douglas Social Credit scheme. In 1907, he founded *The New Age* with Holbrook Jackson and published in its pages Bernard Shaw, G. K. Chesterton, Hilaire Belloc, H. G. Wells, Arnold Bennett, and many other distinguished writers. He was Katherine Mansfield's first publisher in England. He was universally respected and held high in esteem by English writers and critics of his day, and was recognized for doing much to promote the careers of Ezra Pound and T. S. Eliot, who called Orage the "finest literary critic of his day" and "the finest critical intelligence of our age."[8] Orage was an editor and publisher with an unerring judgment for talent. He was socially gracious and generous with his time and energy on the behalf of oth-

---

[6] Ouspensky complained that Gurdjieff's style of teaching in France was markedly different from that which he had carefully documented in Russia. He no longer spoke as he had in Russia in the name of a brotherhood of seekers and of an esoteric tradition, but spoke in his own name as the repository of a new knowledge, and this shift in manner alienated Ouspensky, who went on to establish an independent group in England and, during the war, in the United States. It should be recognized that until his death in 1947, Ouspensky had far more pupils than Gurdjieff.

[7] James Moore's *Gurdjieff and Mansfield* sets the record straight and exposes the sources of the sensational fictions (London: Routledge & Kegan Paul, 1980).

[8] C. S. Nott, *Journey Through this World* (London: Routledge & Kegan Paul, 1969), p. 70, and Phillip Mairet, *A. R. Orage: A Memoir* (Hyde Park, NY: University Press, 1966), p. 121, respectively. The current use of the term "New Age" in reference to theosophical tendencies is probably due to Orage's journal, though Orage had only kept the existing name of the journal he bought. Orage referred to himself only as "O", or "ARO," more formally in correspondence.

ers. He made friends easily, had obvious sex appeal, was an adoring husband and, for a tragically brief period, a doting father. In 1922, upon meeting Ouspensky in London, as his biographer and friend Phillip Mairet notes, Orage was "drawn to a spiritual adventure," which he saw as a path to secular social credit.[9] Ouspensky had the technique and knowledge of a teacher, Orage judged, but not the grace and profound contact with the mysterious which he sensed in Gurdjieff when he met him in London in the same year. When Orage gave up his editorship of *The New Age* a few months later, in October 1922, he announced: "I am going to find God."[10] He was at the Prieuré from October 1922 until December 1923, when he moved to New York as Gurdjieff's American representative. He stayed in the United States, except for brief returns to Fontainebleau and London— where he was in the process of divorcing himself from a childless marriage with Jean Walker—until 1930 when, discouraged and disgruntled with Gurdjieff, he put aside for a while his search for Gurdjieff's secret knowledge and returned to London to found *The New English Weekly*.

With Toomer, Orage directed the English translation of Gurdjieff's *All and Everything*, roamed far and wide to raise funds for the Institute, and established teaching groups from New York to San Francisco. He never found in Gurdjieff's teaching all that he had expected or hoped for, and his devotion to Gurdjieff's ideas was, from the beginning, a detriment to his professional and domestic life. Family, social ideals, and the banal problems of fund-raising finally drove a wedge between Orage and Gurdjieff. To many of Orage's friends, his time with Gurdjieff changed him for the worse, though his return to publishing in London revealed to the public an unimpaired talent. To his friends, who were amazed at a new and uncharacteristic calm in his character, he would say that Gurdjieff taught him patience and tolerance. Despite his personal conflicts with the man, he never renounced Gurdjieff's teachings or lost faith in the existence of a great truth that only Gurdjieff possessed. Gurdjieff's enneagram—the geometrical logo of his esoteric system—is inscribed above his name on his tombstone in Hampstead, where he died in 1934.

Though twenty-one years his junior, Toomer, like Orage, was a self-made man. He was an engaged if impatient student at the University of Wisconsin before World War I, and at City College of New York in the 1920s. Like Orage, he devoted a great deal of his energy to carefully devised programs of self-improvement. He studied body-building, meditation, philosophy, and literature, and took meticulous notes, which he carefully pre-

---

9   Philip Mairet, *A. R. Orage: A Memoir*, pp. 86–87.
10   Philip Mairet, *A. R. Orage: A Memoir*, p. 88.

served as references for future use in what was to become his own teaching. Toomer was 29 years old and a successful author at the end of 1923 when, through his literary mentors, Waldo Frank and Gorham Munson, he became acquainted with Orage's and Gurdjieff's teaching. Unlike Orage, Toomer never intended to sacrifice his writing to a quest for Gurdjieff's "truth." On the contrary, he sought an experience radically different from that in 1921, when he produced his novel *Cane* in order to inform new and fresh fiction. The drunk teacher Kabnis in *Cane*, as he boasts to his friends, echoes something of Toomer's program for his career:

> An as f you, youre all right f choppin things from blocks of wood. I was good at that th day I ducked the cradle. An since then, I've been shapin words after a design that branded here. Know whats here? M soul. Ever heard o that? Th hell y have. Been shapin words t fit m soul.[11]

Like professor Kabnis, Toomer conceived of writing and teaching as complementary, if not identical, occupations. He would teach in order to write and write in order to teach, whereas Orage's commitment to Gurdjieff led him to put domestic, social, and professional ideals aside indefinitely. When he first saw Gurdjieff and talked with Orage in January 1924, Toomer was ready for an adventure of the mind that would complement the extraordinary adventure of the spirit he had experienced a little over two years earlier as a mestizo Afro-American in the racially divided rural South in Georgia. Now he wanted to write from his experiences in the urban North and in Europe. From 1924, when he first met Gurdjieff, to 1939, when he renounced Gurdjieff, he was writing regularly and sending things to editors, but with little success in getting them published.

From the beginning, Gurdjieff seems to have used Toomer as a pawn in a grand scheme to finance and disseminate his teaching. While Gurdjieff saw in Toomer a magnetic personality to "sell" his ideas, Toomer saw in Gurdjieff's teaching a valuable medium for expressing his own ideas. From this perspective, it is understandable why Toomer spent little time in the physical presence of Gurdjieff and Orage compared to most of the other "pupils" associated with them. He needed only enough time to gain Gurdjieff's confidence and acquire Gurdjieff's pedagogical and intellectual authority for his own teaching. While Orage saw marriage as an insurmountable impediment to the continuation of his teaching, Toomer assumed that his role as husband and father would increase the value of his

---

[11] Jean Toomer, *Cane* (New York: Boni and Liveright, 1922), p. 223.

teaching. Nevertheless, Gurdjieff was strangling Toomer, as he was strangling Orage, with a chain of financial obligations. Perhaps it was finally, more than anything else, the matter of money that exhausted Toomer's patience and made him break from Gurdjieff. With his wife, Marjorie Content, he put into effect his own teaching at the Mill House, near Doylestown, Pennsylvania in the '30s. His daughter Margery, nicknamed "Argie," and I, nicknamed "Polo," flourished for a time in that post-lapsarian paradise of Bucks County.

What I recall of my life with Toomer between 1937 and 1954 I wrote, in stages, between 1949 and 1955. I reproduce those recollections here almost entirely in their original form. When I first started writing about Toomer, it was partly to fix in my memory a man I knew and loved. Later, during long nights of duty in the American Army of Occupation in Bavaria, I added to those recollections more recent conversations. Then, during the Christmas season of 1973, shortly before her death, I came upon my mother watching television from a rocking chair by the hearth, feeding the fire absent-mindedly, it seemed to me, with sheets of paper from a scattered heap beside her. To my anxious query about the contents of the papers, she replied that they were things that concerned no one but herself. In effect, she was burning the records of her life. Into the flames went notes on Gurdjieff's talks, her letters from me, old love letters, even letters to me from Jean Toomer and Ann Orage, along with university notes I had stored in the attic of her house when I had moved to Europe ten years earlier. She was even feeding flames with the autobiography she had started five years earlier at my insistence. When she finally paused in her systematic destruction to go to the kitchen during a commercial break and put water on for the tea she would sip just to warm her mouth and feel the flavor—she was unable to hold anything on her stomach—I grabbed what I could of what remained, a few scraps about the Prieuré and a few pages about her youth. After her death two weeks later, I found, in a forgotten box of old address books, a few letters from Orage. Out of these fragments, I wrote a memorial biography of her for my family. A few months later, my sister sent me a small bundle of Toomer's letters that she had found in an old briefcase beside Nick Putnam's transcription of Toomer's translation of *All and Everything*. Twenty years later, I looked into Toomer's papers at the Beinecke Rare Book and Manuscript Library. What I found there filled out and confirmed much of what I had assumed in my earlier recollections of his thought and what I had felt of his being. In August 1996, in Mechanicsville, PA, Susan Sandberg made available the papers of her own mother, Marjorie Content, which included a record of her marriage with Jean.

My recollections of Gurdjieff were recorded first in diary form during the summer of 1949. What I knew of A. R. Orage, the man, was mostly hearsay until the early winter of 1981, when I ventured out to Russell's Water Common in Oxfordshire to renew my acquaintance with his widow, Jessie, in her unheated, nonelectrified farmhouse. It had been over twenty years since I had seen her last. We sat long into two nights with cups of instant coffee before a smoky coal-burning iron basket and talked about my mother, Orage, Toomer, and Gurdjieff. She confirmed many of my mother's stories. Though some dates and orders of events seem to have been garbled by the years, before I left, I had heard in her own voice much of what her diaries contained, as well as a great deal they did not. Jessie's daughter-in-law, Anne Orage, invited me to peruse those diaries in the spring of 1994. At that time, I noticed several dog-eared pages, indicating that someone had marked them before me, and I recognized information I had already read in published materials that had not acknowledged Jessie as the source. Since that time I have also seen what remains of Orage's personal correspondence concerning Gurdjieff and Toomer. With these documents, I have been able to reconstruct a more detailed account of Orage's and Toomer's defection from Gurdjieff.

If my own personal accounts of Gurdjieff and Toomer seem to clash at times with the personal or scholarly views of others, I can only respond by saying that, although I follow my sources closely, both written and in oral exchange, memory is naturally selective and, hence, interpretive. I recall that Gurdjieff once wrote—though I have forgotten where—that one's own account of things past constitutes an "essence of man of giving out as one's own, after having changed some minor detail." Toomer, like Gurdjieff, was a spinner of the fabric of myths and, in encouraging me to write about myself in order to merge the subject "I" with the object "me," he said that there is always value for others in the data of one's experience, but there is greater value in that data for he who imagines he lived it. He went on to say: "Only when you become a part of the story can you achieve its truth. Only then will it be *your* story, different from all other stories, but part of their total truth."[12]

---

[12] Oscar Ichazo, "Letter to the Transpersonal Community." *The Arican*, 1991, p. 99, remarks that "it is well-known that none of Gurdjieff's close followers arrived at any degree of mystical transcendence." This is simply ignoring the authoritative testimony of men like the philosopher P. D. Ouspensky, the teacher John Bennett, the architect Frank Lloyd Wright, the composer Thomas de Hartmann and, among many others, the writer and teacher Jean Toomer. For early writings on Gurdjieff, see J. Walter Driscoll. *Gurdjieff: An Annotated Bibliography* (New York: Garland, 1985).

Chapter Two

Living with Toomer

I also am an ancestor, a source, an initiator.
                                        —*Essentials*

I could taste flavors in a grain of sand,
My eyes saw loveliness,
And I had learned to peal the wind.
                        —"The Blue Meridian"

I have been living with Jean Toomer for so long in my imagination that it is difficult to trace a firm border between experiences of my spirit and of my body. Clearly, the quantity of time I spent with him is out of proportion with its mark on my memory and its influence on my thought. Each moment that I relive with Jean widens to occupy more space in my thoughts. At the moment, my earliest recollection of him is from 1937, and the last from 1959. I was a member of his household from 1937 to 1939, spent summer months with him throughout the war, then visited occasionally for some years until the summer and fall of 1954 and the spring of 1955, when I again "moved into" the Mill House. In 1959, I visited him for the last times in the made-over grange on the hill above the Mill House. I recall my painful incredulity when my mother called me in 1967 from the United States to tell me he had died.

In the early summer of 1937, my mother had taken me out of an uncomfortable and demoralizing environment in a boarding camp in New Milford, CT. Leaving my sister there to suffer alone, she brought me to live with her in a one-room furnished flat near Union Square in New York City. There was no father about, and my mother was working for W. J. Sloane, preparing an exhibit for the New York World's Fair. I was almost 7 years old then. We had been in the United States less than two years, having arrived in New York on the SS Milwaukee in the early winter of 1935. Now my mother was living in makeshift circumstances, having left all her possessions behind in storage in Paris, except for the huge Delage automobile she had brought over with us on the boat. So I slept on a bed made of two armchairs placed face to face and, while my mother worked, I was tended by the teenage son of one of my mother's New York friends.

One hot evening in late August, a tall, slim man with a broad smile and deep bright brown eyes dropped by and talked for some time with my mother. At one point in the conversation, he turned around on his chair and looked me straight in the eye and asked if I would like to come and live with him. My mother said nothing to either encourage or discourage me, but waited silently for my response. I was frightened, and yet I felt easy with this man right away. I can still summon up the smell of him that evening, something like soft leather and hollyhocks; but I was afraid to be separated from my mother once again. The tall man with the broad smile was not in the least put off by my reluctance to respond, but began to tell me of all the pleasures awaiting me in his house. There would be someone to take me to school, someone to pick me up, a playmate at home, a large room overlooking the street where I could play, a backyard garden to explore, parks nearby, and a church on the corner. Even better, I would be in a country home on weekends where there was a farm, fields, and a stream. He then added the ultimate inducement: If I moved in with him, I would be free to do whatever I wanted at his house. "Why," he added, "if you want to go up to the roof of the house to sing and dance a jig, you can, and I'll even join you."

Shortly afterward, my mother and I went to dinner at 39 West 10th Street. A few days after that, I was moved into the house. I was not surprised and did not resist, though I had never told my mother that I wanted it. I could see, nonetheless, that she wanted it, and it had already been decided between her and Jean. I was, after all, used to being sent here and there. The day I moved in, Jean said to me very seriously: "Explore everywhere. A house is like the world, you see, and you should know as much about it as you can." I was immediately struck and intrigued by this big house full of voices, colors, and odors.[1]

I was enrolled in Friends Seminary on 3rd Avenue, not far from Gramercy Park, if I remember correctly. In the beginning, my mother parked her huge Delage automobile near the school, and I would wait in it for her to finish work. Then she would take me to a drugstore for an ice-cream, and we would talk. After a few weeks, she no longer appeared, and an older girl picked me up at school and took me to 10th Street. The brownstone house at 39 West 10th Street was a warm haven for me. I see it clearly still. It was narrow, with a staircase running up the right hand wall

---

[1] Marjorie Content Toomer was the daughter of stockbroker Harry Content, who had given her the house on 10th Street as a gift for her marriage to Harold Loeb, the avant-garde editor and publisher who is probably best known as the model for Cohen in Hemingway's *The Sun Also Rises*. Loeb describes the activities in the editorial office basement of the house in his autobiography *The Way It Was*.

from the entrance. On the left of the corridor was a large living room and, past it, a kitchen that overlooked the backyard, whose shapes are still familiar to me. There was a gravel walk down the middle of the yard, high, dirty brick walls all about, three or four thin trees, many bushes, and a small kitchen garden in the middle where herbs grew. It was a yard of shadows, and I don't think sunlight ever touched much of it.

On the upper floor of the house, at the head of the stairs on the right was a bathroom and, across from that, at the front of the house overlooking 10th Street, was my room and playroom. I constructed there an elevated roadway with wood blocks and I played for hours with the two toy cars my mother bought me just before I moved in. I don't know when I first discovered that there was another child in the house. My earliest memory of her is of playing "train" in a line of wooden chairs on the floor, and sharing the baths we were forced to take every other afternoon, supervised by a tall, blonde, handsome, buxom girl who was in her first year at NYU or Columbia. In the course of our baths that first winter, she taught me and Argie to whistle.[2] Argie was in first grade, a year behind me in school, but she managed to whistle before I did.

My fullest memory of the house, however, is of the kitchen where Argie and I had our meals. There were bunches of Indian corn hanging here and there and, to this day, I associate that heavy spicy smell of the kitchen—curry, mustard, coriander, cumin, ginger—with blue, red, yellow, white, and black corn. Although Jean's wife, Marjorie, seemed to me to be sweeping through the kitchen at all moments of the day, there was a cook, a German woman named Alvina, a short, stout, and soft woman who spoke with a decided accent. She and her husband, Oscar, lived in the basement. Oscar returned to Germany a year later and she stayed on in the house in New York to keep it in order when the rest of the family was in Doylestown. While the Toomers were in India two years later, she visited her husband and returned before the United States entered the war. She was short-tempered with me.

On sunny weekend days, Argie and I rollerskated in Washington Park, just a few blocks away. I remember vividly the water fountain in the middle of the park, like a hub of a wheel with many concrete walks like spokes leading from it. It had a base upon which I could stand to reach the arc of water. In the park, we could buy ice cream on sticks, hoping to find a star

---

[2] Jean Toomer's daughter, born in August 1932, was baptized Margery, after her mother. Jean called her Argie and Arge at the time I lived with them. At secondary school she was Marge, or Margery, and when she took up a career, she preferred Margot. My names for her follow, generally, my relationship with her at any given time.

on the stick that we could return for the bonus of another ice cream. Jean took me around the block to the Episcopal Church on 5th Avenue and enrolled me in the choir, but I sang only once or twice that whole winter and spring.

Argie called her father "Poppy" and, after a few weeks, I did too.[3] In light moments, he called me "Bolo," a variation of my sister's and my mother's nickname for me, "Polo." In serious moments together, he called me "Boy," but I don't remember him ever calling me "Paul." His wife, to whom my mother always referred as Marjorie Content rather than as Marjorie Toomer, called me "Polo" to my face and "Paul" when she spoke to Jean. To me, she was simply "Marjorie," and to Argie, "Mother."

Marjorie did not display much affection for me. She seemed distant and exotic, but always business-like and in a hurry, moving quickly, full of energy, and with a bright vivacious smile, but a smile more of interest and concern than of pleasure. I was struck immediately by the colors she wore, which seemed to blend in with the colors and odors of the kitchen. She dressed in Navajo skirts with colorful designs, blue and yellow blouses, with long silver and beaded necklaces, silver and turquoise brooches and earrings, hair pins and combs. She raised whirlwinds through the house with her twirling skirts.

Poppy, on the other hand, would sit quietly in a loose-belted jacket in an armchair, reading or just meditating, apparently alert to everything going on about him, but saying little himself, compared with the constant chatter of Marjorie. When something caught his attention, however, he would cock his head to the side and downward and look at it, or you, with a quizzical expression. The effect was even more striking when he was reading, for he would lower the newspaper or book in his hand and look over his glasses as if to ask: "What in the world is that?" When there was company, however, Poppy talked and laughed while he paced the floor, gesticulating.

I was too busy with my life with Argie and school and Washington Square to spend much time alone with Poppy that winter. Occasionally he would ask what I thought of one thing or another, but he talked seriously with me only on those occasions when I seemed upset or confused, or did

---

[3] On November 29, 1938, Marjorie wrote her daughter Susan: "Arge seems to me to have matured quite a bit in the 12 days we were gone!! She certainly was most expressively affectionate on our return when I came in the door. She dashed down the stairs—and Polo after her. I hardly greeted them when Polo said: 'Where's Pops?' (meaning Jean). He has sort of adopted Jean as his father since he says that he hasn't seen his own father for 4 years or more—he says Jean is going to be his father now" (Marjorie Content Papers, Doylestown).

something he considered amusing. When I couldn't sit still in his company, he called me "Mr. Fidget." After Argie and I had come in from Washington Square or from the backyard, he would question us as to what we
had seen. If I talked about flowers coming up in the garden, he asked what
they were. When I couldn't identify them by name, he suggested that I
should give them names according to the impression they made on me. So
I mentioned blue star-flowers, and white button-flowers (that I learned
later from Marjorie were chives), and all colors of umbrella-flowers. He
thought about these names, and then said that it would be a good idea if I
made stories about why these flowers had such name-shapes. "Names of
things should reveal something of what they are and what they do. How
can you know those things if you don't know the meaning of their names?
Observe them carefully and they'll let you know by what name they would
be called. There is a story in each name, a plant's own story. Learn to make
your own story out of everything you see. Then you will not forget it."

We didn't go out very often in New York. A few times, Poppy and Argie and I went to Fred Leighton's Mexican shop, where my mother helped
with import orders. That shop, with Navajo blankets on the wall, heavy
silver bracelets with large turquoise settings, and pottery everywhere,
seemed an extension of 10th Street. Fred was one of the few visitors to
10th Street whom I got to know well myself. On my first visit to his shop,
he gave me a little Navajo drum and a straw cowboy whose head had come
off by the time I got him home. I don't remember many of the numerous
visitors to the house, but I do remember a beautiful woman who was introduced to me as "Georgia." The name seemed strange to me, and from
that moment on, whenever I heard the name of the state, I saw Georgia
O'Keefe in my mind.

Very special occasions for Argie and me were the weekends when we
drove down to Doylestown, PA, crowded into a Ford station wagon with
rugs, lamps, books, and all sorts of equipment. After one or two trips, the
routine drive became a sort of ritual that I enjoyed immensely. The land-
marks are still familiar to me today and many of them survive: the pock-
marked asphalt under a sort of one-sided tunnel on Route 22 in New
Jersey, the ship-form restaurant in the middle of the grassy hill median
further south, the huge traffic circle on Route 202 at Somerville, where
Argie would cry out "Half-way House!" Sometimes we would stop there
at a small restaurant for a snack before continuing on the second half of
the drive.

The long winding hill down into Lambertville and across the bridge
to New Hope was Argie's and my favorite moment, not only because New
Hope was only a few miles from Doylestown, but because that hill over

Lambertville and the Delaware River was often full of circus tents, agricultural exhibits, and carnival attractions. After the narrow bridge, the farms and houses built of stone, so typical of Bucks County, were everywhere. Just past a big sign advertising an underground cavern, we turned right, up a dirt road that went up and down over three hills before it passed over a tiny wooden bridge with walls topped with red roof tiles. On the rise of the next hill, we turned right, along a hedged drive to Mill House, a huge white wooden house with blue shutters, on the left. On the right a few yards further was a gigantic square stone barn on the rise of a field that ran down to a stream that passed by the back of the barn toward the wooden bridge. Attached to the upper side of that stone barn was a car shed and, beside it, a broad and leafy walnut tree that smelled musty and damp.

In front of the car shed, the black stone drive turned left up the hill, past the dining room and kitchen of the house, to a large farm yard in the ell formed by the tractor shed, hayloft, and grange. A tractor path continued between the yard and a field to meet another path at the top of the hill and parallel to the front drive. Around to the right, it turned into the barn loft. Before the entrance was an unbroken expanse of cornfield, stretching as far as I could see. This slope was the last all the way to Mechanicsville. Twenty-five years later, this tractor door would be the entrance to Jean Toomer's last home.

On the other side of the road, closer to the bridge and stream, was a farm house, below and in front of a large yard with stables and worksheds whose lower walls were of stone. The stone walls continued in different directions to make enclosures of sorts. One contained a huge manure compost. Up higher on the slope were fields of grain, and between the yard and the farm house was a neat, large, square kitchen garden.

The stone barn by the Mill House was the most impressive structure on the property. It had a low stone-walled terrace with cement floor before a large double door that opened inward onto a wooden platform. Straight ahead in the dark interior was a broad open staircase to a higher platform upon which construction had begun on two or three rooms that remained unfinished for a few years. Down to the left of the entrance platform, a long wooden staircase without bannister hugged the wall and descended some twenty feet to the earthen floor of an enormous room that must have been at least sixty yards square. A narrow wooden platform on the house side held two small toilet compartments. The rest of the room was bare except at the far end, where there was the largest water wheel I have ever seen, blocked still, and with only a little water seeping through the sluice gate from the stream behind into the deep well beneath the wooden blades still in working condition. There was a small wall in front of it to protect us from falling into the well in which it stood. It was frightening to look down into the dark bottom of the mill wheel.

I recall the interior space of the house and the Mill particularly well, perhaps, for one reason. Poppy asked me sometime later if I had carefully noted where everything was. "You want to know the house, and the house to know you. You are two living things who must get to know each other. The kitchen is a stomach. Our bedrooms are our minds when we sleep. The living room is where we talk and listen and read; but the Mill House is the best of all, a place to work and play. Just like your body, everything on this property has something special about it, and something special it allows us to do. If you know this place, or know *any* place, you will always know where you are in it. Whenever you look at something carefully, you are looking at yourself. That way you have a friend in what you see who will help you control it as well as yourself. Know where you are in this house, and you will know what has happened there, what can and what *will* happen there."

I remember the sounds, feelings, and smells of Mill House as well. I awoke each morning to the contented cooing of pigeons. The feel of the blue-black gravel of the front drive under my shoes, the smell of the dry hay in the barn loft, the soft smell of soap and after-shave lotion outside Poppy's bathroom, the smell of book covers along the wall by the study, the heavy smell of the Navajo blankets in Marjorie's workroom downstairs, the flat, cold cement-smell of the Mill House interior, and the warm blend of aromas from the kitchen. My senses seem to have found their enduring forms there. I remember once asking Poppy why the pigeons cooed not exactly at daybreak, but apparently always at the same time after it, and why they cooed so happily. He lowered his head in his habitual thoughtful manner and said, looking at me from under his eyebrows: "They remind themselves at the start of each day who they are. Everything living has a language to use to know who he is and to what family of life he belongs. Think each morning about the first thing you say, and what it can mean to your day." That message stuck and, to this day, the first thing I say consciously identifies a bond with something precious to me.

Another time, he told me to imagine myself a dove flying over the Mill House. What would I see? "Try to imagine your world from the view of other things in it." One day, Argie took my teddy bear, "Fuzzy," and threw it to the bottom of the well beneath the wheel. I was crushed with sadness. In tears, I told my story to Poppy and Marjorie, while Argie stood by defiantly. Poppy said quite calmly, "Well Arge, maybe you were inviting Polo to see what the world looks like at the bottom of the mill wheel, but I don't think Fuzzy's able to do it for him, so you'll just have to go down and fetch it." She was too afraid, of course, but Poppy took her by the hand and the three of us went down the stairs, a descent that itself frightened me, and over to the edge of the pit, where Poppy took Argie with him down two rudders, and then reached her down to where she could go the rest of the way. I recovered "Fuzzy," a little damp, but none the worse for the experience. That evening, Argie got her revenge by spitting in our common bath; and it was my night to clean the tub.

The mill was a never-ending source of terrifying images, whose calm and sunny outer terrace was belied by the immense space of the dark and damp interior just behind its bright wooden entry doors. That large terrace was our favorite play area. From its low wall, we could jump into the grassy field near the drive. From the back of the terrace, we could look down fearfully at the field some fifteen to twenty feet below.

For those several weekends during which pieces of 10th Street were transported, the house that we called Mill House and particularly the mill were places of adventure and excitement that offered relief from the city and a school I did not particularly enjoy. I do not remember much of my mother during that year at 10th Street. She never came with us to Doylestown, and I half forgot about her in my immersion in the life of the Toomers. I don't remember seeing her, even at the end of the school year when we drove out to the Mill House to pack up for a summer holiday. Late that summer, Poppy and Marjorie drove to Provincetown and one of the househelp, May, drove up a couple of days later with Argie and me, stopping for one night in a tourist house in Madison or Old Lyme, Connecticut. The next afternoon, we drove up the Cape, past a stately Inn with a blue wooden ship sign hanging outside, and turned left toward the bay and the cottage in which we were to spend the end of the summer. It had but a single bedroom, so Argie and I had to sleep on cots in the dining room, while May slept on the couch.

Argie and I had a marvelous vacation there. We would run across the back yard onto tidal flats that led toward a dune topped with sea grass. That sandy hill was our archaeological dig and we searched for hours for Indian arrowheads. Argie found one, or something resembling one. The house had no plumbing other than a kitchen pump, no electricity, and there was an ill-smelling outhouse in the back. Some days, we drove up the cape to Provincetown. I remember the smells of the sea and of grilled corn. I remember almost nothing of Jean and Marjorie at Wellfleet except for the drives to markets for food and excursions to Provincetown. In a later reminiscence, Argie reminded me of the crab claws we played with, snapping at each other with them. We kept them beneath our pillows until Marjorie smelled them and threw them out.

After Wellfleet, we settled into the Mill House and left 10th Street behind.[4] Argie and I were assigned to a huge bedroom at the upper end of the house, over the kitchen. The windows gave us views on both sides: over the lawn and rock garden toward the dirt road and farm on one side, and over the drive between the mill and the upper tractor yard on the other. The door to our room was at the end of a long corridor that ran along a number of windows overlooking a flagstone terrrace and the lawn, and at the other end of the room was a door into our bathroom. Just before our room was a wooden stairway between the kitchen and a small galley-like pantry. Under this was another wooden stairway to a cellar with shelves stacked with preserves. Upstairs, on the other side of our bathroom and the stairs, was a guest room and then Jean's bathroom and, at the southwest corner of the house, their bedroom, a mysterious place that I can't remember ever entering, but that I peered into once or twice without daring to step over the lintel. The bathrooms had doors to both the hall and the bedrooms. One day, walking down the hallway with the bright light coming in from the windows over the lawn, the door to Jean's bathroom was open and I turned to see him standing naked at the sink leaning forward against the sink toward the mirror, shaving. It was the first time I had seen a man's naked body, and I noted his long, slim, strong body and penis arched against the side of the sink.

Argie and I went to school at Buckingham Friends in Lahaska, not far away from where the bottom of our road met Route 202. The school house was a square stone building on a steep hill a hundred feet above the road, and across that road was a long one-story house where a woman

4 Cynthia Earl Kerman and Richard Eldridge, *The Lives of Jean Toomer* (Baton Rouge, LA: Louisiana State University Press, 1987), p. 223, say that Jean and Marjorie moved to Doylestown in 1936; Lifon and Eldridge, in "Marjorie Content," *Quasha*, 24, have the date as 1935, and in an article of Marjorie in *The* [Doylestown] *Intelligencer*, 14 November 1983, the move is dated Thanksgiving 1934. Rudolph Byrd, *Toomer's Years with Gurdjieff* (Athens, GA: University of Georgia Press, 1989), p. 85, also gives 1934 as the date for the move to Doylestown. All of these confuse dates of purchase, preparation of the house, and the actual move. The Toomers had probably completed most of the necessary work on the house and had started redoing the mill itself by 1936, as the date on the millstone at its entrance testifies. They had spent some weeks in the house in the summers of 1936 and 1937, supervising arrangements. Nonetheless, 10th Street was their principal residence until the summer of 1938. Robert B. Jones, in his introduction to *The Collected Poems of Jean Toomer*, Robert B. Jones and Margot Latimer, eds. (Chapel Hill, NC: University of North Carolina Press, 1987), p. xxv, has the correct date as summer, 1938. In the Toomer papers, there are letters addressed to both West 10th St. and Doylestown between 1936 and 1940. Marjorie's correspondence to her daughter Susan in 1937 is mailed from New York during the week, and from Doylestown on weekends.

served school lunch. At one of our first lunches, the woman asked me why I had not drunk my milk, and I replied that I didn't like milk. "What do you drink at home?" she demanded. I said "wine and beer." She was furious, but when Poppy heard the story, he roared with laughter.

Next to the school was the Quaker Meeting where Marjorie later served as Secretary. I remember going to two or three meetings with Jean, but I don't recall that he spoke. In fact, the Lahaska Meeting was, for me, a rather quiet and subdued affair, serving as an occasion, in the schoolyard before and after the service, for talking about local events and issues. On Sundays at the Mill House, when guests were present, lunch was served in a dining room that consisted of a wide passageway between the front sitting room and the kitchen-pantry area. There was one imposing piece of furniture in that room: an oval mahogany-colored table, at least ten feet long, with an elaborate sculpted base resembling Brancusi's Bird in Flight. This was the work of a craftsman, Wharton Esherick, who was a frequent visitor to Mill House. Argie and I sat at that table only on festive occasions.

From that long narrow room, between the kitchen pantry and the front sitting room, there was one door out to a flagstone terrace leading to the croquet green and, on the other side, another door out to the drive on its incline toward the barn. I supposed that this door, with slate steps outside, was designed as the house's main entry, but I never saw it used except as an escape route in our play. The family ate almost all meals at a large table in the kitchen that had a door out onto a flagstone walk on that same side of the house. In the winter, the flagstone was enclosed in a wood and glass storm porch to guard the door, and it was filled with hanging herbs, tools on hooks, wooden crates with apples in a corner, and implements of all kinds.

Lin Davenport did all the handy jobs, like raising the winter porch. He and his brother, Don, were the "motors" of the property, especially the farm across the way. The farmhouse itself was lived in by an older man, Ramsey, who did the everyday farm chores. Around the Mill House, Lin and Don were Jean's aides. Lin was my favorite—strong, fast, full of self-confidence and humor, seemingly capable of doing everything from repairing tractors to delivering calves. Don, slighter, wore glasses and was much quieter, though he entered into children's games with Argie and me and participated in the family game of croquet, played every possible weekend on the immaculately kept lawn that stretched out from the dining room slate terrace toward a weeping willow and the field and dirt road beyond.

The croquet games were the highlights of weekend afternoons before supper. Those games gave me my first serious concern with style of play, for no two players used either the same grip or the same game tactics. Marjorie, stiff-legged, weight on the back of her body, bent over at the waist with an interlocked finger grip, swung evenly between widely spread legs, with her head raised, chin right over the end of the mallet. Jean poised his head over the ball, standing almost straight, with a golfer's putting stroke. Lin used a one-handed stroke, knees slightly bent, and laughed with such pleasure when he knocked an opponent's ball out of bounds that it was almost a pleasure to be his victim. Marjorie preferred to play her own ball and not bother with defensive tactics, but Jean would try to put someone else's ball in a tantalizingly frustrating position, on the wrong side of a wicket. There were never arguments among the adults during these games, but a lot of talking, as if the game served the talk.

The Davenport brothers were also our teachers. At the bottom of the mill, under the back of the terrace toward the stream, they set up a workshop where Lin taught us carpentry, leatherwork, knots, woodcutting, and stone-chiseling. When we were about the property, the brothers were guards and companions, and we went often into the fields with them while they worked. I remember Lin supervising the ripping out of the hedge that bordered the front drive. It was quite a production, for the drive must have been a hundred yards long, and he and Jean did the job with a caterpillar tractor and chains, dragging each plant out of the ground one by one. When Lin wasn't driving, Jean was, and once he gave me a turn on his lap. It was easy enough to pull the steering levers, but my legs weren't long enough for my feet to reach the clutch pedal.

In warm weather, Argie and I sat on bales of hay in the upper part of the barn and watched Poppy, the Davenports, and others play basketball between the tractor entrance and the loft doors that opened into space above the tractor hanger. Lin was strong and moved with power toward the basket, but Jean glided rather than ran, and the ball never stayed still in his hands, but seemed only to change its speed and direction on the way toward the basket or toward another player. When he shot a basket, it seemed as if the ball were an extension of his hands that came up from just under his belt to high above his head in one evenly paced glide. At no other times have I seen Jean move so quickly and sweat so profusely. What struck me then, and still strikes me in recollection, is the extraordinary control and balance he had over his bodily movements.

I felt secure at school, and especially with my teacher, Kitty Simmons, who used the Quaker pronoun forms *thou* and *thee* in a soft and persuasive manner. Buckingham Friends had only soccer as a school sport. My friend Guvner Cadwallader played with riding boots and kicked dents into my shins. I discovered science, not only because of the insects that inhabited the dirt and brush schoolyard, but because we were studying the solar system and the history of life on the Earth. I remember telling Poppy one evening that I thought the Earth was nothing but a speck of live dust floating in the air of a giant's room. He asked me to tell him the difference between living and dead dust, why they weren't the same thing. When I didn't do well with that question, he asked me how we might see the giant and how he might see us. I did no better on that one, but Poppy seemed unperturbed and sent me off to think more on "these matters." I did think about all sorts of ramifications of what I considered a bright analogy and, a few days later, I thought I was ready when he asked me about the giant's dust. "I guess the giant is like God," I said, "and this room is his universe." "Good," he smiled, "and what about other rooms?" I thought fast and said that I imagined there would be many universes. "And many Gods?" he wrinkled his brow, as he lowered his head and raised his eyes to question me. "Go and think more." I thought that I'd be more careful next time and be more prepared for complications like this.

On the farm, Argie and I were assigned tasks by Jean and Lin.[5] One was to feed and water the two horses, Dolly and Perry. The sound of Dolly crunching ears of corn was music to my ears, and I loved stroking the velvety-warm front of her nose. She had a mind of her own and often, when I watered her, she would decide to step over the thin cord into the kitchen garden and trample young vegetables. Ramsey would rage, and Poppy would smile and tell Argie and me that we were entrusted with the responsibility to tend the horses for their own good as well as ours; and it was not for their good, he laughed, to have Ramsey striking their hindquarters.

Although Argie and I were expected to assume as much responsibility around the farm as we could handle, and especially those things we could do without supervision, like cleaning out the cow stalls, feeding the chickens, and collecting eggs, we had complete freedom of movement about the property. We gloried in the immensity of space, but lack of supervision occasioned more than one faux pas. One weekend late in the summer or early fall of 1938, my sister Eve, nicknamed "Petey," stayed with us at Mill House just before returning to school in New Milford. One morning, we fed the pigs watermelon rinds in which Petey put some hot pepper seeds. She giggled with delight when a large pig ran around the pen, squealing and shaking his head from side to side. Ramsey ran over and saw what my sister was doing. In fury, he sent us away and complained to Lin and Poppy, who were looking at a tractor in need of repair.

---

[5] Assignment of farm tasks was Gurdjieff's practice at the Prieuré. There, each task had a particular name, so that no two people did the same thing.

Later that afternoon, Poppy confronted us. I do not remember my sister's reply, but it seemed to me that Poppy harbored some ill feelings toward her.[6] He turned to Argie and myself to ask what part we had played in the affair. Our attempts at evasion of responsibility fell flat, but suddenly Poppy paused, smiled softly, grinned, and said: "You know, the situation is not as serious for the pig as it is for you. He forgets quickly the surprise he had today, and tomorrow he might sniff his watermelon rind carefully before eating it, but in a day or two he will have no regrets over his painful experience.

"You are different. If I put a generous dose of tabasco in your soup, you will also squeal. You will wonder what happened, and why it burns your mouth, and you will have respect for that little bottle of tabasco. You will even learn to like tabasco once you can measure the amount it takes to spice the soup to your taste. You will learn what the pig cannot because you have a memory and an awareness of yourself—what you like and what you can do to serve your likes. Memory is a valuable tool. A pig forgets pleasure and pain, but remembering pleasure and pain makes you superior to pigs. You will not tease the pigs any more because you remember how Ramsey reacts, and you will remember not to tease the pigs because their pain gives you no pleasure, just food for your curiosity. Cultivate and refine your memory. Give it things to work upon for your own profit, and not for others' pain. Remember, you become what you can be only if you remember yourself."

Every incident became an occasion for a lesson, always given with a deep, low, and soft voice out of a mouth curved into a sly smile. One day, Lin caught a snapping turtle in the stream and put it into a wooden tub of milk in a corner of the cow barn. The smell of sour milk and the sight of that pointed head and body the circumference of a volleyball rising to the surface of its white sea was terrifying. I stood with Poppy, watching the turtle slowly turn in the milk. "You see," he said, "the turtle is not restless because he has no desire to go anywhere. He isn't the least concerned with where he is as long as his body is comfortable. He's not curious to know what's on the outside of his barrel, any more than the pigs are curious about what is in the next field unless they are hungry. We call the pigs and the turtle lazy, but that's wrong. They aren't lazy at all. They have nothing to occupy themselves with except eating and sleeping.

"You, boy, have plenty to eat, and are curious about other things. That is good, but to know other things you have to start like the pig and the tur-

---

[6] I guessed at a reason for his hostility when, many years later, I discovered that he knew that Petey was Gurdjieff's child. Argie does not recall ill feelings toward Petey on the part of her father at any time.

tle. I mean you have to know what you need for your body, and know how to move your body to get it yourself, if it isn't given you. To take what is given you without questioning your dependence on the giver is to stay the pig, sniffing only to see what might hurt you."

One morning Argie and I came upon a dead cow left in the farmyard after an autopsy. Its inner organs spilled out between its legs, and the stomach and heart looked as if they had been dipped in sand. "It died of eating nails," Ramsey explained, and I could imagine the cows in the pasture beside the Mill House barn licking up nails from a keg. Lin and Jean stood by the carcass like two surgeons comparing notes. Poppy smiled at me after a while and said that not all animals knew what was good for them, but it would have taken a lot of pepper seeds to kill that cow.

We ate cow's tongue often, and Poppy used to kid me about my enjoying the sandpaper-like feel of a cow's tongue on my cheek so much that I would bite out a tongue directly from a cow's mouth. Argie and I watched Lin chop off chickens' heads on a bloody wood block, after which some of them would hop about the yard for a long time before Lin caught them and hung them to bleed dry. Most afternoons, Poppy would take long walks with his dog, Mickey, who was part chow and part something else. Mickey's tongue was almost black and he was slightly larger than most chows, but he had a uniformly reddish-tan coat. He was a quiet and friendly dog, and I could see Poppy striding across the fields on the opposite hill, on the other side of the stream and thin line of small trees, with long steps, stick in hand, and Mickey bounding ahead and then waiting with his brush-like tail wagging. Jean usually took those walks alone with Mickey. He said that they cleaned out his thoughts at the end of the day. Many times I was invited along, and would listen to Poppy point out features of trees and soil in that low even voice of his. One afternoon, I complained that my new shoes hurt. We stopped; he looked at my shoes, then told me to walk in the stream with them until they were thoroughly wet. So I did, while he walked along the bank. He said then that I should walk in them until they dried on my feet, "because a new shoe on a foot is like a new idea in the mind. It must be shaped to the particular form in which it will serve you best."

Often after lunch, Jean would take a nap on the small couch in the front room, just to the right of the front entrance. He lay flat on his back with his head on a small cushion, arms crossed on his chest, and body covered with a Navajo blanket. The only times he lost his temper with me were on the occasions when Argie and I would race from the kitchen area across the bare wooden floor of the dining room and leap down the one step to the sitting room, passing within ten inches of Poppy's body. He would raise nothing but his head and bellow out, "QUIET BOY!" We would scurry either out of the front door or up the front stairs to race down the hall to our room. At other times when Poppy would get angry over something I had done, or more often *not* done, his anger was in his aspect and his glaring eyes. Rarely did he have to speak. His look terrified me, but a few minutes later everything would be back in place. He never held a grudge, but shifted out of moods as rapidly as he went into them.

One late afternoon a week Argie and I were allowed to listen to "I Love a Mystery," whose theme music was Sibelius' eerie "Waltz Triste." At that time, most of the adventures were taking place in Sumatra, and I was fascinated by the jungle island, reading everything I could about the Dutch East Indies. Jean furnished maps and suggestions, and soon I was memorizing statistics on the East Indian islands and eventually the whole Orient. Jean warned me that I would end up with a head like the straw cowboys in Fred Leighton's shop. "If you keep putting in facts, they will mix up with ideas and your mind will start to resemble an attic full of junk. Learn to order things in your mind. Put all the facts you want in there, but put them in a place that can be cleaned out now and then without disturbing the essential machinery. And, be careful not to memorize things you will be unable to forget." I said this seemed funny, since at school we are forced to memorize facts.

"Yes, and that is fine, but new facts have to take the place of old ones, sometimes, and you must make room for them. To do that, you have to erase parts of your memory just as you have to erase chalk marks on the schoolroom blackboard when you need room to write more. Treat facts like food. Once food is digested it becomes part of your body, your strength, your sight and hearing. Facts are the same. Digest them, have them strengthen your mind the way food works on your body. Facts that have to do with things that you cannot join to yourself weigh you down. Ask yourself what these 'facts' mean to you personally, and you will find good ways to use them. Just remember that what you forget *consciously*, can be recalled in fresh form for use at a later time. But, if you cannot remember yourself, you will forget others unconsciously."

One day, I told Poppy that, looking south from the Mill House toward the ridge of the hill on the other side of the stream and sensing countless ridges of hills one after another on the other side, it seemed that the entire earth could be traversed ridge by ridge all the way to China. I said I'd like to walk there one day. He liked the idea and encouraged me to hold on to it as a plan, because, as he said, "knowledge is in China." There would be no sense, however, in undertaking the voyage until I was old enough to recognize what I might see there. From that moment on, every project I expressed to him became measured by the China Walk. I tried to calculate how long it would take, and if I could take Mickey along with me. Poppy suggested that the walk might do more good for Nina, the German police dog Lin had bought as Mickey's mate, because she needed the discipline of the journey. Nina had a wild spirit and trusted no one.

Nina began making a pest of herself. She would leap at Argie and me to snap at the top of our heads. She caught a weasel one evening and played with it on the croquet pitch. I was horrified, but Jean, instead of rescuing the weasel, said simply that Nina would learn with age to discover the proper place and purpose for her hunt. Next, she started raiding Ramsey's chicken roosts, and Lin and Jean took one of her mangled victims and tied it about her neck. For days Nina loped around the property uncomfortably. Argie and I thought this punishment both disgusting and unfair, but Jean explained simply that to have to live constantly with the thing you want only occasionally is a good way to make even a dog consider if he wants the thing at all. In the spring of 1939, Nina gave birth to pups. Argie and I adopted Smokey, who looked very much like a giant collie.

I was sitting with Poppy listening to the radio one evening in the fall when Orson Welles made his "Invasion from Mars" broadcast. I was confused and frightened by the tone of panic, but Poppy never stirred. He bent over slightly from his seat, as he was used to doing when listening intently, and smiled through the whole thing. The weekend papers were full of illustrations of Martians in the streets of New York, and I told Poppy that I would walk to New York to find my mother. "It isn't necessary," he replied, "your mother can take care of herself. If she wants you, she'll call. Besides, what do you think you could do? You have to know what you are up against when you set out on adventures, like your walk to China. You have to plan your route, but more importantly, prepare yourself."

So Argie and I started planning adventures together. We borrowed hatchets from Lin's workshop and began cutting down, as best we could, clumps of sweetbriar along a stretch of the stream. Then we began to widen and deepen the stream bed to make what we planned as our swimming hole. We never got very far, because the opposite bank of the stream was overgrown with a thick briar patch, but the project interested Poppy, who strolled by to inspect our labors on his walks, while Mickey came and sniffed along the stream. Each evening, he asked for a progress report. In an offhand remark, he wondered if either of us had considered that it would be useful to know how to swim before we finished the pool.

That fall, sure of our growing skills, we set out to build a tree house. We gathered wood, made a design, found tools, and set to work. Well, we tried to set to work. But we couldn't manage working in the tree, and the ladder we built on the tree trunk kept collapsing. We had more success with our projects later, when it snowed for a whole day. When Lin could barely open the kitchen door (the kitchen patio had not yet been enclosed for the winter), Argie and I burrowed out, and then built a marvelous igloo on the croquet pitch. Poppy remarked that, often, improvised projects were more successful than those well planned. "It is a question of knowing what your are doing," he observed, "and if you don't know, instinct works better than plotting."

We became daring in our escapades as we became familiar with the area. One morning, we climbed through Ramsey's kitchen window after he had left to plow a distant field. I remember my surprise and envy when I caught the lingering odor of the porkchops and fried potatoes he had eaten for breakfast. We raided his bread box and found a loaf of raisin bread with a sugar-glazed crust. I had never smelled anything so warm and sweet, or tasted pulpy raisins in soft dough before. We weren't caught and were not repentent, but I always suspected that whenever we did such things, Jean knew about them. I can't remember him ever scolding us for such pranks, and neither he nor Marjorie ever raised a hand in anger against either of us. Instead, he found something amusing in everything we did, an occasion to get a thought across to us. For example, some days later when we were crossing a neighboring field in the direction of Mechanicsville, a grazing bull looked up at us, and we taunted it to charge by waving our hands. To our frustration, the bull resumed its meal placidly. Argie's story to her father that evening was of our narrow escape from a ferocious charge. "China is the other way," said Jean with a wry smile.

Argie and I were given two miniature play wagons that we pushed about the huge cement terrace in front of the mill entrance. Poppy told us to make a city out of the terrace, and he gave us a piece of chalk. Argie and I marked off streets and, kneeling on the wagon bed while pushing with one foot and steering with our hands, we raced through our labyrinthine designs for hours on end. It was our favorite play area, and it was ours alone. On the lawn, Poppy taught us a variety of exercises. The one I remember best involved supporting the body upside-down on a tripod of neck, shoulders, and elbows. He had me do that for many minutes at a time, explaining that it was good for blood circulation and breathing. One day, all alone in the field, perhaps fifteen feet from the mill terrace, naked, I trampled a small circle in the grass and did my exercise there. Suddenly, I felt the urgent need to piss and, feeling it perfectly logical to do it upside-down as well as standing up, I pushed forth a fountain that, unfortunately, did not quite arc clear of my face. I crumpled to the ground, sputtering, and then heard a roar of laughter. There above me, not six yards away, was

Poppy with one foot on my wagon, bent over, with his hand under his chin, and a huge smile on his face, laughing. I lay there ashamed and afraid to race for my clothes, while he just turned, still laughing, and strode up the drive trailing a loud "Ho, Ho" behind him in the air.

Two or three times that winter, Jimmy and Susan Loeb, Marjorie's children by Harold Loeb, came for visits. They were both at the University of Chicago, he in "another freshman year," he once joked. He was full of cheer. Susan, a year or so younger, was a tall and slim girl with striking, sharp and delicate features. She was intensely serious. She adopted me as a younger brother and I was flattered by her care. Jimmy got along well with everyone, but Susan seemed reserved around Jean, respectful, but modest and unassuming. Mother Latimer, Argie's grandmother, also visited, and I was struck by the softness of her almost purplish white hair. She was gentle and quiet, and spent a lot of time with Argie. I assumed at first that she was "Mother Lavender," a name that perfectly fit the impression she made on me.

There was always something happening at the Mill House, and I can't remember either Argie or myself complaining of boredom. There were projects afoot and constant talk. There were frequent visitors, mostly artists like Wharton Esherick, several small gatherings, but nothing resembling gala parties. In the evening, Jean would go to the kitchen pantry where the beverages were stored and take out a bottle of wine or beer. I remember so well the smell of his mixture of ale and stout, just one glass before bedtime. For me, odors of food became markers of events and ideas. One day, in late fall I think, while we were all at the kitchen table eating a lunch of lentils and frankfurter slices, two hunters stopped at the kitchen door to offer some of their catch, two or three game birds, as payment for permission to hunt on the land. I associated the smell and taste of the lunch with the colorful birds; but, when we had them for supper a day or so later, I couldn't distinguish any particular taste to them, aside from the unpleasant shock of biting on buckshot. At Christmas, we had a goose with thick fat.

Suppertime at the kitchen table was a time for talk. Arge and I were not expected to start conversations, but to be alert to questions posed. We broke the rule all the time, of course, but order was always restored with humor. I earned the name Fidget most often at the table. Once when I was asked about a book I was reading, I summarized the story of a Highland boy with a name like Angus McIntosh who had to master two skills. First, he had to learn to sit absolutely still while waiting on the heath for deer or rabbits to approach close enough to catch; second, he had to learn to control his breath to play the bagpipe. Jean approved of the boy's education, and I too hastily said that it shouldn't be too hard to sit still on a heath. Poppy gently challenged me to back my chair up to the wall behind me and remain absolutely still for five minutes. He promised me a nickle if I succeeded, and gave me a hint of how to do it. "Think about one thing, but think about it in a way that will not distract you from what is going on at the table. Listen to what we say while you think about something else— let's say, about how a Turkestani bandit divides his attention between his own bodily functions and the vastness of space before him as he sits motionless on a grassy knoll on a plain where he can see and be seen for miles. He will be seen as a rock by a caravan miles away, but if he even twitches an eye he will frighten off his prey and live hungry for another month. What does he think of for hours while the caravan inches across the steppes toward him? More important, think how he breathes, for time is in one's breath, and breath controls thought and speech." This last remark intrigued me and, as I sat there I became nervously aware of my breathing patterns and the itch at the edge of my nose. I'm sure I lost the challenge, but I did experience a strange new sense of detachment from the rest of the family, as if I were not there at all.

I mentioned this to Jean a day or so later, and he said in a very serious tone that I had learned something important and should work on detachment, from my fidgeting particularly, but from myself as I see myself from day to day. "That Turkestani bandit is able to leave himself completely, even watch himself watching the caravan route; and then he joins his body again at precisely the instant he must move to attack. You see, he has learned how to become *part* of the terrain, not just an object *on* it. Try this exercise: Look at yourself in the mirror," he continued, "until you no longer see any feature of the face before you. When your image leaves you and becomes part of the mirror, only then will you see something deeper in you that your fidgeting hides. When you sit at the table, as you did so badly the other night, join the space of the chair, and then you'll see that you'll be able to control the space it and you occupy. Try the same thing with words. Repeat a single word until it is but a sound without sense, and then you will begin to sense the range of potential meaning in it, and gain power over it. Do the same with breathing and you will see why Angus had to learn to control his breath. Think of breathing as a function you control by thought and will, and see how hard the very process of breathing will become for you in a very short while. Make it hard, and imagine that if you stop willing yourself to breathe, you will stop breathing. Then slow down your breathing until you take only three breaths a minute. Take these three breaths for six minutes and then forget your control. Then come and tell me after a while what happens."

We ate well at Mill House. Our diet was nutritious, with lots of soups and vegetables and cheeses, though there were some things I did not appreciate at the time. We had okra soup at least once a week, made with okra grown along with herbs and tomatoes in the little garden just above the kitchen. There was no question of not eating anything served us, but I did express something less than pleasure at seeing my okra soup one day, and Jean quite calmly challenged me to explain what I did not like about it. I said that it was "slimy" and the skin was rough. "Hmmm," he replied thoughfully, paused, and then said, "but let's pretend that these are the two things you like most about it. How would you tell me why you like the *slimy* pulp?" I said I didn't know, and then he advised me to think carefully each time I particularly liked or disliked anything and to practice the opposite feeling. The exercise, he said, is not much different from looking in the mirror, or hearing the same word over and over, because all of these exercises can reveal a deeper understanding of yourself and the thing before you.

Every meal, like every game, was an occasion for observation. Jean even taught me the art of cracking walnuts, not just to preserve the halves of the nutmeat intact, but also to admire the shell. "Everything has uses that one can discover," he said, as after supper one evening he showed me how to drip wax into the bottom of a shell, place a match stick in the molten wax, and then attach a small paper sail to it. In this way, I made an armada for the bathtub, and Argie and I threw out our foul-smelling celluloid fish and boats.

The bread was homemade, and there were always lots of crisp, broad, flat crackers that we ate with local cheeses. We ate lots of corn products, barley, and rye. I do not remember many meats besides the chicken and the squab that were our own farm products. Marjorie was a good cook and made no concessions to Argie and myself. I do not remember eating anything not prepared for the whole family, except on those occasions when there were guests and the adults ate in the dining room while Argie and I stayed out of the way, playing in our room or listening to the radio downstairs in the front sitting room.

I liked the other sitting room to the left of the entrance hall that was really Marjorie's library, sewing room, and workshop. It had a desk and lamp and a single couch-bed laden with Navajo rugs against the interior wall, under suspended book shelves. On the window ledges and floor were always piles of work materials, mostly textiles. Right over this room, on the second floor, was Jean's study, at the end of a narrow gallery whose wall was lined with books. I rarely went in there, but I remember how bright it was, with windows on three sides. There was a narrow extension of that gallery under a window at the front of the house that led to his and Marjorie's bedroom. Only when the door was standing open did I ever see anything of that room.

Visitors were received in the small sitting room where Poppy napped. There was a fireplace on the east wall, separated only by a small window from the dining room entry and step. It was a small room, made even smaller by Mickey's presence on the scatter rug in front of the fireplace and Jean's chair beside it; but there were rarely many people in it. On the left of Jean's chair was another leather chair where Argie and I often sat together to listen to the radio that was on a small end table by the entry from the front hall. On the wall that separated the room from the front stairs was a simple couch with cushions, and another on the wall separating the room from the dining room. This was Jean's napping couch. Larger and more formal gatherings took place around Wharton's table in the dining room, or on the lawn on the west side of the house.

Marjorie and I did not always get along well and, many years later, after Jean's death, she and I exchanged stories about the way we treated one another in those days. She commanded the house and set little domestic chores for Argie and myself, surveyed our every-other-day baths, took care of the kitchen, sometimes alone, but usually with one or two women who helped with the cleaning and washing. They were usually recruited by Lin from neighboring towns like Washington, where one girl, named May, lived. Marjorie administered our discipline and monitored our school work. She had extraordinary energy and resources.[7] I felt later that she had resented something of my adoration for Jean. For me, he was a father; but Marjorie was only a replacement for a mother I missed terribly. From her point of view, I was undisciplined and insubordinate.[8]

Our relations came to a crisis just before Christmas of 1938, three weeks shy of my 8th birthday, when I came home from school and told Marjorie that she had to make me a white cape with blue trim for the Christmas pageant. She looked at me stonily and replied, "I don't *have* to do anything of the kind," and turned away to her tasks. The pageant was only two weeks away, and I was confused and sad. Marjorie worked on

---

[7]   According to Kerman and Eldridge, she was pregnant when I went to live at West 10th Street, and so I must have been an extra burden to her. She lost the child in the winter of 1938. Susan Sandberg told me, August 2, 1996, that she did not know herself that her mother had been pregnant.

[8]   My presence with the Toomers in both New York and the Mill House was a nightmare for Marjorie, who saw in me a sort of grotesque caricature of her husband, displaying what she felt the worst of his traits, an ego which related everything to self. Awaiting my mother's arrival to pick me up, she wrote Susan that Argie will miss me, but "I shall not weep."

whatever Argie needed for her part, but ignored me, and I didn't know what to do. Finally, I had the courage to go to Jean, as he sat in his chair in the front sitting room with Mickey on the scatter rug before him, and explained what I had said and what she had responded.

"Hmmm," he nodded gravely, held his head slightly bowed as he so often did when thinking seriously, then gave me a stern lecture: "Boy, she is absolutely right. She is not *obliged* to do anything for you or even for Arge. No one likes to perform tasks under compulsion. Marjorie *wants* to do things not just *for* you, but *with* you, but she knows that to do the best for you, you have to show her that you know how to do the best for yourself. This way, both she and you will be working together. Only a slave works alone, and consequently works badly. You spoke to her without *thinking* what you were saying, but, more importantly, without *knowing* what you were saying. It isn't only the words you used, but the spirit in them to which Marjorie reacted. She felt what was underneath them, their spirit, or rather lack of spirit. You gave her empty words, like the empty command to a slave whose only force is the power behind it but not the reason *in* it. Go and ask her in what way you can work *with* her to get the costume made, and tell her what you will be doing with it in the play." It was not easy to do so, but I did. Marjorie smiled and said, "of course." While I was still with her in her work room, she measured me, took an old sheet, cut it to size, and sewed a neat blue border onto it. It was beautiful, and I felt proud of her.

For Easter, Arge and I wrote a skit to present to the whole family. Susan was home, and Lin and Don would be there. With Argie's play typewriter—consisting of a typewheel that one had to press for each letter individually, I composed a two-page script that took Argie and myself about ten minutes to rehearse. We prepared a little stage in the mill by the bottom of the stairs and found chairs and stools for our select audience. As usual, Poppy showed interest in our preparations and repeatedly reminded us that he expected some worthwhile entertainment. Neither Argie nor I fully appreciated our responsibility, but were happy to be the center of attention for a while. When the crowd was assembled and someone called for attention, we started our lines. My story was not really inspired. Argie played the part of a little girl who wanted a rabbit for Easter, and I was her boyfriend who promised it to her; but on Easter day it was not there. Disappointed, she began to cry. I said that she'd have to look for it; and there it was, just under the stairs beside the audience. I proclaimed the end of our all-of-three-minute drama, to which Marjorie gave a long quizzical look. Poppy rose to calm a disappointed gathering, saying: "Well, I think we have a little work to do."

He took us half-way up the stairs, and said: "I think you two need to work a bit more on this. I have some trouble understanding what this play of yours is about, and I don't think anyone else does either. Listen, when you present something like this to others, make sure that you are giving them something that they do not have in their own experience. Give them something particular to yours. Drama should expand the visions of others. Now, go back and finish the play."

Well, Argie and I ended up going back before our select audience and singing our school song to the music of "Alexander's Ragtime Band," concluding with:

We can play a soccer game,
that is always full of fun;
We've never lost a game
And we've always won.
We are the best school what am, Buckingham.

The audience applauded, politely. Poppy grinned from ear to ear, but I knew I had failed him.

For Easter, Argie and I were each given large chocolate rabbits, about a foot high from ear to tail and hollow inside. We went under the willow tree where the boughs formed a bower and ate our gifts without even being disturbed by Nina, who was with her brood of pups over at Ramsey's farm. After a while, I felt sick, and I'm sure Argie was not feeling well either. We couldn't look at our supper that evening and Poppy took the occasion to mock me, saying not only that my eyes were bigger than my stomach, but that I had lost sight of the different appetites within me, each of which had particular functions to perform for my body. "Which of your centers gave up control?" he teased me. I could say no more than that Argie and I wanted to eat the chocolate. "What is it to want something? Was it your stomach alone that wanted?" he asked with a smile.

Whenever I did something stupid, Poppy would challenge me to identify which "center" of my being had "forfeited" its control. "You know," he once said, "I can live with any of your selves, but you have to learn to live with them too. Whatever being you want to be is no problem for me, if you can harmonize its partnership with the others. Be as many things as your imagination yearns for, but beware of getting lost in any one of them alone."

I complained to Poppy once that Argie spit in the tub during one of our baths—one of her favorite ways of getting back at me for some cruelty of mine. He looked sternly at me and reminded me of control. "That word doesn't only mean self-control, but it refers to your control with others. You have to keep not only yourself awake to things, but you have to keep others around you on their toes, cautious of their own balance; and if you are in balance yourself, they'll reach for you to help you and not to hurt you. Use other people as an alarm clock to wake you to things. Then, if you fall asleep, they will wake you; and when they sleep, you will wake them."

In late June of 1939, my mother came down to the Mill House to take me to Westport, CT, where she had moved with an associate at W. J. Sloane's.[9] She negotiated with Lin on the spot to buy one of Nina's puppies for five dollars. I wanted Smokey, but mother and Lin decided on "Bucky," Smokey's pitch-black brother who looked enough like a Belgian police dog to take a blue ribbon two years later at the Longshore Country Club Dog Show. We drove back through New York City and into the country. When we reached the sign, "This is Westport on the Merritt Parkway," the Mill House had passed out of my mind and, within weeks, the Toomers had themselves left for India.

---

[9] In Marjorie Content's letters in the Toomer Collection at the Beinecke, I discovered one contributing factor which made my presence in the Toomer household less justified. When Gurdjieff came to New York City in the spring of 1939, Jean took a vacation alone to Bermuda to get out of harm's way. On April 29, Marjorie wrote to Jean there, noting that Fred Leighton and Edith had been in New York working for Gurdjieff, a situation which would have been felt by Jean as moral treason. On May 1, Edith came down to Doylestown to see about registering me for school the following year along with Arge, and Marjorie wrote Jean to say that she was going to "disillusion" her. It is understandable that she was reluctant to continue a favor to someone who had knowingly acted against her husband's wishes, and both Jean and Marjorie may have thought that Edith persuaded Fred to join her with Gurdjieff. Jean had projected a trip to India as early as October 1937, just after I moved in with him. At that time, he wrote a letter to a contact in India asking about appropriate schools for Argie, mentioning that he might be there within a year. It wasn't until after the Bermuda vacation in 1939 that he finally decided to go ahead. Kerman and Eldridge speak of this vacation as a "rest cure" (*The Lives of Jean Toomer*, p. 42), but mother told me years later that he didn't want to "be on the same soil as Gurdjieff." For Toomer, this period marked the end of his relations with Gurdjieff. A letter of Marjorie Content to her daughter Susan (see chapter 5) explains deeper reasons for the trip.

Chapter Three

Growing with Toomer

I am of no particular race. I am of the human race,
a man at large in the human world, preparing a new race.
                                                —*Essentials*

Surely there are such sights
In the many-colored world,
Or in the mind.
The strange thing is that
These people never see themselves
Or you, or me.
                                                —"People"

I left Mill House secure and happy, sure in my ties to Jean as a father, touchstone, and foundation. His were values which I would emulate and guard as moral and intellectual underpinnings. I had been a very unhappy and insecure child at age 5, in 1936, and my mother had been desperate in her search to find someone to take care of me when Jean Toomer came to her rescue. He was the only father I had ever known, and I knew love by loving him. He never for a moment put my trust in him in doubt. And yet, since I left Mill House, I have wondered more than once exactly what I was doing there in the first place. My mother spoke of Toomer as a treasured friend she had known for many years. She always referred to Marjorie, on the other hand, in neutral tones as "Marjorie Content." Marjorie herself had hardly, if ever, mentioned my mother at all, but had let me feel that she thought Edith a bit frivolous. My mother once explained that Jean had taken me into his house as a companion for Argie, but that didn't answer the question of why Marjorie accepted me, and I wondered, quite naturally, why my mother should ship me off to a stranger for *his* convenience. I reasoned that she was in no position to take care of her children at that time, and let the matter drop. After all, my sister and I had been sent to a number of homes to live after our arrival in the United States. The summer before my mother brought me to New York City, I had stayed with Thelma Wood in Sandy Hook, CT, but I was all alone there with no friends and no one to look after me except a soft-spoken valet. Thelma Wood was a lovely woman known for her various love affairs in Paris in the circles of Djuna Barnes and Natalie Barney. She and my mother had a brief love affair in Paris in the 20s, and they continued to be friends. To me, she was stern and intolerant. To keep me out of mischief, she assigned me tasks like tying twigs into fireplace-size bundles. And she took exception to the way I played with her collection of lead soldiers. Almost ten years later, when Thelma and my mother went into business together selling herbs and exotic foods, Thelma told me, with a wry smile, that she had thought of setting up a household with my mother and herself. The business failed and, after mutual recriminations, the friendship faltered.

My two years of living with the Toomers in New York and in Doylestown had left an indelible mark on my character, but I found myself quickly lost and confused outside of the Mill House and Buckingham Friends environment. I had left Jean after two years, comfortable with myself, confident in myself, and eagerly anticipating a new life with my sister and mother in the vision of Westport I had made in my hopes from my mother's encouraging description. Unfortunately, few of the things I had taken for granted in Doylestown were available in Westport. My self-confidence was ill founded, for, although Jean and Buckingham Friends had stimulated my thought and my imagination, I was ill prepared emotionally and socially for what awaited me in Westport. Where I had nothing to fear physically in Lahaska except an occasional stray kick from Guvner Cadwallader's riding boots, I found myself a handy punching bag in the rough and tumble of public school playgrounds, a target for the boys who wanted an easy and amusing tussle at recess. The teachers seemed distant and unconcerned, and the principal an insensitive tyrant. In short, I was a misfit and, instead of trying to fit in, I aggravated the situation by distancing myself from my peers even more. Though I showed up for scheduled fights, and even made truces with some of my antagonists, I was a "case." I rebelled against schoolwork by simply scribbling instead of writing and by answering questions with an air of being from another world. I had heard Jean's lessons, but I could not use them in this strange world.

Things were hardly better at home. My mother was playing housewife to her companion, and my sister and I were an uneasy audience to their quarrels. Since my only previous family life had been with the Toomers, I took to making comparisons between Marjorie's and my mother's ways of doing things. She took all of this as unflattering criticism. She had never had to manage children before and found it difficult to know how to mediate between my sister and myself, who were strangers to one another to begin with. In short, the absence of father and brother figures like Jean and Lin became more and more crucial in my adjustment to a different sort of domestic and social environment. On the other hand, my sister had come from a difficult experience where she had been boarded and schooled, and found Westport a decided improvement in her life. If she was sensitive to our psychological plights, she seemed untouched by them.

For my part, I still thought of Argie as a sister, because we had shared so many things and so many happy moments together, so much mischief around the property, and most of all a complicity of affection for Poppy. Even now, after seeing so little of each other over the past thirty years, we share a recollection and affection unmatched by any of my other youthful relationships. In the first weeks of our separation, I received postcards from Argie in India with scenes of a Bombay boy button seller, an elephant dragging tree trunks, and others that my mother later threw out. Just before Christmas of 1939, I received a box with an Indian bell and a small teak elephant with tiny ivory tusks and eyes.

My mother moved about Fairfield County society as if she were one of the wealthy emigrés who had settled there and who continued to settle during World War II. She joined a number of various war-relief groups, such as Friends of France and Bundles from Britain (assigning housing to children evacuated from English cities), and was prominent for a while in civic activities such as the Women's Club. At home, her standards of reference were stubbornly faithful to the artistic life she had lived in Paris and to the life of ideas she had known at the Prieuré. Within a very short time, I began to seize upon her stories of the good old days in order to fabricate a new past for myself. I began, that is, to invent stories of my background and about my own social and intellectual status. My school mates mocked me, my teachers scorned me, and, as time passed, I became more adamant in insisting upon my difference from, and even a superiority over, my peers.

School officials contacted my mother at the end of January of 1940 to discuss my discipline at school. She was lost, and was forced to face the choice of psychiatric counseling, transferring me to another school, or having me put back two grades. In March, she finally told me this and I was terrified into applying myself enough in my math and English lessons to make my teachers feel that I could be promoted to the fifth grade. I discovered that she had consulted Jean for advice, a practice that she would continue until the 50s, not only concerning her problems with me but for all of her own personal problems. On this occasion, she had questioned Jean about the cause and treatment of the stories I was inventing. Jean told me a few years later that he had turned the question back upon her, telling her to analyze the stories in terms of her personal relations with me. My fictions in school, he had said, are not as important as hers to me at home.

My mother listened, but retreated all the deeper into a world of her own where she felt comfortable and important. In a way, though she continued to influence my social conceptions with constant reference to her own past, she never found, or perhaps never sought, a way to move herself closer to the immediate needs of either my sister or myself. Within a year or so, I began to write to Jean myself and, whenever I did, I quickly received in response a long and thoughtful letter written in a small neat hand on yellow drawing paper and signed "Poppy."

Sometime in 1940, I read *A Fiction and Some Facts*, Jean's brief declaration of identity, or rather, a declaration to refuse racial identification. I can date the pamphlet confidently because I had started to teach myself Morse code and, too lazy to search out paper, wrote it out on the end papers of this seven-page manifesto, printed privately in early 1940 in response to local gossip among his Bucks County neighbors about his racial background.[1] I was confused by the issue at stake, because I had not and could not distinguish Jean's "color." I suppose that, at the time, I had not been conscious of the term "Negro" except in magazines or newspapers, but the tone of Jean's declaration was thinly disguised anger. "This story, this trumped up ghost,"[2] it began. Only years later, after reading biographical

---

[1] When I saw the pamphlet, it had just arrived for my mother from Jean, and it lay on her reading table in the living room, where I appropriated it for my use. I cannot imagine a reason why he would wait to send it to her three years after printing. My mother added the date "1940" in pencil on the title page. Kerman and Eldridge (*The Lives of Jean Toomer* (Baton Rouge, LA: Louisiana State University Press, 1987, p. 31), citing interviews with Marjorie Content, date the composition in 1937, but it would seem unlikely for Jean to distribute such a statement in Bucks County before he had even taken up permanent residence there. It was in his early contacts with the Friends and with his daughter's school that the issue of his race began to be raised. The opening of his statement—"Well, it comes into the half-light again, this story, this trumped up ghost"—alludes quite clearly to the persecution of Margery Latimer a decade earlier. This polemical *apologia* contains a very equivocal statement of his racial identity: "I am not prepared to state as fact that there was, or that there was not, some Negro or Indian blood in the family" (*A Fiction and Some Facts*, p. 4). It is hard to imagine the kinds of social and moral pressure weighing on him that would force him to such a defensive position. He goes on to say that he has not claimed or disclaimed having Negro blood (*A Fiction and Some Facts*, p. 5), which is fairer, and concludes with a call for respect for his life (*A Fiction and Some Facts*, p. 7). Bucks County was not, perhaps a very welcoming community to Jews and blacks, and it is even possible that Marjorie had suffered some reproach on her husband's behalf, since she had tried to dissuade Jean from publishing the pamphlet (Kerman and Eldridge, *The Lives of Jean Toomer*, p. 231). Perhaps in 1939 he was reacting to Quaker questions about his background, questions that he felt posed a threat to his daughter's security. For a discussion of Toomer's carefully-worded responses to those who asked of his racial identity, see Byrd, *Toomer's Years with Gurdjieff*, pp. 56–57.

[2] *A Fiction and Some Facts*, p. 3.

accounts of Jean, did I begin to understand something of the complexity of the situation he had put himself in, not just for the color of his skin—for the beauty of blackness in *Cane* is paramount—but for the refusal of his neighbors to look past skin color to the spectrum of character.

Jean Toomer said repeatedly that color doesn't matter. It is a wrapping of being, but not its substance or essence. But, color *did* matter for Toomer, despite his efforts to neutralize the issue. "He passed" was a remark I heard later, even in the mouths of those who admired Jean. From an opposite perspective, it is more accurate to say that Jean Toomer was a white who "passed" for black in the deep South.[3] I've never heard of a black who denied Jean's right to claim black blood, though many whites denied him the right, despite his appearance, to "pass" as a white. The careful research of Kerman and Eldridge discloses an African blood strain in Jean of between 6 and 12 percent. I, who couldn't measure blackness or whiteness on either a social or a biological scale, used to ask critics of Toomer's "passing" if, upon entering a hotel, he should announce to the clerk that he wasn't eligible to be given a room because of a color that others could not see. I never received answers, just stony stares.

This may seem like a flippant and dilatory consideration, but between the mid-30s and mid-50s when I knew Toomer well, he was constantly plagued by the color issue. He wasn't blamed for denying his blood, but for not declaring it.[4] He told Gurdjieff that he was classified as a Negro, though Gurdjieff, who probably had as much if not more exotic blood in him, had never asked him to identify his blood. Gurdjieff "read" something of Jean's "African" essence in him, as Toomer himself relates in his autobiographical writings, and that pleased Jean, because it wasn't color that Gurdjieff had read, but a value beneath it—the same value, undoubtedly, that Toomer associated with the Afro-American community in Sparta, GA, that he had joined briefly in 1921.

---

[3] In *The Voice*, 15 May 1990, Roby Selman writes: "Shortly after I published an essay on the Harlem Renaissance poet Jean Toomer, I received my first piece of hate mail. A Group in Madison, Wisconsin, attacked the editors for allowing me to review the work of a white poet whom 'guilt-ridden negroes' like me were trying to kidnap for their own depraved history." Selman is Jewish.

[4] Most recently, Byrd (*Toomer's Years with Gurdjieff*, pp. 58–60) shows how Toomer sought to have his blood identified in other than racial terms. Further, as Richard Wright has said: "Black Literature" exists only because of white racism; remove the latter and the former disappears" (cited by Henry Louis Gates, Jr., "Introduction," "Tell me Sir . . . What is 'Black Literature?'" *PMLA* 105 (1990), p. 20). Charles T. Davis, ("Jean Toomer and the South: Region and Race as Elements Within a Literary Imagination," *Studies in the Literary Imagination* 7 (1974), p. 27) says that "Toomer chose to be black" when he went south. "It was not something that he had to accept because he was trapped, as many Americans were, by history or family or caste or race." In other words, Toomer chose the "nature" of his being in service of his literary imagination.

When Jean and his family moved to Bucks County, the locals accepted him without question as another urbanite moving into the country. When rumors started circulating that he was "colored," people began to notice a color, took note of racial characteristics, and, in some cases, even invented them to fit conventional readings of racial stamp.When I read the Kerman and Eldridge biography of Toomer, I was struck by accounts neighbors near Doylestown gave of their first sight of Jean at the time I was joining his family. The difference between their informed views and my child's perspective shocked me. One retrospective eye-witness view of him when he first moved to Mechanicsville, PA, recalled: "I thought when I saw him he must have been from either Ethiopia or India. He was narrow, and tall, and black-haired, and walked rather slowly, pondering as he went, meditating, I should say. He always wore a white leather jacket and a black hat, and generally he had on beautiful, what we call Santa Fe trousers that were creamy whipcord trousers—the luxury pants of a cowboy; and he had a black and white coach dog."[5]

Although the informant was a friend and admirer of Jean's over a period of many years, her testimony suggests that he was exotic, perhaps even out of place. So was his wife Marjorie, if one were forced to make a snap judgment from outward appearance only, and this is confirmed by the same informant's recollection of her. She was "intrigued with Marjorie's colorful long skirts and distinctive carriage, judging her a gem in a conservative town."[6] Marjorie *was* a gem, exotic as much in her kitchen as in public, with her long Indian skirts and bright silver and turquoise jewelry. With her short body, broad hips, dark complexion, and slightly bowed nose she looked more like a Tiwa squaw from Taos than a suburban Bucks County housewife. What makes these two descriptions contradictory is the suggestion that Marjorie's exotic appearance was inviting, while Jean's was alien, strange. Why? Because he was black.

Though my retrospective view is biased, I would say that the description here seems somewhat invented, or perhaps "enhanced," to accord with an interviewer's expectations. I say this only because neither I nor Toomer's daughter can recognize Jean in this description. It is obvious that Toomer was hard to read, though a detective of fashion might pierce the mystery of the sartorial details if not of the man. I walked these rural roads with Jean often, precisely in those days just after he and Marjorie took up residence in the "Mill House." I have tried to rediscover something distinctive in my own visual image of him then, but I was too young

---

5   Interview with Dorothy Paxson on 24 January 1975, reported in Kerman and Eldridge, *The Lives of Jean Toomer*, p. 227–228.
6   Kerman and Eldridge, *The Lives of Jean Toomer*, p. 238.

a boy to have cultural models against which to measure the view I had of that tall man who moved so smoothly and effortlessly over straw-stubble fields and high-grassed hills, along worn and rutted tractor tracks.[7] That image resembles nothing I have known before or since, either in dress, deep reflection, stooped glide, or lean and yet soft body that seemed to contain a reservoir of power whose only gauge for me was the extraordinary register of a voice. I have carried untutored images of him for almost sixty years without feeling that they might someday grapple with other "truths." But can one undo the hammerlock of the first impressions of another, seen or read?

We have, in this testimony, a mysterious mosaic made up of incongruous parts, one whose figure suggests a past in India or Ethiopia and whose present array suggests a mixture of luxury cowboy from the New Mexican highlands, a Bucks County country esquire, and a slow-stepping thinker. Such a testimony might be read as a concern about the direction the neighborhood is going. Take his clothes, to begin with. Clearly, Toomer is described as over-dressed for the occasion,[8] but next to Marjorie he seemed to me negligent and disheveled in his baggy trousers, rumpled shirt, unpolished shoes, and unkempt hair hanging out from under a battered brown hat.

Clothing is, perhaps, a minor detail, but I do recall a long-haired, white wool, belted jacket with a blue and brown patterned band across the chest that he wore often and proudly. In my closet now hangs the tattered brown tweed Norfolk jacket that he wore outside on balmy fall and spring

---

[7] The single detail in this portrait that points most obviously to social pretension is the "black and white coach dog." Now, while coach dogs tend in period novels to be Dalmatians, Dalmatians are not coach dogs unless they run along with coach horses and their carriages. Jean was driving only a beat-up old Ford station wagon that no self-respecting coach dog would permit himself to be seen in or beside. It may be that many people call Dalmatians coach dogs as a matter of local convention, but in this context of Toomer's motley attire, the identification, intentionally or no, makes Toomer look socially presumptuous, like an upstart or arriviste. Actually, when I took walks with Jean, besides an occasional curious farm dog trailing along for a field or so, the dog that accompanied Jean regularly from the time he moved into the Mill House was the mongrel Mickey, succeeded in the 40s by his son Smokey, whose mother was the German shepherd Nina, and in the 50s by Mickey's grandson Whitty, short for Whittituck. The Dalmatian, Margot Latimer reminds me, was Skippy, Susan Loeb's dog that the Toomers took with them on their earlier trips to the Mill House.

[8] Kerman and Eldridge quote Toomer in 1930–1931, saying: "All my life I have dressed well, in fact, have looked like a million dollars" (*The Lives of Jean Toomer*, p. 185). If this were so before 1931, this was certainly not the case after. No photo in the book of Toomer from this time or later displays anything of sartorial splendor. Besides, it is easy enough for me to imagine this statement uttered in a whimsical tone inaudible in the printed word.

days, but more usually inside instead of sweaters, whose feel made him uncomfortable. In the winter of 1938–1939, he preferred a thick wool white-and-black jacket when it wasn't raining. The cowboy luxury trousers say nothing to me, but then I can't tell Santa Fe from Sears and Roebuck in trouser cut; and what kind of cowboys hang around the Governor's Palace in Santa Fe? To me, Jean's trousers seemed more often to be loose, baggy affairs, fit for the kind of lounging and working he did around the farm. His crumpled felt Knox hat was in sad need of reblocking. His shoes were, apparently, out of sight in the low grass. And they weren't Fred Leighton cowboy boots, mind you, but what we used to call clodhoppers, ankle-bone-high, leather, thick-soled shoes of incomparable comfort and durability. In general, neither my own photos nor those I've seen of Marjorie Content do honor to Jean's sartorial splendor. As far as the view of his color and general racial features, he had nothing of the form of Mahatma Gandhi or Haile Selassie that might suggest he was Indian or Ethiopian, despite the moustache and the hat shading his face. In this case, silence and distance between an eye and the sight of Jean Toomer on the landscape instilled mystery and suspicion. Biographical "facts" pass ineluctably through an ideological screen that projects an abstract form of a person which fits in a dialectical design.

Perhaps the color issue in relation to Toomer has faded in importance as his novel *Cane* has gained in esteem, distinct from the biographical accounts of its author. But it is hard for me not to feel that the consensus on Toomer's attitude toward his own ethnic origins, whatever they really were, is unnecessarily slanted, unjust, and, to some extent, mistaken. I conjure up here what Toomer called the "trumped up ghost," to offer a view of Toomer's life-long struggle—one that deeply touched his work— to reconcile his liberating vision of self with the restricted vision others had, or wanted to have, of him. Toomer himself was impatient with epithets unearned or unexperienced. Perhaps that is why he took such pleasure in the game of giving and attracting nicknames. Gurdjieff too gave descriptive names to all those who entered his school, and he tested his pupils' self-perception by challenging them to name themselves. I remember Jean saying once to me that tags of identity are liable to exclude others, while one's own pride of entity includes all others.

Toomer says, in *A Fiction and Some Facts*, that his blood had strains of Welsh, German, English, and Native American, as well as Negro. He saw no reason to claim any of these to the exclusion of the others and, to the outward sight of others, he was not clearly one or the other. Toomer's communal identity was American, and his vocational identity was an artist. I would argue that, for the thirty years I knew him, Toomer lived with *no* color. His skin had no relevance to his being, and so he refused, with honest directness, to submit to the claims upon a racial identity which others would have skin color represent.[9] We would call Toomer "black" to enlist him in the ranks of the cultural war of the races, even if he didn't look black and even if he dissociated the cultural confrontation in his writing from his own personal experience.

Experience, and not blood, he argued, makes one's being. He moved from one experience to another, and would not have "blood" determine his direction. In distant retrospect, I can regret that he did not indulge himself further in the experience that shaped *Cane*, but it is clear that Toomer refused to force another experience of the same kind in order to write in the same mode.[10] I regret more that his directions, first toward Gurdjieff and then toward the Society of Friends, failed to inform his writing with the power and beauty one experiences in *Cane*. No matter such regrets. Toomer knew his options for moving across racial, social, cultural, and intellectual boundaries. He indulged happily in the roles each new territory demanded of him, and he had a facility for drawing value out of each context he moved into. The context of *Cane* was not any more "native" to Toomer, in his view, than the context of *Portage Potential*. Both were as "natural" to him as the respective landscapes of the Prieuré and Bucks County.

Call him hybrid or mestizo if you will, but it was others—whites during his lifetime—who insisted on attaching him to a single cultural and racial matrix. His refusal to be bound to a color in the spectrum of humanity was not meant as disrespect to any one formative force, but as a respect for all informing agencies of culture. The intensity of love Toomer had for the world could not be restricted to a single direction. James Baldwin speaks for Toomer as well as for himself when he says that "white people in this country will have quite enough to do in learning how to accept and love themselves and each other, and when they have achieved this—which will

---

[9] The history of this issue in Toomer's life is long and complex. Toomer's *A Fiction and Some Facts* is dedicated to the problem. Darwin T. Turner, editor of Toomer's *The Wayward and the Seeking*, cites Toomer earlier expressing his frustration at being accused of denying his race (Washington D.C.: Howard University Press, 1980), pp. 132–133.

[10] I question Rampersad's statement that to build upon the success of *Cane*, "Jean Toomer would have had to emphasize his links to black culture. This he was not prepared to do. Nonetheless, his links to black culture were weak until the Georgia experience, and Jean was uncertain about the success of *Cane* very soon after its publication." I think Rampersad is closer to the truth when he says that "he had no staying power as an artist. Writing was always uphill work for him" (Arnold Rampersad, "His Own Best Disciple," *New York Times Book Review*, Aug. 30, 1987, pp. 7–9).

not be tomorrow and may well be never—the Negro problem will no longer exist, for it will no longer be needed."[11] In his autobiography, Langston Hughes echoes this cry when he says of himself: "I am not black . . . here in the United States the word 'Negro' is used to mean anyone who has *any* Negro blood at all in his veins. In Africa, the word is more pure. It means *all* Negro, therefore, *black*."[12]

These considerations were confirmed for me when I found in the Toomer papers evidence of his long struggle to tackle the Negro problem head-on. Even before *Cane*, as he was about to leave for a trip to Mississippi, Toomer wrote with force about racial hatred in response to a letter asking him about Southern social views.[13] After the publication of *Cane*, in reply to a request for information about "race, social, art" from the editor of *Prairie*, in Milwaukee, Toomer wrote: "Racially, my bloods are mixed to the extent that it is stupid and absurd to call me anything other than an American. And yet, American is still too loose a term . . . it cannot be used for racial definition. . . . My bloods are black and white. . . . When I live with the blacks I'm a Negro. When I live with the whites, I am white, or, better, a foreigner. My concern is with the art of literature. Call me what you like." In the same letter, Toomer goes on to speak of early literary influences on him, notably Victor Hugo, and then explains the making of *Cane*:

> I went south to Georgia, and there, beneath the mask of black and white life, deeply touched by the old folk-songs, something happened to me. It was one of the revelations, a particularly appropriate disclosure to which the gods at some moment treat the artist unless they happen too perversely to conspire against him, which Henry James writes about. Whatever stuff of any consequence I have done, dates from that trip (the fall of 1921).[14]

In 1930, Toomer wrote with angry impatience to correct his identification as a Negro by Suzanne La Follette, the editor of *The New Prairie*: "The fact that I am not a Negro is a negative, and not of main importance. I am chiefly concerned with the positive which is a positive above the hypnotic divisions of Americans into white and black. (The hypnosis has such a

[11] James Baldwin, *The Fire Next Time* (London: Michael Joseph, 1963), p. 33.

[12] Langston Hughes, *The Big Seas: An Autobiography* (New York: Hill and Wang, 1963), p. 11.

[13] Toomer Collection, The Beinecke Rare Book and Manuscript Library, Yale University, Box 8.

[14] Toomer Collection, Box 6, Folder 211.

hold on us that even our literary men are taken in by it, and literature, which should be on the plane of art and intelligence, becomes an unwitting agent in fostering fictions and absurdities.) I feel that this positive has importance not only for me, but for the people of this country who have been tugging futilely at the racial bone these many years."[15]

In this context, Toomer's "I am not a Negro" is not a denial of blood, but a denial of a prejudicial and dilatory racial tag. I can find no record of Toomer ever telling someone he was German, English, Welsh, or even "white" in opposition to "black." A year later, to the Chief Librarian of the Negro Division of the 135th Street branch of the New York Public Library (was there an "Anglo-Saxon" division?), Toomer wrote: "This is in reply to your kind letter concerning a gift copy of *Essentials* to your division of the library. In *Essentials* there is a line that reads: 'I am of no particular race. I am of the human race, a man at large in the human world, preparing a new race.'

"This is an accurate statement of my position as regards race, I am dissociating my name and self from racial classifications as I believe that the real values of life necessitates it. This is my stand, not only for myself but for all Americans and for people in general."[16]

In February 1932, Toomer wrote Nancy Cunard, the editor of a special issue of *Color*—a woman whom *Time* magazine later branded a "negrophile"—to say that, "though I am interested in and deeply value the Negro, I am not a Negro. . . . In America I am working for a vision of this country as composed of people who are Americans first, and only of certain descents as secondary matters. In order to establish my view I have had—for a time—to swing into a rather extreme position which has not allowed me to be associated with any race other than what we may call the American race."[17] Meanwhile, Toomer did not refuse to associate himself with black cultural organizations, such as the Friends of Harlem's Negro People's Theatre, of which he was listed as a regular member, along with Adam Clayton Powell and Countee Cullen.[18] He supported several such groups over the years.

During the war, in my very proper New England haven where no blacks were permitted to own property, and where no black had been a

---

[15] Toomer Collection, Box 6, Folder 191. Orage remarked in a talk on 6 April 1926 that "The way to transcend identification, both with oneself or another, is to die each morning. . . . Imagine that you are leaving the Earth for the planet Karatas, perhaps forever" (Toomer Collection, Box 68, Folder 1544).

[16] Toomer Collection, Box 6, Folder 191.

[17] Toomer Collection, Box 1, Folder 24.

[18] Toomer Collection, Box 3, Folder 78.

student in a Junior or Senior High School until the 1950s, issues like these meant nothing to me, and I had no basis for racial judgment when, in response to my questions about what I was doing with Jean, my mother began to speak freely about Jean's color and his background. She had told me that Marjorie Content was not Argie's mother, another detail that confused more than enlightened me, because my sense of "mother" was more affective than empirical, more illusory than real. In fact, it had always been obvious to me that Argie and I were pretty much equal in Marjorie's care. Mother also said that Margery Latimer's death in childbirth may have been precipitated by the persecutions of those who accused her of marrying a black.[19] This also confused me, but it explained at least what Mother Latimer's blood relation to Argie was. My mother also began to speak of Jean's career and fame as a writer, something Poppy himself had never alluded to. It seemed natural to me that he could be famous for anything, but she placed that fame in a past as distant as her own fabulous life in Paris in the 20s, her period of involvement in the lives of the famous. The essence of my mother's life was situated in her remembered or imagined participation in a Golden Age. She constantly looked backward and yearned for a past to which she would return.

Little by little, I could piece together her allusions to that past, but I simply didn't know what questions to ask, and I could never be sure that her stories were "factual" or a desired fiction of self. Her version of the beginning of her relation with Jean goes as follows. She met Jean with Waldo Frank in a train from New York City to Albany in 1923; she was attracted by his good looks and manner. In January 1924, she saw him in the company of A. R. Orage and the part-owner and manager of the Sunwise Turn Bookshop in New York, Jessie Dwight of Albany.[20] Orage had arrived in the United States in December 1923 to arrange a tour of Gurdjieff's danc-

---

[19] This is a careless exaggeration. Kerman and Eldridge (*The Lives of Jean Toomer*, pp. 292–294) detail the circumstances of Margery's death, caused primarily by a heart leak.
[20] It was indeed a small world, for Harold Loeb and Marjorie Content bought a third share of this shop on 38th Street in 1919, and helped manage it until 1921, when they sold their interest, probably to Jessie. Orage met Jessie there, and Jean Toomer met Orage there in 1923, when the bookshop had already become a meeting place for Gurdjieffites. Stanley Nott worked for Jessie in 1923 and met Orage at about the same time Jean Toomer did. Harold Loeb's autobiography describes his ownership of the shop at the time when he was launching *Broom*, a journal that published some of Jean Toomer's early work. It is difficult to imagine how Marjorie Content could have avoided seeing or meeting Toomer in New York between 1922 and 1924, since she spent long hours managing the shop with her husband, though she claimed not to have met Jean before 1933 (Kerman and Eldridge, *The Lives of Jean Toomer*. pp. 214–215). It is not unprobable that much of Marjorie's later distaste for Gurdjieff was incited by her experiences in the Sunwise Turn. She admired Orage but shied from his followers.

es that would raise money for maintenance of the Institute. Just after New Year's Day 1924, Orage gave a series of lectures on the "work" to a small audience at the Sunwise Turn Bookshop. During the evening of his second lecture, he met Jessie. Born in 1901, five years after Edith, Jessie was almost thirty years younger than Orage, who had been separated for some time from his first wife, Jean Walker. Within a few days, Jessie became Orage's secretary, and they remained together for the rest of his life.

A month later, Gurdjieff and his troupe arrived and gave a number of demonstrations, first to sparse audiences, and then to larger ones, after sensational reports circulated about them.[21] Edith brought some of her New York friends to the dances, but remained on the sidelines. When Gurdjieff returned to France in March, she tried to talk Jessie into going to France with her, but Jessie, who was already somewhat skeptical about Gurdjieff's teaching, wanted to stay with Orage, who had been commissioned by Gurdjieff to expand the group in New York.[22] Orage himself talked her into going to the Prieuré that summer of 1924, and she arrived just before G's accident. In the calm interlude before Gurdjieff resumed

---

[21] Roy Finch, *Les dossiers H.:Georges Ivanovitch Gurdjieff*, Bruno de Panafieu, ed. (Paris: L'âge d'homme, 1992), p. 34, quoting Edwin Wolfe, says that when a reporter asked Gurdjieff what he wanted to do in the United States, G replied "to show people that when it rains, the streets are wet." About the dances, one popular story is worth recalling here. Gurdjieff made it a rule that when he entered the scene of the "exercises," he would watch for a while just off stage before striking the floor with his cane. At that instant, all the dancers would "freeze" no matter what position they found themselves in. During one exhibition, Gurdjieff walked in from the wings upstage to one side and raised his cane. The audience waited while the dancers continued their movements. Gurdjieff made a slight movement of his head and all the dancers ran toward the front of the stage. Gurdjieff and the audience watched as the front group leapt off the stage over the orchestra pit, and then he struck his cane loudly on the floor. Crashing down on the chairs in the pit, the dancers froze. Gurdjieff struck the floor again, and they got up, unbruised, and calmly took their places on the stage for the next exercise. The audience roared "Bravo." James Webb, *The Harmonious Circle: The Lives and Works of G. I. Gurdjieff, P. D. Ouspensky and their Followers* (London: Thames and Hudson, 1980), pp. 268–269, cites William Seabrook's newpaper account of this incident. The more reliable James Moore, *Gurdjieff: The Anatomy of a Myth* (Rockport MA: Element, 1991) p. 198, repeats the account. For a description of the origins and of Gurdjieff's use of these exercises for self-discipline, see Kenneth Walker, *The Making of Man* (London: Routledge & Kegan Paul, 1963), pp. 136–140, Thomas de Hartmann, *Our Life With Gurdjieff* (Harmondsworth: Penguin, 1972), pp. 185–186, and Moore, *Myth*, pp. 351–353.

[22] Fred Leighton quotes Betty Hare on the relationship: "Gurdjieff needed Orage just as Orage needed Gurdjieff, that Gurdjieff was the great intellect, Orage the great formulator" (Toomer Collection, Box 4, Folder 138). Until the summer of 1926, when he returned to the Institute for almost the rest of the year, Orage held group meetings regularly in New York.

his work, Jessie and Edith Taylor, both "single women," became his fast friends and gadflies. My mother did not mention Jean's presence there that summer, but she had an apartment in Paris, where Jessie stayed now and then. After Gurdjieff's accident in July, she made only occasional day trips to Avon. Jessie rejoined Orage in New York in November, and for the next five years they were constantly on the move in the United States and across the Atlantic. Edith often shared their New York apartment.

Throughout the war, in New York and in Westport, I saw many of my mother's friends from those days. We spent six consecutive New Year's Days with Rita Romilly and Martin Benson on Sutton Place South, though I escaped the bulk of conversation by listening to the football Bowl games on the radio. We spent several summer days with Peggy Matthews at Louise March's farm in Bloomingburg. In trips to New York, we saw Muriel Draper, Payson Loomis,[23] Paul Leake, and the Stanley Spiegelbergs. In Westport, we saw much of Sherman Manchester and Daly King. Stanley Nott, Nick Putnam, Eugene McGowan, Philip Lasell, and Fritz Peters were occasional houseguests in Westport, both before and after my mother left her companion and moved with Petey and me into a large and frail wooden-frame house that she rented for thirty-five dollars a month, perched precariously over the Saugatuck River above a huge and stinking sewage outlet. Before he entered the army, we would drive over the New York State border to Brewster with Fritz Peters, to visit Wim and Ilonka Karasz Nyland. Nick Putnam, who taught me to play chess, rented a different house in the Westport area each summer during the war, where he spent weekends with successions of impressionable and giggling young women; and Philip Lasell stayed with us on the way from his Mexico and California opium and gambling bouts to his mother's house in Whitinsville, MA. One winter night, we were visited by a small, furtive man my mother introduced as "Metz," with whom she spoke only French. Just after the war, Marcel Duchamp spent weekends in Wilton with Jean Guerin, another Paris friend. In 1943, Orage's widow, Jessie, came from Santa Fe with her children, Dick and Ann, to wait for a freighter convoy to take them back to England.

Most of these people had nothing in particular to do with me, and my sister and I were nothing much more than captive audiences to their numerous anecdotes about the good old days and endless gossip about those who had lived them together. They talked, laughed, ate and drank, told jokes, and had fun together, but never gave me any reason to appreciate their talents or public reputations. The only reason I recall these names

---

[23] It was Loomis who brought Nick Putnam and Philip Lasell, as well as Lincoln Kirstein into the Gurdjieffian circle in the summer of 1927.

here is to suggest how widespread was the universal interest of all of these people in one subject of conversation—Gurdjieff. Even Marcel Duchamp had tales to tell of the rumors that spread through the cafés on the Left Bank in the early 20s about the infamous charlatan Gurdjieff.[24] Those who had not gone themselves to Fontainebleau had stories to tell of their friends who had. All of these "exiles" wondered now how Gurdjieff was managing during the occupation, but no one doubted that he could deal as cunningly with the Germans as he had with others. Those who had not known Gurdjieff had their appetitites whetted with sensational stories about the ageless power of the man. I had heard stories of how he picked up the front end of a car to release someone trapped underneath; and about the time he surprised two burglars in his apartment and smashed their heads together. A more likely story was told me by my stepfather, Philip Lasell, who was in Gurdjieff's car on August 9th, 1948, when a truck crashed into it on the road south of Paris near Montargis. Gurdjieff was pinned in the wreck by the steering column. Philip was thrown clear and tried, though injured himself, to pull Gurdjieff clear. Gurdjieff told him to stop making his pain worse and sit down and listen; then, until help arrived over an hour later, he told stories.

He was known also for his amazing cures that often consisted of re-hearsing the cause of the illness. To treat a kitchen burn on a hand, he would thrust the hand back into fire. More than one person had told me how he often transferred his own energy into the body and mind of anoth-er. Ouspensky reports that Gurdjieff could communicate with him by thought, could receive Ouspensky's thought in return, and could exercise the power of making himself invisible to others.[25] Gurdjieff had been seen on more than one occasion in two distant places at the same moment.

Normally, Jean Toomer's name entered conversations only if I men-tioned him. Besides Nick Putnam, who had an endless repertory of racy stories about the sexual intrigues at the Prieuré, few had much to say about Jean, simply because he was not a member of their social circle. I

[24] For typical American tabloid journalism, see the full page spread in the *New York World* magazine section for 25 November 1923, headlined "Behind the Scenes at Gur-djieff's Weird Château of Mysteries."

[25] My mother says that Gurdjieff treated one of his own burns this way. Fritz Peters, *Boyhood with Gurdjieff* (London: Victor Gollancz, 1964), p. 124; and Luba Gurdjieff in her memoirs (Luba Gurdjieff with Marina C. Bear, *Luba Gurdjieff: A Memoir with Reci-pes* (Berkeley, CA: Ten Speed Press, 1993) record the same treatment on themselves. Stanley Nott, *Teachings of Gurdjieff: Journal of a Pupil* (London: Routledge & Kegan Paul, 1961), p. 63, gives an account of energy transfer, citing Hartmann, *Our Life*, and P. D. Ouspensky, *In Search of the Miraculous* (New York: Harcourt, Brace and World, 1949), p. 325, speaks of Gurdjieff's shape-shifting, plasticity, and invisibility.

was rather pleased with this, because I couldn't conceive of Jean swapping stories of the old days. Nick was ready with anecdotes about Jean because Jean and he had worked briefly together on the English translation of *All and Everything*, but, as far as I could tell, Nick hardly knew him, and the stories were obviously secondhand.[26] When I realized that stories about Orage did not circulate either, it became evident that the "inner circle" of Gurdjieff's group was immune from gossip and rumor. My mother's friends only talked about themselves with Gurdjieff.

I had not yet seen a copy of *Cane* and, besides Gorham Munson, whom my mother saw in New York once or twice, none of these people seemed ever to have read Jean's work. My mother did not speak about *Cane*, except to say once that she had named me after a character in the book. Since my older sister, Eve, Gurdjieff's daughter, was known as "Petey," I assumed that "Paul" was just completing an apostolic duo. Our mother never spoke then of Jean at Fontainebleau, though all of her stories of the early days of my sister and myself included anecdotes about the Château du Prieuré and Gurdjieff. Curiously, in all of these festivals of reminiscence, even when she had had a great deal to drink, my mother was very guarded in speaking of her personal relations with either Gurdjieff, Orage, or Jean. I suspect she thought she was guarding secrets, or that she would rather not have people talking about these things in front of Petey and myself.

Meanwhile, I corresponded with Jean and yearned to return to Mill House, first in order to escape my Westport life and restore some health to my damaged pride, and then because I missed the sights, smells, and good feelings with Poppy and Argie. For some time after I left Mill House, my mother was not in touch with Jean. He didn't write her from India or contact her after his return in 1940. After his kidney operation in late 1940, my mother talked with him on the phone and pleaded with him to talk to me. I was, apparently, beyond her control. Jean and Marjorie invited me to Mill House for short stays over vacations, and I even returned to school at Buckingham Friends for a month in the spring of 1943, before returning for several weeks during the summer. I remember feeling guilty that summer about something I had done during my spring stay. At Buckingham Friends, during a picnic-outing, I had spun tales of how I had been in the blitz bombing of London before coming to the United States. My classmates were fascinated, so I kept the fabrication going far too long. Argie must have heard about it at school, and I was sure that the story had

---

[26] I find Nick's name mentioned in published literature only by Louise Goepfert March, in Beth McCorkle, ed., *The Gurdjieff Years 1929–1949* (Walworth, NY: The Work Study Assoc., 1990), who uses the form "Putnamm."

reached Jean's ears. I felt I had to say something to him. So one day, I told him what I had done and asked him if he could explain *why*, and how I could stop inventing stories of myself. He seemed not the least surprised, angry, or puzzled. Without any tone of scolding, he gave me a lesson in self-control that I recall quite well, for I was painfully alert in my shame.

"Listen Polo," he started,[27] "you are, as everyone is, not one, but many people. It is one thing to tell stories about 'I,' but another thing to know who the 'I' is that is speaking. When you tell stories about 'I,' you don't realize which 'I' is talking. What *you* think is 'I' is really a collection of 'I's; and the one 'I' you think is *you* does not really exist. You have many 'I's. At one moment there is one 'Polo' on stage, and at another moment, another one. Because these various 'Polos' contradict one another, you do not function harmoniously. You are like a violinist who plays only on one string, because you use only a very small part of the instrument of your being. You do not realize that you are just a machine whose parts and operations you are responsible for, but have no control over.

"So you tell stories because, like a machine, you are run by external circumstances, and you act along the line of least resistance. To be a *good* liar is an art, because a good lie can force a truth, so to lie successfully, you have to make a truth, because only the truth fits together beautifully. Machines lie badly, because they operate like machines, making things automatically without caring how their products profit users. Only wise men can lie beautifully, so beautifully that they can have others believe a truth which is good for them. Do you know what I mean? Can you master the machine 'Polo'? No. You can just turn it on and watch what product comes out. One time it will grind out one 'Polo' truth, and another time another 'Polo' truth; but you have no control over which operation the machine is performing. If you say 'I did this, or this,' and do not know what *you* are doing, that is a sad state of affairs. If you know that it is *you* who are doing it, then you have some control of things. If you know how to harmonize *all* the 'Polos' in you, then you are in full control, aware of the right times for one and for another 'Polo,' and aware of how *all* your selves collaborate in the operations of any one self you show. The more things you can be, the greater your wholeness can be, just as the more instruments there are in a symphony, the greater the sound, so long as they all play in tune with one another. You have this to learn, to recognize the particular qualities of each of your beings, and to have each work for the *whole* of you.

---

[27] I recorded this and the other talks in this chapter as accurately as I could from memory in the summer of 1951, after a visit to Mill House. The language and tone is certainly his, but I may have mixed at times the content of one talk with another.

"I don't mean that you lack strength of character. There is both strong and weak in you, and you must be aware that, as you increase your strength of character, your self-control for example, your weaknesses of character will tend to diminish accordingly. You are full of negative as well as positive forces, and the negative will overcome you unless you prevent it. What is negative is uncontrolled; what is positive needs instruction how to gain control.

"Since you were here last, conditions haven't changed for you. Only circumstances have. It's not suprising that tales and truths take turns in you, because both are mechanical. Perhaps you invent tales because you cannot tell the truth, and perhaps you tell the truth because it is easier for you to do so at the time. Both tale and truth are mechanical operations in you, and so they are the same thing. What is true is what can be used profitably. What is false is waste. You can't see the difference in them unless you study and analyze what they do for *you*; and then you will begin to understand what they do for you and *others*. After all, what is intelligence, essentially, but the capacity to adjust oneself to circumstance, to *use* for one's own and for others' good the potential in external influences.

"Listen, there are three centers in this *mechanical* 'Polo.' He is physical, he is emotional, and he is intellectual. Look at yourself and ask what you are right now. Which 'I' is in charge. Each time you do so—and when important occasions arise in which you must act, it is essential for you to do so—you will discover in yourself something different from what you expected to be, but you will always be one of the three.

"There is something you must do to change this, for you must, you *must* change. You must become a conscious 'Polo.' You must learn to recognize which you is the machine running now, and then you must learn to switch levers and change operations, and finally you must learn to perform all your mechanical operations at once. Then they will stop being 'mechanical' because they will be under your conscious control. Do you see what I am getting at? You will be able to harmonize all those forces which belong to one or another operation in one act. Change begins with understanding, and understanding rules the capacity to act for your conscious self.

"It will take time. Begin by consciously applying yourself to controlling one center at a time, and you will be surprised with the result. You *can* apply a desire for control to one or another center. The Caucasian bandit must strike from his hiding point at precisely the right moment or lose his life. If he misses, he has no second chance. So it is when shooting a basket in the last second of a basketball game. Both are exercises in an absolute control over the physical center of your being.

"The important thing right now is to realize that you cannot change by yourself. Bandit and basketball player rely upon the training only another person can give. You need help, just as the circle of your being needs a stable center in order to be drawn correctly. The first thing to learn is that you need the knowledge only another can give you. Think of what I have taught you, what Lin has taught you, what the farm and your school have taught you. These things do not become knowledge until you make an inner change in yourself, until you begin to know yourself, become self-conscious. You are unconscious now, asleep. Some things get into your head even when you are asleep, but not enough, and who can profit from the experience in your dream? Once you know the difference between sleep and waking, you will know something of the difference between lies and truths. And you will know which of your beings is in control of things, and then, maybe, you can start controling the levers yourself. Right now is the time to decide whether you are going to live completely mechanically or completely consciously. It is easier to be mechanical. Almost all of mankind is, but unless you become conscious you will never love life, the real life, instead of the lie. So use me now as your alarm clock. I will keep you awake, but you have a responsibility to that clock. You have to wind it up, keep it where it is needed, and set the alarm to wake you up. You did it now, and that is a good thing. It is one thing to sleep too late once, but a worse thing to invest in a clock and then continue to sleep late because you don't know how to use an alarm clock." What I did understand from Jean at that moment was what I should have understood long before: that "self-control" is not an exercise in inner concentration alone, but involves control of relations with others.

I saw less of Jean and Marjorie than usual that summer, because my life with Argie extended its space to movies in Doylestown, visits to girl friends, and trips to Stover Lake where we both struggled to learn to swim. I tried vainly, until Jean finally succeeded in getting me to relax sufficiently to float on my back. "Just a question of concentrating on your physical mechanisms," he said with a sly smile, as he slowly withdrew his supporting hand from under the small of my back. Jean himself was a strange animal in the water. He swam like nothing I've ever seen. He seemed to combine the Australian crawl with a breaststroke and sidestroke all at once, arms and legs moving underwater in different directions in different rhythms. Only his head, almost straight up and pointed forward like the prow of a ship, and his hands, like tips of seal flippers, appeared above the surface of the water. His movement through the water reminded me of a watersnake whose body parts seemed to go in all directions while the whole of him kept going straight ahead. He gave no appearance of tiring himself in the least. He was in complete control of every movement, in control of every particle of water that enfolded him.

Except for a weekend or two, it wasn't until the summer of 1947 that I managed to return to Mill House for an extended stay. I noticed that the upper rooms in the mill were completed and that Susan, Marjorie's daughter, was living there with her children. There was a nice feeling now about the mill, unlike the damp chill and musty smell of cement that used to permeate it; and there was a good feeling throughout the property. Everyone seemed happily occupied that summer. Jean was talkative, Marjorie kind and unusually attentive to me. Argie had a horse up in the old tractor shed and, with another one borrowed from a friend, we went riding together over the same fields we had played in years earlier. She had grown slim, tall, and strong. I found her a strikingly beautiful young woman; but she had never lost a bit of the light and playful streak that made it impossible for me to be serious with her about anything. Later that summer, I tried to write a poem for her, but that didn't work, and I'm not sure she ever saw it. I tried telling Jean what I felt about her and, true to his style, he cocked his head and looked up from his newspaper and over his glasses with that look of questioning puzzlement that always made me feel I had invited a death sentence, though he never delivered anything like one. "You think you know your self, perhaps, but how well do you know her? Do you think she will, or can, receive what you offer? What kind of gift do you imagine your affection is?"

I was left to ponder this, because I lacked the questions to keep the discussion going further. Back home, I repeated some of my thoughts a few weeks later in a letter to Jean, feeling helpless to write directly to Argie, who would have laughed. For to her, as to her father, laughing was a way to keep a thought from going unnecessarily deep into consciousness. Later, in the course of conversation, Jean asked me about my plans for the future, what I was thinking of for college. I told him of my mother's hope that I would go to the military academy at West Point, to which he gave one of his low "Hmmmm's." I said that I wouldn't mind leaving school for a year to study with Gurdjieff. He replied with a quick and firm, "Above all, don't do that!" Then he paused, smiled and said: "Better to go to China." That was the only time I mentioned Gurdjieff's name in his presence, and I never heard that name from him.

A few evenings later, the subject of learning came up again, and I confessed a general lack of motivation in high school that made it hard for me to concentrate. He reminded me with amusement that very little had, then, changed for me. I told him that whenever I tried out one of his exercises it only tired me. As an example, I cited the exercise of trying to go to sleep by relaxing my whole body piece by piece. Every time I did this, my body seemed to relax, except my mind grew so much more alert that I found it impossible to go to sleep for hours. "Yes, and you are Mr. Fidget not only in your bodily gestures but in your thoughts," he replied, "because you only did part of the exercise. If you concentrate all of your mental energy on one thing, let's say, your right arm, there are wonderful things it is able to do, but only once you leave the energy there. As long as you keep your mind on the arm, it is locked to your thoughts, but your thoughts are continually jumping here and there. Let's say that you want to write from one to ten on a blackboard with your right hand. That's easy. But let's say you want to write from A to Z with the left hand at the same time. To do that, you have to withdraw your thought from your right hand and put it on the left. What happens? If you have taught your right hand what to do and practiced it enough, it will go on easily enough by itself and you will be free to place your mental energy elsewhere. When you learn how to swim, you have to practice first your kick, and when that becomes automatic for your body, you can shift your attention to what your arms do.

"The point is, you have to be taught how to do these things. They do not happen by themselves. We have to teach our natures to do what we want them to. It's the same with putting oneself to sleep. You can place all the mental energy where you wish, but you must know how to remove it and let the organism do its own instructed work. So go ahead and concentrate on your toes in order to withdraw all sensation from them, move up through your body, applying and then withdrawing your concentration to relax each muscle in turn. Then, when you get to your head, to your brain, the last muscle to work on, you find you cannot apply thought to where it *is*. So, you have to learn to withdraw thought from your body, make your mind a void, turn its motor off, separate it from its energy. If you can do this, your thought can leave the body to rest, and then return to it to be rested by the body.

"It is possible to rest the body as much this way in a few minutes as most people do in hours. Try this a few times: take a pencil between your fingers and sit back in a chair and *relax*. When the pencil drops, wake up. If you practice this enough, you'll discover that the moments before the pencil drops are enough to restore your bodily energy. There is an art in joining concentration with relaxation. It consists of using feelings to relax sense, thought to relax feelings, and sense to relax thought. All your three centers need the others, just as each of your beings depend upon the others. You'll be suprised when you discover that even your dreams will change. This won't happen overnight. Try it for ten, fifteen, twenty days, and see what happens. You want to accomplish everything at once. If you have trouble, imagine me telling you these things. Concentrate, if you like, on my voice until your own inner voice takes over from mine. You have to learn to listen, and when you listen well, you will find rest for your own thoughts. When thinking tires you, you are thinking badly." For nights, I practiced dissociating myself from my body. I could get as far as the head, but besides my jaw, I could not numb my senses. I told him this one day, and he said that my problem was perfectly normal. "Now try concentrating on your face *first*." After a few nights, this seemed to work, but the effort was so strenuous that, after a time, I gave it up.

Another time, after I twisted my ankle slightly, I complained about the pain that prevented me from sleeping or from concentrating. He said that if I couldn't forget the pain, do the opposite: remember it. "Make friends with the pain that makes you more aware of your mind and body. Think about it, analyze it and think of ways of describing its variations, its ebbs and flows. Pain is not unlike pleasure, and you can give yourself up to either. Pain 'hurts' because it gets in the way of other activities, while pleasure separates itself from other thoughts and activities. Try having pain exclude other things so that you can concentrate on it. You will find that if you consider pain objectively, you will be able to move it in and outside of yourself. But remember, pain is good when it makes you aware of yourself. Pain has a rhythm. Think of your breathing when you are in pain, and its rhythm will master the rhythm of pain.

"Another thing: whenever something hurts you, physically or mentally, do what wise men have always done, retrace the event. Go backward over it. You know, the yoga goes forward with an exercise, and then, *always*, to leave the exercise, goes backward through it. The American Indian does something of the same in his ceremonies, and the effect is that time disappears, because as far as you move forward in an event, retracing it backward brings you back to the beginning, and therefore erases the time the exercise moved through. You see, you can *be* and *do* without spending time. This is a power belonging to the yoga and to what the Christian calls a Saint."

Little by little, I began to understand what Jean was driving at, but I didn't have the patience to practice these things consistently, and I found that exercising them often isolated me from the rest of the family. In school, I was having a hard time "training" my mind to concentrate on the painful studies that bored me. Little by little, though, I found that, if I thought about my own performance in things I didn't like rather than in the things themselves, I could enjoy my engagement. I remembered Jean telling me once that the secret of survival is learning to like what you have to do, rather than wasting time doing what you like. Somehow I managed in my last year in high school to raise my grades to the point where I could count on having a choice of what university I would attend.

In that year of 1947–1948, I wrote a few times to Argie and Jean, but my principal pleasure was playing basketball and my goal was college entrance. Another success in applying Jean's teaching came on the winter night my appendix became painfully inflamed while I was dressing for a basketball game. The pain kept me doubled up, and I was even put in the ambulance in a tucked position, but as I began the long trip to Norwalk hospital, I concentrated all of my thought on my abdomen, which seemed only to make me more aware of a hurt in which I found nothing of personal interest, but when I moved my thoughts to the sound of the siren, the reflection of the lights, the bumps in the road, the pace of my breath, and particularly the touch on my wrist of the attending nurse, the pain changed. It was still there, but I felt it from a distance, where it was not troublesome.

In the summer of 1948, I worked in the shipping department of the factory where my mother was receptionist and telephone operator (from that privileged position she spoke frequently to Jean on the telephone), and in the fall entered Brown University in Providence, RI. I was already making plans to go to France for my sophomore year. I wanted particularly to see Gurdjieff there, but just before Thanksgiving I found out that he was coming to America in a few days. In my excitement and anticipation, the image of Poppy faded momentarily toward the back of my consciousness.

Chapter Four

The Ascent: With Gurdjieff
1924–1926

Gurdjieff represents a fourth Yoga with no school and no teachers . . . but an addition of the three Yogas, Raj, Bakhti and Hathi,
the wholeness that is something more than the three parts which
make it up.

—A. R. Orage

She was going where I was going,
We together,
And a buried being was called to life,
A beauty and a power, a revelation
Of what life is for, and why we are.
　　　　—"The Blue Meridian"

Men like him can fascinate. One is not
responsible for fascination.
　　　　—Cane

To each his own Gurdjieff. I have never heard anyone who knew him to
have the same opinion of him as another's, or even to have the same versions of stories about him. As for myself, I carry few conscious impressions from my direct experience with him as an infant. A rare memory I
have of my stay at the Prieuré des Basses Loges in the early 30s is of the
games we children—perhaps eight or nine in all—played under Gurdjieff's direction or under his personal surveillance. Gurdjieff was open and
generous to children and he organized a community for us free from the
surveillance of mothers and fathers. We had no ordinary "family" setting,
but lived a rather free life.[1] I remember best the game of "Stop" that we

---

[1] Except for mealtime, when the children had their own table apart from the adults,
they enjoyed an almost pastoral freedom. Gurdjieff opposed public schooling, and
only Dimitri's force vis-à vis his brother permitted Luba, Genia, and Lida to eventually get to the local school. Lida (for Lydia), the youngest, had more schooling, therefore, than her older sisters. According to Nikolai de Stjernvall, Toly (Anatole
Mercourov) escaped school altogether.

played regularly on the huge lawn sloping down from the main house.[2] Another game was a version of "Simon Says," in which positions and movements of a leader were to be imitated. Both of these games, I realized later, were preparatory to Gurdjieff's "rhythmic movements." I can also hear dimly in my memory music from the Study House that Gurdjieff composed and played himself.

While I was there, I was the youngest, the baby, "used" by my elders as their servant to beg a snack from the kitchen, or ask someone busy in the garden or working on the Study House decorations for some favor.[3] In short, I became recognized by the conscientious and dour "pupils" as a pest. I remember being sent by the gang to ask G (the name most of us used except to his face, where we would call him "Monsieur") for something to eat from his tea tray. In real or mock fury he would throw a bun or piece of fruit at me, accompanied by a stream of Russian expletives. The others were always close enough to hear and laugh as they looked at what I had retrieved. Perhaps this was a game between us. I have seen Gurdjieff hurt even children's feelings, apparently on purpose, but never without giving some indication, if only in his eyes, that there was a lesson in self-reflection involved.

My sister and I were often in Gurdjieff's company in Paris before my mother packed up and left for the United States in the autumn of 1935. From the time I was 9 or 10 and living with her once again—though I could not recall that I had ever lived with her before—I was curious about

---

[2] Stanley Nott, *Teachings of Gurdjieff: Journal of a Pupil* (London: Routledge & Kegan Paul, 1961), pp. 12–13, cites Orage's explanation that the purpose of the exercises is to force one to "stop in a position it has never stopped before. This enables a man to observe himself better. He . . . can sense differently." P. D. Ouspensky, *In Search of the Miraculous* (New York: Harcourt Brace and World, 1949), pp. 351–356, has a much fuller explanation, the essence of which is that the exercise forces the body to find and feel the transition between two "automatic," or conditioned positions. The exercise forces the will to restrain the body from finding its usual position. Ouspensky recounts some amazing anecdotes about the exercise. In his notebooks, Toomer says "The 'stop' exercise is simultaneously an exercise of the will, attention, thinking, feeling and motion" (Toomer Collection, Beinecke Rare Book and Manuscript Library, Yale University, Box 48, Folder 989). Rudolph Byrd, *Toomer's Years with Gurdjieff* (Athens, GA: University of Georgia Press, 1989), p. 70, analyzes this description.

[3] It is not easy for me to conjure up the images and names of the children at the Prieuré when I was there. There must have been ten or more. I can think of myself and my sister as the youngest. Valia, Anatole, Lonia (son of Lenotchka Savitsky and Rachmielevitch, and grandson of Ouspensky's wife, Sophia Grigorevna), Lida, Genia and Luba Gurdjieff, and Nikolai were all ten years or more older, all born during the exodus from Russia between 1917 and 1920. Michel de Salzmann and Dushka Howarth were born in 1924, and my sister in 1928.

my mother's contacts with Gurdjieff, if only because almost every visitor to our house from afar talked about Gurdjieff in those days.

Why and how my mother became involved with Gurdjieff in the first place is a question that continues to intrigue me, as it had intrigued me throughout my youth, even before I became involved with Gurdjieff myself for a brief period just before his death in 1949. She was not a seeker after truth, nor was she an intellectual, though she had a broad cultural background and philosophical interests. She spent her lifetime, it seems to me, in search of affection and security. I knew little about her life in the twenties, and nothing of the circumstances that might have played a role in her drift toward Gurdjieff's teaching and his person. What I discovered later of her life saddened me, not only because of the "facts," but because she would not share those facts with me or with my sister.

She was born, I have gathered from an application for life insurance, in Providence, RI in April 1896, to Mary Ann Fitzgerald Taylor (who was en route from her home in Saratoga, NY to a summer occupation in Newport). Her father's name is listed as "James Walter Taylor," but the name is an *ad hoc* nomination for the circumstances. Mary Ann was a *fille de joie* who followed the excitement and money of the late 19th-century racing crowd. Upon returning to Saratoga, she surrendered her daughter, Edith, to a Catholic orphanage that remained her home during her early school years. She cavorted with children of wealthy Saratoga families, like the Formans and the Putnams, who descended directly from General Israel Putnam of War of Independence fame.

When she was 15, she ran away to Baltimore, where she found a place dancing in a musical review. The troupe traveled to England in the late spring of 1914 and, on a weekend visit to the regatta at Henley, she met and fell in love with a boy on summmer vacation from the University of Pennsylvania who was a member of one of Philadelphia's most prominent families. When the War broke out, they both enlisted in the Morgan Harjes Ambulance Company. In 1917, he was commissioned in the American Army, and they were briefly separated. After the war, they traveled through England, France, and Italy, until he returned to Philadelphia to enter the family cotton business. Edith stayed in Europe, traveling on her own, but, in 1922, they were together in London, where they heard Gurdjieff talk. They separated when he returned to the United States to marry a girl of his social class in Memphis, TN, a girl that his family had picked for him.

Depressed, Edith settled in Paris with some money "Johnnie" [MacFadden] had left her as consolation. She made contact with her mother, who came to France to visit, and they spent some time together in the south of France, where Edith became acquainted with Esther and Gerald

Murphy and Scott Fitzgerald. Back in Paris, she was part of a "crowd" of acquaintances including Djuna Barnes, Jane Heap, Natalie Barney (who had written a poem for her in 1921), Gertrude Stein, Man Ray, and Marcel Duchamp.

It is not easy to reconstruct the chain of events that first brought my mother to the Institute, and even more difficult to explain why she kept returning there, even as a resident for months at a time. She talked freely to me and my sister about her adventures during the war and in the Paris of the 1920s with a certain measure of exaggerated self-importance. To questions about Gurdjieff, she told us that she had gone to the Institute "on a lark" with Kiki Vanderbilt in a fit of depression after her mother had died in Saratoga in 1926. This information contradicted the stories others told about her life in Paris in the early 20s, as well as the anecdotes she exchanged with houseguests who had been with Gurdjieff earlier. After she died, I found among her papers notes taken from Gurdjieff's talks in London in February 1922 and from talks at the Prieuré on 24 May and 21 August, 1923. Even earlier, packing books for our move to Weston, CT in 1946, I discovered in the back page of her copy of the *Journal of Katherine Mansfield* a pencil-written, eyewitness account of Mansfield's last evening of life in January, 1923.[4]

It is clear, nonetheless, that our mother felt lost after Johnnie left her and, with the money he gave her, she led a rather disorganized life in Paris, on the lookout for some sort of stability. Her own mother married after her visit to France and Edith did not feel comfortable with her stepfather, though she hardly knew him. At any rate, Saratoga was out of the question for her. The only places she really knew well now were Paris and London; and London, where she and Johnnie had split up, was for the moment uncomfortable. She may have visited Gurdjieff's Institute in late 1922 or early 1923. She saw him in New York in January of 1924, shortly after she had met both Orage and Toomer, but the papers she left after her death include a fictionalized account that place her first meeting with Gurdjieff in

---

[4] *Journal of Katherine Mansfield*, edited by John Middleton Murry (New York: Alfred A. Knopf, 1927). To Murry's closing description of her death at the Prieuré, my mother added the following: "*Note*: Katherine Mansfield sat in the study-house for over an hour listening to the music, looking happier than I had ever seen her, holding her husband's hand. It was unusual for her to stay up so late, she was especially anxious to have J. M. M. hear the music which she enjoyed so much. We all felt she had used too much energy, was too excited & over taxed her strength. ET" Though this may be a record of someone else's recollection, my mother also left notes of talks given at the Prieuré in 1923. For a clear picture of the events leading up to and following Mansfield's death, see James Moore, *Gurdjieff and Mansfield* (London: Routledge & Kegan Paul, 1980).

mid-summer 1924, shortly after his automobile accident. It is entitled "This Wizard of Ours: How it all came about. Chapter 1." I present it here not as fact, but as an imaginative reconstruction. She may have written it as a sort of exercise in observation that Gurdjieff and Toomer alike had pupils compose. Nonetheless, it is a picture of the environment Jean Toomer found himself in when he arrived at the Prieuré at almost the same time, a few weeks after Jessie Dwight, Orage's future wife, had arrived on her first visit.

> We were stitting, meditating, at a table on the half-deserted terrace of Le Dôme when Marta Dennison strolled along; neither Curtis [Moffat][5] or myself showed any signs of recognition for we were both enjoying our own thoughts, but Marta was no one to be considerate and apparently there was no one else seated on the terrace at that time to attract her, so she approached our table and timidly asked if she might join us. . . . While I watched the terrace filling up and the choosing of tables given as much care as the choosing of a horse at Tattersalls, Marta was entertaining Curtis with her exploits in the Near East Relief, but not until she mentioned the name of Gurdjieff could I give my attention. "Tell me all you know of this Gurdjieff," I asked her, for it was only that morning that Dorothy Ireland, whose house guest I was, started telling me of her own and Lady Bea Rothemere's [Lady Mary Lilian Rothermere] extraordinary sojourn at Gurdjieff's institute near Fontainebleau, so naturally I was interested to hear another version. Marta began by telling us that she had first seen him in Tiflis, her Russian prince companion had pointed Gurdjieff out to her, describing him as an Armenian rug merchant, but who was clever enough to have gotten out of Russia during the revolution with about forty followers. Since that time he is being considered a kind of god.
>
> "At a night club in Montmartre the other night," continued Marta, "who should I see there but this same Gurdjieff and I was informed that he was the brains behind several of these cabarets and besides food, drink and entertainment, opium could be bought at a price.[6] He has a château," she told us, "where human derelicts and sex-starved old maids went hoping to save their souls. The treatment was first to make them do just the very thing they disliked doing the most of all,

---

[5] A not-very-prominent portrait photographer who was briefly associated with Man Ray and Marcel Duchamp in Paris.

[6] In fact, according to his own authobiography, *Meetings with Remarkable Men* (London: Penguin, 1963), p. 288, Gurdjieff owned two restaurants in Montmartre and had some financial interest in other places there at this time.

such as washing dishes, scrubbing floors, etc. Just the place for you to spend a vacation, Curtis," and she laughed loudly at the thought. "And why pray?" he asked, "when I can do that very same thing right here in Paris?" "How do you mean?" she inquired. "If you must have it," he said, "sitting here, talking to you, drinking a drink I don't either like or want seems to me a fair example." "Enough," I piped in, "let's be off to the Jockey and sample its wares."[7]

I could hardly wait to get back to tell Dorothy [Ireland] what I had heard about Gurdjieff, for it was certainly quite a different tale from hers, and I was anxious for her to convince me that it was the same man. She assured it could be no other, and commented on my interest in him, saying, "Surely after telling you Bea's and my experience, I cannot understand what there is to attract you to him. It would be a jolly good lesson for you to go down to his filthy institute and learn all you want to know first hand. It's easy enough to be admitted; just get out your best clothes and with a right amount of rudeness they'll take you for an American heiress and throw the gates open wide." I fell asleep that night planning my visit, but it would certainly not be as she suggested.

At a loss for something better to do, I accepted an invitation to weekend with Marta in Samois where she had rented a cottage for the season. A promise of a visit of Jane Heap was used as bait. How well she knew I'd bite, for Jane had my greatest admiration, not just because she was early to recognize the masterpiece of James Joyce's *Ulysses*, and daring the printing of it to the extent of going to jail, but for her never-tiring efforts to protect her beliefs and ideals, her courage, her faithfulness to her friends, besides being a talented writer. She was an editor of the avant-garde magazine *The Little Review* published in New York; Margaret Anderson was her associate, and she was as talented as she was beautiful.

The day I visited Marta, Jane came to lunch. She had called at Gurdjieff's Institute, "Le Prieuré" to visit some friends who were staying there. They joined us at tea and it is from them that I got quite a different impression of the man and his work. He had recently returned from a successful demonstration tour in the United States, and was now recovering from a serious automobile accident.[8]

---

[7] The Jockey was the name of a restaurant opened in the spring of 1923 by Hilaire Hiler. It soon became a Mecca for Americans in Paris.

[8] Thomas de Hartmann, *Our Life with Gurdjieff* (London: Penguin, 1972) pp. 199–202, describes the circumstances of the accident and Gurdjieff's injuries. No one seems to agree on the extent of them. Hartmann minimizes the gravity of his injuries, while James Webb, *The Harmonious Circle: The Lives and Works of G. I. Gurdjieff, P. D.*

Before taking his troupe to New York, he gave a performance in Paris at the Théâtre des Champs-Elysées. It must have been quite unique. The two fountains in the theatre lobby were spouting wine, one was white and the other red wine. The performers' costumes were made by themselves from G's design, assisted by M. Saltzmann [de Salzmann] who was a well-known scenario painter in Germany before the war. It was said that he was among the several painters attached to the Imperial Court of Russia. He was extraordinary looking, a head very much like a death skull, a mass of heavy iron-white hair, parchment-color skin drawn tightly over his bony structure. His hands were monstrous, abnormally long fingers with the biggest thumb imaginable that he used instead of a brush for painting murals.

The Paris demonstration troupe was made up of Jacques Dalcroze pupils headed by Jeanne, the French-Swiss wife of Saltzmann, an ex-ballet dancer with an Armenian name, and G's Russian wife, Mme Galumian, and the Russian wife of Frank Lloyd Wright, about forty-five dancers in all. The demonstration consisted of exercises and various Eastern dances all taught by G, who composed the music as well.[9]

The expenses for the American trip were collected by subscription, principally among the English members who had previously financed the purchase of the magnificent château at Avon near Fontainebleau called "Le Prieuré," where he established his Institute under the title of "The Harmonious Development of Man."[10]

When I suggested to Jane that she take me to visit this extraordinary man of whom I had heard so many varied accounts, she chuckled softly and eyed me, coyly saying, "All right, if you want to, I don't know if he'll even see us." However, she agreed to take me. Beside the château gates I was surprised to find a conventional 17th-century châ-

---

8 (cont) *Ouspensky and Their Followers* (London: Thames and Hudson, 1980), p. 296, conjectures that Gurdjieff "staged" the accident to give him an occasion to observe his pupils without his personal direction.

9 The wife [mistress at the time] of Frank Lloyd Wright was Olgivanna Hintzenberg, a Montenegrin dancer who attached herself to Jeanne de Salzmann during the exodus from Russia. She met Wright in 1924, and they were married in 1928.

10 The facts here are obscure. Gurdjieff leased the Prieuré with an option to buy and, with the help of English money furnished by Ouspensky's students, did manage finally to buy the château for 700,000 francs, according to Webb, *Harmonious Circle*, p. 233. Moore, *Gurdjieff and Mansfield*, p. 155, is clearer on the transactions. The American trip was probably financed heavily by English money, but Orage had already exacted promises of support from his new American acquaintances. Gurdjieff's own story of his money-raising appears in "The Material Question," the coda to *Meetings with Remarkable Men*, where he implies that he raised the money himself.

teau in a magnificent park designed by a Fontainebleau architect. I don't know honestly what I expected to find. We were not disappointed and were escorted to what was known as the "Study House," and told that the master would receive us there.

This Study House was constructed from an abandoned airplane hangar, the glass roof was covered with a painted parachute depicting the Koran and painted by the resident pupils. The dirt floor was carpeted with many oriental rugs that had been carried out of Russia by G and his followers. There was a raised platform used for dance practice, around the sides of this fantastic room were placed goatskins for sitters, the backs were cushioned by pillows covered with colorful materials supplied and made by the pupils. There was also a small round cement pool with a spouting jet d'eau, lighted by hidden colored lights on festive occasions. In an alcove sat G, half-sitting, half-lying amongst a mountain of silk cushions, his shaved head glistening like varnished sepia, his deep set black eyes seemed to be tender yet menacing and terrible. He appeared to look through rather than at one. He acknowledged our presence with a bow without changing posture or expression. He waved to Jane and me to be seated on the goat skins near the railing.

Seated, or rather squatted at G's right was Dr. Sternval [de Stjernvall], who with his very queenly Danish wife were among the people G had brought with him from Constantinople during the revolution in Russia. Mr. Saltzmann, with drooping head, was next to the doctor. On the left sat the women of the entourage, Mme Galumian, Mme Saltzmann [de Salzmann] and Mme de Hartmann, wife of the musician; she acted as secretary and interpreter.

A small smiling perky Jew named Metz was busy serving black coffee in small bowls that he placed on the floor in front of the guests. G's brother Dmitri Ivanovich and his sister Sophia and her husband Capananci [Kapadnadze] were also present. Little did I dream as I sat there on my first visit that I was to spend many days and many more nights in this same Study House, nor could I realize through what stages of emotional tension I would pass, yet even to this day that Study House holds for me a sacredness that no church has had for me.

(Eight years after my first visit, tears came to my eyes seeing such magnificence in a state of decay, the prayer rugs showing huge rat-chewed holes and dog and cat remains, smelling of damp rotting wool. The roof supports had given way under the weight of winter snows, windows were broken, and the light cast shadows like wounds on the stained patterns of the rugs.)

I was interrupted in my meditation by G calling to me, "Miss, I sick man, truth very weak, now institute die for everybody, but necessary something, do you agree? So like ordinary man I to think how be, many years much do, but never before one thing I do, I wish write book. Surprised? No? Some time in life every man must write book, but such book already I begin, and if you very much wish we can even English read." This was said with the broadest of smiles, the scene for the reading must be corresponding, he informed me, so we filed out of the Study House, he leading the way leaning heavily upon a stout walking stick. We were taken along an avenue of plane trees around a circular pool to the end of the garden to a small tea house up a few stone steps into the one room about three metres square.[11]

This is as far as the script goes. She made a typed copy in the years just before her death, with only minor changes and some repetitions. The exact date of the visit is not given, but it must have been between mid-August and 5 September 1924, when she went to England to visit friends. Her first impressions were probably not very different from Jean's and Jessie Dwight's. Jessie left a poignant but unpublished record of her first impression of the Institute, and Jean recorded his initiation into Gurdjieff's world in an unpublished essay, entitled "In Memory and a Devotion and a Hope." "It must have been towards the end of 1923 that the events began," he wrote, "events that were to claim me and, in a sense, chain me for the rest of my life. I am claimed and I am chained. . . . When I die you will find Gurdjieff written in my heart? Yes? No?" The sixteen years between 1923 and 1939, he went on to say, included six years of intensive involvement [1924–1930]. "And now I swiftly look back over all that, and I say—I do not know Gurdjieff. I have never known Gurdjieff. I never will."[12]

Toomer's involvement began when Waldo Frank told him that Orage was giving a series of lectures on Gurdjieff at the Sunwise Turn Bookshop at the beginning of January. He was involved in a love affair at the time with Margaret Naumburg, Waldo's wife, with whom he attended an Orage lecture where he saw Edith again. Orage's lecture explained then that the purpose of Gurdjieff's teaching is to have each human being acquire his own "I," by correcting a lack of control over his moods, reactions, and passivity to events about him.[13] Man has four personalities, he explained. The first is the sense perception he shares with other animals, the second is his

---

[11] Edith Annesley Taylor, unpublished memoirs, estate of Edith Taylor.

[12] Toomer Collection, Box 46, Folder 953.

[13] See G. I. Gurdjieff, *All and Everything* (London: Routledge & Kegan Paul, 1950), p. 1237.

reaction to those perceptions, the third his motor reflexes, and the fourth is the sense of self that characterizes his particular "I" or being. The average man, Orage went on, is a slave of the entire service to all universal purposes that are alien to his own personal identity.

Several days later, Toomer saw Gurdjieff for the first time at a dance demonstration in Webster Hall in New York, and thought he looked like "a monk in a tuxedo," but he was impressed by the spectacle and by Orage's talks. At the end of January, he wrote Orage saying that he and Margaret had missed a talk, and asked for a personal interview in order to get authorization to go to the Institute.[14] No answer came immediately from the request and Jean went to Chicago until July, when he returned to New York and wrote Orage from the Hotel Albert to say that he regretted missing the work at the Institute and looked forward to seeing Orage. Toomer's recollected explanation for his letter states: "The fact is that on July 9, 1924, I was all set to go to Gurdjieff's Institute at Fontainebleau. Only a terrific set-back could have stopped me.[15] I wanted that life there, that work. I wanted and needed it as all of me had never before needed any work, any way of life. This had become clear to me, a deep and inevitable conviction, before my return to New York; and I had come back to book passage to France on the first possible ship. I did not want to see Orage. I did, as said in the letter, want to get a sense of him. But, if Orage had been out of [the] city, or had he not wanted to see me, or if, on seeing him, my impressions of him had changed and had become unfavorable, I'd have gone away. . . . It had taken me about six months to decide to go to Fontainebleau, and now that the decision was made, I wanted to be off. Orage's reply came promptly. He asked me to come to his place and have a talk. . . . I went."[16]

After seeing Orage and approving of what he heard, he wrote Gorham Munson to say: "I suggest that we apply the Gurdjieff outline which we have both accepted."[17] He urged Waldo to come with him to France, and Waldo replied promptly: "It is the right move for you now—a dip into the digested and easeful life that is French culture. Get in touch with Orage,

[14] Toomer Collection, Box 6, Folder 205.

[15] Curiously, C. S. Nott (*Journey Thruogh This World* (London: Routledge & Kegan Paul, 1969), p. 74, says that he sailed for Europe in April of 1924, and went almost immediately to the Prieuré where he started a long stage of work with Gurdjieff, and recorded lengthy conversations that took place between them that spring and summer. Of course, Gurdjieff was in the United States until June, arriving back in France a few days before his accident.

[16] Toomer Collection, Box 6, Folder 205.

[17] Toomer Collection, Box 6, Folder 186.

150 East 54th St. before you go. He is the American agent and Americans are supposed to apply for admission through him. It is *important* to see him first."[18]

Jean replied on the 17th of July: "I am off to Fontainebleau. But not simply to Fontainebleau; rather to a place where someone whom I believe to possess adequate knowledge had conditioned things that I may the better examine myself." Then, to reduce the tension that Gorham felt, caught between his friend Waldo Frank and Waldo's wife Margaret, Jean's mistress, Jean added: "No Gorham, I did not *ask* you to choose between Waldo and Gurdjieff. I simply stated an opposition as I saw it [Waldo had returned from France without being admitted to the Prieuré]. . . . I too see directions. Orage gives the figure of the incline. But on this incline there are two directions. I judge that Waldo is determined by his inclinations and involuntary motors. I judge that Gurdjieff controls. And to this extent I see an opposition, or rather, a contrast, a quite different placement on the slope."[19]

Jean had in hand a descriptive brochure translated into English by Orage, titled *G. Gurdjieff's Institute for the Harmonious Development of Man*, consisting of an eleven-page history and description of Gurdjieff's teaching, the program of work at the Institute, and a seven-page form for pupils, titled "Historometrical Individual Record (for pupils and patients of the first category)." The introductory paragraphs of the brochure validate Gurdjieff's authority.

> The Institute for the Harmonious Development of Man by the G.I. Gurdjieff system is practically the continuation of the Society that went under the name of the "Seekers after Truth." This Society was founded in 1895 by a group of various specialists, including doctors, archaeologists, priests, painters, etc., whose aim was to study in close collaboration so-called supernatural phenomena, in which each of them was interested from a particular point of view.
>
> During the existence of the Society, its members undertook many very difficult journeys, mostly in Persia, Afghanistan, Turkestan, Thibet, India, but also in other countries. They also undertook a good deal of work of various descriptions in connection with their object that involved much labour and organisation.
>
> Throughout the period of travel and work, many of the Society's members lost their lives, while others from time to time

---

[18] Toomer Collection, Box 6, Folder 186.
[19] Toomer Collection, Box 6, Folder 186.

abandoned the task, and only a small number returned to Russia in 1913, under the leadership of Mr. Gurdjieff.[20] Their first stop was at Tashkent, but Mr. Gurdjieff subsequently set up his headquarters in Moscow with the intention of arranging the material that had been collected and of putting to practical use such of it as was adapted to the purpose.

A course of lectures given by Mr. Gurdjieff resulted in a number of men of science, representing all branches, rallying round him, and the number of people interested in his ideas began rapidly to increase.[21]

He then resolved to give effect to the plan that he had long entertained of founding a training establishment under the name of "The Institute for the Harmonious Development of Man" for the study of his ideas and in order to put into practice his system of training.

But the war and the subsequent events in Russia hindered this plan and, being compelled by circumstances to leave Moscow, he travelled from country to country and at last settled in Europe.[22]

Notwithstanding the enormous difficulties arising out of the events of recent years, Mr. Gurdjieff nevertheless contrived to organise several scientific expeditions and to form groups in various cities with a programme for the study of the theoretical part of the work.

The site he had long been looking for was at last found in France, at Fontainebleau, near Paris, where Mr. Gurdjieff in 1922 acquired by purchase the old château called Le Prieuré, and where he founded a permanent centre for the Institute according to his original plan.

Although the period of organisation is not yet complete, the main branch of the Institute is already capable of accomodating two hundred attending and one hundred resident students and in a short time these numbers will increase.

---

[20] These events are recorded in *Meetings with Remarkable Men*, but their status as fact is not verifiable.

[21] The development of the Moscow group is described by P. D. Ouspensky, *In Search of the Miraculous*, the work best known as an explication of the Gurdjieff "system."

[22] Gurdjieff and his group of close followers spent some time in Constantinople after leaving Georgia, and settled first in Berlin from the spring of 1921 to the spring of 1922, when they decided to establish the Institute in France. Thomas de Hartmann recounts these adventures in *Our Life*. There was a rumor circulating in the 40s that, while in Berlin, Gurdjieff had suggested to the incipient Nazi party the use of the Swastika as their emblem, but the party had chosen its symbol before Gurdjieff's arrival.

The circle of those interested in the ideas of the Institute is continually widening, while the members of the Institute in all countries is now not far short of 5,000, of all nationalities and religions."[23]

The brochure goes on to outline his theoretical base and pedagogical principles, and it mentions instructors who are specialists in medicine, psychology, etc., and speaks of laboratories and a medical center, as well as a journal "printed in the Institute's own special characters," that records "not only all lectures and talks, but also all the events of Institute life." The extent of these facilities seems to represent more a goal than a reality, though many pupils had assumed roles as "instructors," and some were known to represent themselves as having been appointed G's teaching agents to treat particular disorders.

Jean arrived at the Insititute with a certificate of membership issued to him by Orage,[24] and so was a bit surprised at the indifference of others to his presence: "They were ignoring me. You must recognize that a thing exists in order to ignore it. These people, so it now struck me, simply were not aware of any existence. To them I wasn't present."[25] It took some time for him to learn that activities had been cut back because of Gurdjieff's almost fatal automobile accident on Saturday, 5 July, the news of which was calculatedly slow in reaching New York.[26] Hartmann cabled Orage on the

---

[23] G. Gurdjieff Institute for the Harmonious Development of Man, n.d.

[24] Toomer Collection, Box 60, Folder 1404: Jean's certificate number was 619, and was valid initially from January 6, 1924 to January 6, 1925: "The bearer of this, a member of the GURDJIEFF INSTITUTE, has the following privileges.

'First, residence, with all rights of permanent members, at the chief centre of the Institute at Fontainebleau, as well as the Institute's boarding houses in other places; Free attendance at all classes, lectures and conferences, wherever held under the auspices of the Institute, except those lectures, etc. specifically held for personal members; Free subscription to the Institute's journal and all the literature issued by the Institute.

'The right of enquiry and reply concerning the ideas of the Institute, any member may, if he or she wish, use any of the sanatoria or hotels of the Institute for him or herself, and family, at one half the regular rates.

Annual membership subscription $120.

(Signed) Georges Gurdjieff
A. R. Orage"

[25] Toomer Collection, Box 47, Folders 982 and 984.

[26] This is the date Thomas and Olga de Hartmann cite in Our Life, 120, and they fix the hour shortly before 5 P.M. In private communications, James Moore tells me that 8 July is the correct date, but I haven't seen his sources.

16th with the news and, in his call on the 21st, he said that "as for G's accident, it is absurd to suppose that it is self-directed."[27] Orage received Jessie's cable about the accident on the 24th.

Toomer finally saw Gurdjieff one day walking on the grounds helped by two women. A short time after, Gurdjieff called everyone together and announced that the Institute was to be liquidated, and that the property was to be called henceforth simply the Prieuré (an order that had little effect, since pupils continued to call it the Institute until its closing in 1933–1934). In Gurdjieff's voice, Jean sensed a touch of humor (six years later, Gurdjieff wrote that his closure of the Institute gave him the occasion a year later to open eighteen sections in different countries).[28]

Though his recovery from the accident on the road from Paris to Fontainebleau seemed to go quite well,[29] several changes took place in his personal work program in the summer of 1924, as if his confrontation with his own mortality had made him realize how fleeting was the time he had left in the world. First of all, he decided that time was pressing to get his wisdom into print in English. The publication and dissemination of his ideas outweighed any other professional consideration for the rest of his life. He began dictating the "First Series" of *All and Everything* to Madame de Hartmann during his convalescence in late July or early August, beginning with "It was the year 223 after the creation of the World, by objective time-calculation or, as it would be said here on 'Earth,' in the year 1921."[30] There

---

[27] Orage Papers. The Orage papers are in the possession of Anne B. Orage and consist of Jessie Orage's diaries and Orage correspondence.

[28] G. I. Gurdjieff, *All and Everything*, p. 1187.

[29] C. Daly King, *Oragean Version* (New York: Private Printing, 1951), p. 17. who does not hide his antipathy toward Gurdjieff, assumes frontal lobe injury from his accident that reduced his capacities considerably, and feels that Gurdjieff was not the same man after the accident. De Hartmann says that although Gurdjieff was unconscious for four days, he sustained no concussion or serious injuries. Gurdjieff himself, in his "Second Talk" to the New York group in 1930, recorded in *Life Is Real Only Then, When "I Am"* (New York: Dutton for Triangle Editions, 1975), p. 92–93, says he was without memory for three months and bedridden for six. This apparent contradiction in fact should be understood as a pretext in the context of restructuring the American groups.

[30] Thomas and Olga de Hartmann, *Our Life*, p. 126 quote only part of this opening of *All and Everything*, p. 51. By my rapid calculations, the year 223 would have the creation of the world 83,711 solar years before the birth of Christ. Curiously, Gurdjieff himself, in *Life is Real*, p. 32, says that he started dictating on 1 January 1925. James Moore reminds me that the American edition of de Hartmann's *Our Life* cites Tuesday, 16 December, as the day work began on *Beelzebub's Tales*, but I suspect that Mme. de Hartmann 'chose' this day to reflect 16 December 1916, when she and Thomas met Gurdjieff, and 16 December 1922 when the Prieuré almost burned down. Jessie Orage, who left the Prieuré on 3 October, mentions his working on the book, and Gurdjieff himself mentioned the book to my mother in late August or early September.

were to be three "series" in all. The first—*Beelzebub's Tales to his Grandson*—
was "to destroy and clear away the rubble"; the second—*Meetings with Remarkable Men*—would "provide constructing data for new building"; and
the third—*Life is Real Only Then, When "I Am"*—was to "disclose objective
information." The writing required the organization and training of a
number of teams. Gurdjieff himself would often dictate to one or two re-
corders in Armenian, which was then translated into Russian; or he dictated in Russian and had the Russian translated into English.[31] Orage, and
eventually Toomer, earned the confidence of Gurdjieff for editing and polishing the prose of those who turned the Russian into a literal and rough
English. There were many Americans and English working simultaneously
on the text, and Orage was considered by Gurdjieff as the one who could
best collate the versions into a single definitive text in English.

Associated particularly with the plans for teaching centers was the arranging and recording of the music he had composed for the exercises
known as the "Movements," and this task was entrusted to the pianist and
composer Thomas de Hartmann, while Jeanne de Salzmann, who had
studied with Jacques Dalcroze, taught and trained teachers for the movements.[32] Further, soon after his recovery, his automobile excursions multi-
plied greatly in frequency, always with a small entourage. These motor

---

[31] There are different versions about the making of the text. C. S. Nott, *Teachings of
Gurdjieff*, p. 92, says that the work was *written* by Gurdjieff in Armenian, translated
into Russian by Madame Galumnian, and then into English by Russians. James
Moore, *Myth*, p. 198, repeats this, but those I have talked to who were there in those
years—Nick Putnam (who made an entire translation into English on his own), my
mother, Philip Lasell, Bernard Metz (who was G's amanuensis for letters in English
and French) and Jessie Orage who was Gurdjieff's personal "offical typist"—say that
Gurdjieff rarely wrote, but dictated most of his book, though he endlessly scribbled
notes for dictation in cafés. What Orage received was, then, not only written in broken English, but at two removes from the original. Mme. de Hartmann, in the epilogue to *Our Life*, says that G dictated to her in Russian and then had Hartmann find
the English equivalent in a dictionary!
[32] Byrd, *Toomer's Years with Gurdjieff*, p. 75, cites Toomer's recollection from that summer. The music for the movements, or dances, must be distinguished from the music
that Gurdjieff himself played on a harmonium, some of which has been transcribed
and recorded. There are several descriptions of the dances, most recently that of
Pauline de Dampierre, "Les mouvements," pp. 129–134, and Marthe de Gaigneron,
"Danses sacrés," pp. 152–156, in Bruno de Panafieu, *Les dossiers H.: Georges Ivanovitch
Gurdjieff* (Paris: L'âge d'Homme, 1992). In *Meetings with Remarkable Men*, pp.162–163,
Gurdjieff recounts his first acquaintance with the sacred dances. They resemble the
dances of the whirling dervishes, and Peter Brook's film has a scene with them. Dushka Howarth has always insisted, rightly I believe, that the movements became a central concern in Tblisi at a time when staging them was a valuable means of raising
money to support his entourage.

trips would last usually two or three days, sometimes as long as a week, but they were frequent and took place until just before his death twenty-five years later, after one last trip to southwest France. I have never been able to discern a particular purpose for these voyages. They seemed primarily to visit sites or persons, but were also a teaching experience, a testing of others under controlled conditions.

The major logistic problem for Gurdjieff in these activities then, as it had been since his exodus from Russia almost a decade earlier, was money, what Gurdjieff himself styled at the end of *Meetings with Remarkable Men*, as "the material question." Gurdjieff had assumed charge over a large entourage at that time, and his burden was increased by the refurbishing and maintenance of the Prieuré. There were his wife and mother to care for, his brother Dmitri, with his wife and three daughters, his sisters, Sophia and Anna, and their families, as well as the pupils who had followed him to France, notably the de Salzmanns, now with two children, the de Stjernvalls and their son, and the de Hartmanns.[33] This group numbered in all about twenty and added to the number of "permanent" residents—such as Metz, the house manager, Ethel Merston,[34] "director" (as Gurdjieff called her) of the children, and the English Miss Gordon—there were rarely as many pupils as there were members of Gurdjieff's entourage. Fifty-five was the comfortable limit for the accomodations at the Prieuré, including those who lived in the Paradou. Toomer remembered that the dining room, with tables for the children, held between forty and fifty persons. At times, Alexander de Salzmann and Thomas de Hartmann earned money in Paris, but Gurdjieff seems to have held control over the fast-dwindling treasury these people had brought with them to the Prieuré. Where Gurdjieff found the money to first rent and then buy the property with all its annexes is a mystery, but he borrowed on the property almost as soon as he secured it.

The men at the Prieuré were assigned specific tasks about the property, usually in one construction project or another. They also had roles in the administration of the Institute. De Salzmann painted walls and tapestry, de

---

[33] De Hartmann, *Our Life*, recounts in detail the period from the war in Russia to Gurdjieff's accident in 1924. In his memoirs, Nikolai de Stjernvall presents his mother's recollection of the exodus from Russia of Gurdjieff and his entourage. Moore, *Myth*, reconstructs the period carefully from all the sources available to him.

[34] Ethel Merston retired to India after the closing of the Prieuré, but kept in touch with people in the Gurdjieff movement. Denis Saurat, the French literary critic, visited the Prieuré in late winter of 1923, and wrote an account of that visit ten years later in *Nouvelle Revue Française* with the improbable statistics that there were seventy Russians there, seventy English, and no French. Saurat also reports that Gurdjieff at that time had no command at all of either French or English ("Visite à Gurdjieff," Nouvelle Revue Française, 1 Nov. 1933, pp. 686–698).

Stjernvall was the house doctor, Metz was a sort of valet for Gurdjieff, delivering messages, interpreting, translating, and writing letters. De Hartmann transcribed Gurdjieff's music and played for the Movements. Orage and Toomer, along with their work on the property, directed translation, for it was decided early that the first publication of Gurdjieff's book would be in English. Women had ancillary jobs that changed often, according to need. By turns, they milked the cows, worked in the kitchen and laundry, taught the Movements, decorated the salon for parties, served as secretaries, typists, teachers, baby-sitters, and ran errands. Even Katherine Mansfield worked while she was there, giving drawing lessons to the children. Some older women in frail health were exempted from tasks.[35]

Since there was no steady source of funds, the pupils were on the lookout for financial support. Nonetheless, all those considered worthy were welcome at the Prieuré. Those who were able to pay were expected to. Some paid for equipment like automobiles, others financed trips, and it is clear that Gurdjieff also took in pupils who had little to learn, but had means to support others. Gurdjieff himself preferred to leave the financial "details" of bookkeeping to his secretaries, first to Olga de Hartmann, then to Ethel Merston, Bernard Metz, and Jane Heap, and finally to Jeanne de Salzmann. He handled small amounts for daily need, but for the most part, everything from château maintenance to trans-Atlantic trips was financed on a day-by-day basis. Upon arriving at a restaurant or hotel, for example, someone would go among the rest of the entourage to scrape up what was needed. There were many who paid nothing during their stay at Le Prieuré, but everyone was expected to work.

Financial matters became all the more complicated with the urgency of raising funds for publication and to finance the training of teachers for the establishment of a number of "centers" in the United States and Canada that would function as conduits for money. After his first trip to the United States in the winter of 1924, Gurdjieff decided that the United States was the most fertile ground for his teaching and fund-raising. Orage was already there gathering money and looking for favorable locations, and so it was fortuitous for Gurdjieff that Jean Toomer arrived on the scene at such a crucial moment with Orage's particular recommendation. Nonetheless, Gurdjieff seems not to have taken any special notice of him that first summer. Though Toomer wandered about the main house and grounds freely enough to describe in detail the routine of the Prieuré—the

---

[35] Despite Gurdjieff's appeal to women, he held them inferior to men in the process of self-perfection. Women were "passive," men "active" elements. Women rose on the ladder of improvement on the coattails of men.

dress, the meals, the ritual toasts to idiots, and the conversation—he didn't exchange a single word with Gurdjieff personally.

As if Gurdjieff's condition seemed not to impede the work from the perspective of New York, Orage wrote Jessie on 1 August, asking: "How is Toomer doing? I hope you will like him despite the touch of colour. He appears to me to be very sincere—and desperate; but perhaps his desperation is not deep. It may perhaps find an easy solace: I don't know."[36] Orage himself had already booked passage on the Mauretania for 20 August, but he complained that he hadn't heard from Toomer, whom he hoped to have direct the New York group until his return. Jean was still at the Prieuré when Orage arrived and explained his plans, and they left within days of each other.

Back in New York, Orage authorized Toomer in Gurdjieff's name to conduct groups in the city, a remarkable turn of events for a man who had seen Gurdjieff only on two occasions and had not yet exchanged a word with him.[37] Orage's confidence in Toomer was based not only on Toomer's progress in studying and grasping the "method," but in his feeling that Toomer was a kindred spirit, a writer like Orage, student of literature and philosophy, and possessed obvious teaching skills. Furthermore, Jean had already won Orage's trust as a teacher and fund raiser in the spring of 1924, before his first visit to the Prieuré. So, in New York during the winter and spring of 1925, he found himself directing a group in Harlem and consulting regularly with Orage and Israel Solon, the subdirector of Orage's group. Meanwhile, Orage was a regular visitor to Jean's Harlem group. The Harlem writer Langston Hughes recalls Jean's presence in Harlem with lightly disguised amusement: "One of the most talented of the Negro writers, Jean Toomer, went to Paris to become a follower and disciple of Gurdjieff's at Fontainbleau, where Katherine Mansfield died. He returned to Harlem, having achieved awareness, to impart his precepts to the literati. Wallace Thurman and Dorothy Peterson, Aaron Douglas, and Nella Larsen, not to speak of a number of lesser known Harlemites of the literary and social world, became ardent neophytes of the word brought from Fontainbleau by this handsome young olive-skinned bearer of Gurdjieff's message to upper Manhattan." Hughes goes on to say that few in Harlem had either the leisure to pursue the teaching or the money to pay the teacher, "so Jean Toomer shortly left this Harlem group and went downtown to drop the seed of Gurdjieff in less dark and poverty-stricken fields."[38]

---

[36] Jessie Orage Papers.

[37] Rudolph Byrd, *Toomer's Years with Gurdjieff*, p. 78, attributes this event to Orage's faith in Jean, and even suggests that, for the next several years, Orage gave Toomer an allowance to keep him going. I doubt this, but it is true that Toomer did not earn very much from his own teaching. It is more likely that some members of his group contributed to his support.

In the summer of 1925, with Orage off to the Prieuré in August, Jean decided to work on his own writing and took a vacation with Paul Rosenfeld in York Beach, Maine. In October he stayed at Lake George, in Alfred Stieglitz's summer home. Late in the summer, Edith Taylor joined Jessie in New York, having returned from Paris, where she had regularly attended Gertrude Stein's and Natalie Barney's literary salons. In the fall of 1925, she spent almost equal time in New York and Paris. The funds Johnnie had left her were dwindling fast, so she was looking for work. For a brief period, she was a consultant for Buckwalter, a decorating firm, but was drawn back to Paris and the Prieuré. Throughout most of the winter of 1925–1926, she moved between Saratoga, where her mother was ill with cancer, and New York City, where she was seeing more and more of Orage, Jessie, and, hence, Toomer.

Orage had returned to New York in October with a draft of Gurdjieff's *Beelzebub's Tales*, and he and Toomer prepared a collaborative teaching program based upon its material. In mid-November, they dined together with Mabel Dodge Luhan, who kept an apartment in New York. After a number of meetings, on 1 December Mabel invited Jean to visit her in Taos over the Christmas holidays. He decided to scout other places on the way and, though he was still closely involved with Margaret Naumburg, he invited Edith to go with him as far as Chicago.[39] After a few days, she returned to New York and he went on to Mabel Luhan's in Taos.

Mabel (b. 1879) and Tony Luhan had met Jean earlier at an Orage meeting in Jane Heap's New York apartment in the winter of 1924, and Mabel had been charmed by his voice and manner. When Jean arrived in Taos, she offered a large amount of money toward the work as an inducement to Gurdjieff to establish a study center on her property, and called the money a loan to "cement" her affection for Jean.[40] A few days later, after returning to Chicago to begin organizing a group, Jean sent the news

[38] Langston Hughes, *The Big Sea: An Autobiography* (New York: Hill and Wang, 1963), p. 241. Charles R. Larson, *Invincible Darkness: Jean Toomer and Nella Larsen*, gives a detailed and sympathetic account on this group. Moore, *Myth*, p. 360, notes Toomer's "self-bestowed leadership role" and "disastrous" teaching of the dances, but Jean was working closely with and taking direction from Orage.

[39] Kerman and Eldridge, *Lives of Jean Toomer* (Baton Rouge, LA: Louisiana State University Press, 1987), p. 139, have Jean in New York City from fall 1925 through April 1926, but Orage wrote to him in Chicago in early January to ask about his affairs there that concerned contacts for a group after his visit to Mabel Dodge Luhan in Taos. So, he must have been out of New York for some time that winter.

[40] Lois Palken Rudnick, *Mabel Dodge Luhan: New Woman, New Worlds* (Albuquerque, NM: University of New Mexico Press, 1984), pp. 226–228. Peter Washington, *Madame Blavatsky's Monkey* (London: Secker and Warburg, 1995), p. 257, remarks that Mabel "was besotted by Toomer."

to Orage with a check, and Orage sent him in return a chapter of the first book of *Beelzebub*, writing: "My dear Toomer G proposes *not* to publish vol 1 until vols II & III are completed in both Russian & English. . . . I am very much interested to know how affairs are proceeding with you in Chicago." He then reviewed the money problems at the Prieuré, explaining that he had sent Gurdjieff $500 out of the fees he collected from pupils, and had promised another $950, noting, "I think this ought to carry over the Prieuré past even the Russian Xmas." Orage assumed that he could manage to raise $1000 per month for five or six months and asked about Jean's accounts, adding: "I don't recall how matters stand between you and the N.Y. fund, however I *do* know that present reckoning . . . is as follows; to Gurdjieff $2000, to Toomer $1050 [respecting Mabel's intention to accord Jean a personal loan of $1000 out of the $15,000 total]. This is to say that you can, if you like, receive in due course the $1050 you loaned."[41]

Ten days later, Toomer lunched with Orage and Jessie to discuss the Luhan investment in the Gurdjieff Institute. The next day, Jessie wrote in her diary: "Mabel [Dodge Luhan] has taken a share in the Gurdjieff Institute for the sum of $12,000, that makes our $20,000 certain. Hurray!" Though the figures seem inconsistent, Toomer received $15,000 from Mabel Dodge Luhan, sent $3000 to New York, out of which Orage designated $2000 for the upkeep of the Prieuré, and reserved $1000 for Jean's expenses (the $50 is the difference between Orage's promise of $950 and the $1000 he expected to get from his own group). So, the other $12,000 of Mabel's donation, added to what Orage had raised and projected he could, made up the $20,000 Jessie mentioned. Since Orage was Gurdjieff's American negotiator, the treasurer of the New York group, Gorham Munson, was entrusted with the accounting of the funds. He forwarded the $12,000 to the Prieuré through Jean.

On 26 January 1926, Jean wrote directly to Gurdjieff to announce the offer and to give his assessment of the situation in Taos. First, he explained, the property is as large as the Prieuré, and the hard life in Taos would be a stimulus to the lazy; but, it is far from public transportation; and, the vice of Mrs. Luhan's ego outweighs the virtue of her energy.[42] On 11 February, Olga de Hartmann, acting as Gurdjieff's English secretary, replied to "Mr. Tunmer" in a curt note, saying that Gurdjieff was too busy to write, but he knew of the offer. She enclosed a copy of a letter from Gurdjieff to Mabel written by Elizabeth Chaverdian, thanking her for the money (though the amount is not specified) and adding that Taos was not

---

41 Toomer Collection, Box 6, Folder 205.
42 Toomer Collection, Box 3, Folder 96.

suitable for the work. Besides, she added, assuming that the offer was to move the Institute itself to New Mexico, it is difficult to liquidate things in Fontainebleau. The book is of paramount importance right now, she concluded. Olga also thanked Jean for the $1000 (undoubtedly Jean's own "expense" money sent as a token) given to Gurdjieff, but Gurdjieff reiterated that there is no question of establishing a branch in Taos. She reminded Jean that he had closed all the others [which others?], but the money arrived at a good time. She suggested that the remaining $14,000 be used for Gurdjieff's own needs. "Speak only with Orage about it. I will not mention your letter to Mr. Gurdjieff until I get a response."[43]

This exchange reveals the misunderstanding that eventually eroded Toomer's patience with Gurdjieff's financial demands eight years later. De Hartmann assumed Luhan's free gift for the Prieuré was $15,000. Orage calculated it at $12,000, with $2000 set aside for the New York group's publication fund and another $1000 for Toomer's expenses. Having given his portion directly to Gurdjieff, Jean expected the New York group to reimburse him, and Orage had assured him it would. Mabel Luhan was already victimized, for although her gift was her investment in a center to be set up in Taos with Toomer, Gurdjieff took the money, but not Taos with it. So, with obvious logic and caution, on 18 May, anticipating Toomer's summer talks with Gurdjieff, Orage wrote to Jean in Chicago with a pact: "My dear Toomer, in the event of your becoming responsible for the English writing of Gurdjieff's book 'Beelzebub,' I promise to place at your disposal for that purpose, the sum of $2,000, Yours sincerely, A. R. Orage." Some years later, Toomer attached to this letter a note to the effect that: "I made a similar pledge to Orage in writing. The $3000 he promised to place at my disposal was, presumably, the part of the $5000 collected in N.Y. for the book. The $3000 I promised to place at his disposal was part of the $15000 given to me for Gurdjieff by Mabel Dodge Luhan. As neither Orage nor I became responsible for the English version (or any other editions) of 'Beelzebub,' there was no turning over of these specified funds" (Toomer cites "$3000" here because he is thinking of Orage's pledge of $2000 added to the $1050 still owed him). The plot thickened. What the New York group raised on its own became confused here with the Mabel Dodge Luhan "contribution," all but $2,000 of which had been delivered already to Gurdjieff.[44]

---

[43] Toomer Collection, Box 6, Folder 206.

[44] Kerman and Eldridge, *The Lives of Jean Toomer*, p. 146, sum up their impressions: "Through a series of misunderstandings and poor bookkeeping, Toomer's money, that is, the remaining $2000 was thought by many, particularly Gurdjieff, to have been kept by Toomer." I don't for an instant think Gurdjieff thought this. He took advantage of the confusion of transferring credits in order to claim that he was owed money

Encouraged by his success in teaching and raising funds for Gurdjieff, Jean was in a buoyant frame of mind to get directly from Gurdjieff the wisdom he had caught glimpses of in Orage's talks. This desire to get to the "source" was made all the more urgent by a "mystical" experience he had in New York in February 1926 which he describes in a draft, "Realization of Existence," a chapter in *From Exile into Being*."[45] He calls the moment "my first day in Being-Consciousness." In the next chapter, "Being Conscience," he explains: "I had been in Being-Consciousness about a week . . . a new center, utterly unlike anything I had experienced before, awoke in my being. Suddenly it made itself felt . . . Being Consciousness, as it were, was relegated to second place . . . To call it an inner sun is to use the most appropriate symbol I can find. . . . I call this power Conscience. I call it Being Conscience."[46] Jean read his epiphanic suspension as a momentary conjoining of his being with what Gurdjieff called "Objective Consciousness." In the weeks following, he decided to postpone his Chicago plans in order to join Gurdjieff for an indefinite period. Coincidentally, it was about this time that he and Margaret Naumburg were breaking up and he and Edith were falling in love. They decided that they would go to Gurdjieff together.[47]

Throughout much of the spring of 1926, in preparation for his move, Jean met with Orage's group and moved within Orage's circle of acquain-

---

[44] (cont) that no longer existed. Beth McCorkle, *The Gurdjieff Years, 1929–1949: Reflections of Louise Goepfert March* (Walworth, NY: The Workstudy Association, 1990), cites Louise Goepfert March, p. 51, on the kind of pressure Gurdjieff brought to bear on people under circumstances he manipulated. Fritz Peters, *Boyhood with Gurdjieff*, p. 65, has Gurdjieff raising money in New York at this time, adding that the amount Gurdjieff raised for himself was in excess of $100,000.

[45] Toomer Collection, Box 17, Folder 469 and Kerman and Eldridge, *The Lives of Jean Toomer*, pp. 154–158, locate the event on the 66th Street El platform. The state lasted for several days, and another ecstatic moment occurred outside a shop window on 23rd Street. Such liminal experiences are called "transformations" by Gurdjieffites.

[46] Toomer Collection, Box 17, Folder 470. He sent the book off to publishers later, and received harsh criticism. One reader reported: "This is a very dangerous book . . . a very dangerous system and unless directed by one of an exceptional power and sanctity will cause great trouble" (Toomer Collection, Box 17, Folder 472). A second reader scoffed: "Toomer is no philosopher, nor student of philosophy. He writes about himself."

[47] Kerman and Eldridge, *The Lives of Jean Toomer*, p. 169, interviewed Gorham Munson, who said that Edith Taylor was rather pretty and had "considerable means." This surprises me, since Gorham knew my mother very well, and knew that she was surviving on hope and a shoestring most of this time. It was Gorham who talked me into taking a degree at Wesleyan in the 1950s when he was still in contact with my mother, but his recollection of her must have been blurred at the time of the interview.

tances. With Jessie and Orage that spring, he met I. A. Richards, Zona Gale, Muriel Draper [mother of Paul Draper and later notorious for her outspoken support of Soviet Russia], and Betty Parsons [proprietor of the Parson's gallery on 57th Street]. Orage, however, was trying to dissuade Toomer from going so soon to Gurdjieff, first because he felt that there was no urgency for the trip, and secondly, fearing that Jean would be coaxed to make promises to Gurdjieff that he couldn't keep. Giving in to Jean's insistence, Orage carefully coached him with his counsel, while he decided he could profit himself from the situation by sending Jessie over at the same time, both as a companion for Edith and as a check on Toomer until Orage, too, could get there.

Edith sailed in the middle of May with Betty Parsons to prepare the ground for both Jean and Jessie. Jean had already decided to use Edith as private test pupil for his teaching, as well as to use his teaching as a test method for bringing two people into one harmonious relationship. It is curious that he used a Gurdjieffian dialectic as an amatory strategy, as if he could, on the one hand, shape the subject to fit the idea of a woman he would love; and, on the other hand, as if the dialectic were itself a *philtre* to attract the subject to both the idea and its formulator. The timing of his attempt is also curious, since Orage had warned him in personal conversations that winter that the "work" has no place in relations between the sexes, and should not be used as a tool for relations,[48] a counsel Orage heeded scrupulously himself in his relations with his future wife, Jessie.

On the day Edith sailed for France, Jean sent her a letter from New York to the dock on plain yellow paper. The envelope is postmarked New York, 14 May 1926, 7 P.M., and is addressed to "Miss Edith Taylor, on board S.S. 'France,' French Line, Pier 57, N.R., New York. Sailing Saturday, May 15." The postage was insufficient, and there is an official stamp on the envelope "FEE CLAIMED BY OFFICE OF FIRST ADDRESS." The reverse of the envelope has the return address: "Jean Toomer, 439 W. 23, N.Y. and a postoffice mark notes "rec'd May 14 7³⁰ P.M."

---

[48] On 6 April 1926, he told Jean: "The only types of sexual relations possible are with someone who is as advanced and capable as oneself. In either case, there will be no feeling of responsibility in regard to progress in the work to interfere. Such a feeling of responsibility should not cut across a sexual relationship. Real sex is impossible if it does. We are not entitled to entertain ideas of development or reform for another person" (Toomer Collection, Box 68, Folder 1544).

Friday

Dearest Edith,

Our talk this morning was so clear and deep and beautiful, we touched so marvelously then, that the inevitable pain and straining that accompanied this period completely left me, and my whole being was unified and free to tell me how much I love you. And it was free to tell you also.

Now that this phase has ended—a strange, muted, phase for me—and ended in a calm, deep love for you, I am thankful that it was just as it was. In one sense, it was a test, and then it told me things that it might have taken years otherwise to learn. It tested and crystallized what I felt for you. In this ordinary life of ours, we are so accustomed to living <u>less</u> than we are, we are so habituated to meeting others with the mere surfaces of love and feeling, we are so accustomed to accept and to pretend that these give us what we really want, that when the possibility of the real thing presents itself, we either cannot recognize it and <u>live</u> it for what it is, or else the recognition comes so slowly and entangled with gross matters that it never really comes to birth, or is stillborn. During this past week or so, there has been a purifying fire burning in me, and I knew, by its strength and intensity, that it must either destroy my feeling for you or else create it, give it birth and being beyond and much deeper than any superficial contact. Had it been destroyed, I should have been glad. For then I would have known that what I felt for you was merely on the surface. And from the moment I first saw you, I either want more than this or nothing at all. The world is full of weak and transient contacts. You could never have meant this [to] me. But just what you did and could mean I could not clearly realize until that first glow took form and substance, and had been tested. It has been. From some pure source I love you with calm intensity.

At first, there was a part of me which saw you connected with my life only for a short period, during the week or so you would be in New York, perhaps on a passage over, maybe now and then in Paris, or now and then sometime or other in New York. I would have been glad of this. And at the same time, of course, there was another part of me which wished to really live and work with you, giving you the deepest and best that you have in you. The idea of motoring with you to Paris appealed to both aspects. But already I was clear to what you, Edith, and I, Jean, together, could and must and would mean.

In you, dear, I have seen, felt, and understood an inner quality, an inner being, of soft and luminous beauty. There is that in you—and I have rarely seen the like of it—which really <u>aspires</u>, and which is capable of faith and love and reverence. When you live in it, you are religious and have the capacity to be religious in the pure and ancient meaning of this term. You have the stuff of a soul. You have the wish, I think, to give this stuff a solid, conscious form, in order that you may live and manifest in it, not intermittently as now, but always and continuously. This is our really common basis. This is our center. And from it we can make excursions into whatever else seems desirable. And it is the seed, the source, of the possibility of our really engaging in a mutually giving and receiving life and work.

I have in mind the outline of a plan of real serious work and real joy which includes both of us as necessary factors. The geographical setting is not essential. It may be Fontainebleau, or Paris, or Italy, or some remote land, or it may involve a constant moving from one set of circumstances to another. Nor is there any arbitrary limit as to time. It is elastic, and can live as long as we can give life to it. The essential factors are you and I, and the essential element is that it will make it possible for us to give and receive what we need from each other, and what we need from life. The essential quality is that it will be at once interesting and stimulating. And it will and does include a purpose. Already I have seen and thought out many details, but I wish to leave them fluid, and the plan itself elastic, until I see you and we begin to live.

So dear, till then I say goodbye, good passage over and week in France. And, dearest, my deepest love to you.

Jean

Until the 22nd
439 West 23rd St.
After that:
S.S. Paris
Second Class, Room 638

These details may not be necessary, but everything seems so when it is a matter of seeing or hearing from you.

Jean himself arrived on Memorial Day, armed with a personal recommendation to Gurdjieff from Orage. Edith met him at the boat-train in Paris with an automobile she had borrowed for the summer from an American friend in Paris who was back in the United States. Jessie arrived a week later at the Prieuré at 10 P.M. in time for the regular music in the Study House and reading in Gurdjieff's room with Jean and Edith. Within two or three days, all three had settled into assigned tasks in the garden and the Study House and settled into a routine of work. Jean rose early to landscape, and the women in the late morning to plant and weed. While Jean worked through the day, Jessie and Edith shopped and walked in the afternoon, before everyone gathered for the late supper, reading, and music. Edith, who was a rare resident with a car, was soon performing taxi service for Gurdjieff, the de Hartmanns, and Jessie for trips to Fontaine-bleau and Paris, where Gurdjieff kept an apartment. On the 14th of June, Jessie recorded in her diary that she and Jean spent the afternoon and evening in Avon, where they had drinks at the Café de la Forêt and talked. She was relaying news from Orage and his concern about Jean's promises to Gurdjieff about money. Jean himself was now consulting with Gurdjieff on a daily basis. His notebooks, written that summer, record some of Gurdjieff's talks and analytic questions, as well as his own conversations with him. Once, I asked, "then for whom are you doing all this work?"[49] "I will live for coming generations," he said. "It is for them." Gurdjieff said he was like God, but his job was harder, because God did not have to destroy first in order to create. When Israel Solon, another of Orage's pupils at the Prieuré in the summer of 1926, warned Jean that Gurdjieff stole money, Jean replied in his defense, "He asks and takes."

Just as Orage had advised Jessie to keep a diary account of her impressions, Jean had instructed Edith to observe others and, as an exercise, to record some of the things she saw and heard. "Everyday," he told her, "be aware of what you have seen and what you have learned from it." Her notes on a lunch early that summer record Gurdjieff's public play with Jean's "African nature." Toomer's own notes recall that Gurdjieff analyzed him as a mix of African psyche and American character, and promised to make him ruler of Africa,[50] On one particular occasion, however, Gurdjieff seemed intent on publicly humiliating Jean. As Jean ate his watermelon dessert, Edith remembered, Gurdjieff asked:

---

[49] Toomer Collection, Box 46, Folder 954.

[50] Kerman and Eldridge, *The Lives of Jean Toomer*, p. 221, quote the last direct exchange between the two on 2 March 1935, during which Gurdjieff repeats this analysis to a credulous Toomer.

"Mister, you like such fruit?"

"Why yes, very much."

"Then eat like, how you say, black baby . . . special name, eh? Yes, picaninny; you know how picaninny eat?"

"You mean with both hands?"

"Good. I see you know very much."

Toomer picked up the piece of melon and ate it. When he had finished he put the rind down and looked at Gurdjieff with a satisfied smile. Gurdjieff remarked, "You finish, mister? You not finished. Eat *all*, even white part."

Toomer looked puzzled, but picked up the rind and continued down to the green, then put the rest of the rind back onto his plate. Gurdjieff said:

"Get up, you finished. Go back to garden work like you eat. When you are finished in garden I send you to America where big little picaninny live. You show them very special picaninny you are. You live there, work there, enlighten such men how you live, and if you fulfill, I give a substantial commission."[51]

Besides the public ridicule, his speech was a typical Gurdjieffian ploy to shock his victim into self-awareness, but Gurdjieff was also testing Toomer's sense of self in relation to a standard white racist caricature of the infantile black. On the positive side, an obvious implication of this exchange is a decision to send Toomer soon to the United States to teach the "system," as Gurdjieff's teaching was often called. It was clear to Gurdjieff in the middle of 1926, through communication with Orage and in consideration of the Luhan "gift," that Toomer was suited not only to stir interest and provide basic organization, but to persuade potential students to contribute funds.[52] Gurdjieff wanted Jean to go to Washington, DC to form a group, but Jean persuaded him that Chicago would be more lucrative.

On 17 June, Edith, Jessie, and Jean went to Paris together to meet Orage at the Gare du Nord. By then, the Prieuré was almost filled with resident pupils, and guests from Paris attended the formal lunches to which

---

[51] *Picaninny*, "small child," derives probably from Portuguese *pequeno*. Edith later dated this exchange "1927," but it seems to fit better into the 1926 context of Toomer's assignment.

[52] Ouspensky, out of the picture now, even if his wife and members of her family spent time in the Prieuré, had set up his own headquarters at Lyme, in England, and later, would do the same to a very modest extent at Franklin Farms near Mendham, NJ, where his widow continued the work well into the 1950s. Tanya Ouspensky [Nagro] sold the property.

the pupils were not always invited. Edith recorded a guest list for one such occasion at the Paradou (a residence on the grounds often used for special occasions): "Lucy [G's niece Lucia], Dimitri [G's younger brother], Capananci,[53] Sofia [G's sister], Nicolai [de Stjernvall] and Jeanne de Salzmann, Jean Toomer, Thornton Wilder, [R. P.] Blackmur, Aleister Crowley." Crowley, the celebrated "witch," known popularly as "the Great Beast," was often in trouble with English authorities because of the goings-on in his witch's coven. Orage had known him in London and thought well of him as a writer. Someone had invited him to the Prieuré in anticipation of a combat of magical powers, but apparently both he and Gurdjieff behaved well.[54]

Another of Edith's notes is titled "After-Bath Feast," dated June 1926, and it tells the story of Waldo Frank's break from Gurdjieff.

> Among those present were Margaret Naumburg, Gorham Munson, Waldo Frank, Elsa Munson, Jean Toomer, Richard Orage, and several others. Gurdjieff sat in silence before a table laden with a variety of exotic dishes. Tom and Fritz Peters went about filling glasses with marc,[55] Genia, and Luba passed the plates, everyone sat in mute attention, all eyes focussed on Gurdjieff. While his eyes wandered down the table, he said, "What you wait for, idiots? Who say toasts? Begin, *bolda!*"[56]
>
> The tension broken, the first toast was announced "to candidates" in Russian, then translated into French, and last of all into English.

---

[53] Kapadnadze. My mother did not see many of these names written and assumed their spelled forms. Nikolai de Stjernvall tells me that Gurdjieff detested this Armenian husband of his sister Sofia, though he adored their daughter Lucia.

[54] Fritz Peters, *Boyhood*, p. 67, notes that although the other guests expected Gurdjieff to put Crowley in his place, neither challenged the other's powers. James Webb, *Harmonious Circle*, pp. 314–315, however, probably drawing upon Nott's account (*Journal*, pp. 121–122) says that Crowley was viciously insulted by Gurdjieff and left like a whipped dog. He places that meeting erroneously in the summer of 1927. James Moore, *Myth*, pp. 219–220, has another version. Crowley was notorious as the English leader of the Ordo Templi Orientis.

[55] Tom and Fritz were Margaret Anderson's nephews. Jane Heap adopted Fritz, who later won some renown as a novelist—*World Next Door, Finistère*—and wrote two published accounts of his experiences with Gurdjieff. He sent his first writings to Jean in Chicago in 1933 for comment and encouragement (Toomer Collection, Box 6).

[56] The Saturday night baths were one of the few activities in which the sexes were divided. The women usually went to the baths first, and then the men. Nikolai de Stjernvall told me that the men used the occasion to compete in telling the dirtiest stories they could recall or invent. Doctor de Stjernvall had, apparently, the most salacious wit.

Everyone raised his glass and drank. Gurdjieff then looked to see that all had drained his glass, and commented briefly on those who had sipped a part of the strong and unsavory liquor.[57] After examining the display of dishes before him, Gurdjieff carefully picked the eye out of the sheep's head before him and tossed it someone across the table, and called "Blondine, eat! Very special properties it has, necessary for you." The Blondine lady was horrified; this was her first meeting with Gurdjieff. Waldo Frank had brought her and had introduced her [Alma] as his newly wed. Between mouthfuls, G would berate the couple. To Waldo he said, "You not marry Blondine, why you tell me so? Better you stay with Jewish wife, for Jewish man only Jewish woman corresponding. In bed he use her like handerchief, truth I tell; woman squirm, she know truth I tell."

The following Monday at the Café de la Paix, Gurdjieff was seated at a front table on the terrace; several pupils had left, only I remained, having been told by G, who was going shopping, that he wanted me to guide him across the street to a shop I had recommended. Breaking the silence he said, "Uneasy now, writing hindered, one idiot I see wait for man to go, he wish speak with me alone. He not know I see him wait, but he not have much time. Miss, you sit." Then he took his pencil and began to sharpen the point, although he had a breast pocket filled with finely sharpened ones. Up to the table came Waldo, shaking with rage. He raised his fist, shaking it at G and yelled, "Go back to your hell, you devil, and leave us alone." G looked up with the innocent eye of a child, turned to me and asked, "What angry man say? I not understand." Waldo, exasperated, walked off into the passing crowd. "Now we can fulfill commission, go buy necessary. Miss, you pay, eh?"[58]

---

[57] Gurdjieff preferred armagnac for his toasts, but often served cognac or homemade pinkish peppered vodka. James Webb, *Harmonious Circle*, p. 320, gives his own version of the toasts to "idiots." There were twenty-one in all, but I have never heard more than eight proposed at a single meal. It would be awkward to perform the ultimate, which would be a toast to himself as the "unique idiot." Orage was a "super idiot."

[58] James Moore, *Myth*, p. 221, gives a version of this confrontation, and dates it a year later in the summer of 1927, but Orage was not there that summer, and my mother's notes were made on the spot. As those who spent any length of time learned, usually painfully, Gurdjieff stripped "masks" off of those who approached him. As the translators of the 1960 French version of *All and Everything* (note pp. ix–x): "People could not forgive him for having seen through them and as soon as they were out of his sight, went to great lengths to justify themselves. This was the origin of the most fantastic legends. . . . He even went so far as to provoke them, at times, if only to be rid of curiosity seekers.

During the night of 25–26 June, Gurdjieff's wife, Julia Ostrovska, died,[59] and Jessie accepted nervously Gurdjieff's offer to move into her room. Caesar Zwaska, Margaret Anderson's right-hand man on the staff of *The Little Review*, arrived on the 26th, and on the 27th, twice during the day, Gurdjieff came and took Orage away from Jessie for confidential talks that she supposed had something to do with Gurdjieff's grief. After the funeral of Julia on the 28th, Gurdjieff gave a vodka party and on the next day, Jessie and Edith were assigned new jobs. Jessie was appointed principal typist for the English translations of Gurdjieff's work (there were different teams working independently, often on the same text), and Edith became Orage's and Toomer's editorial assistant for French texts. In early July, Edith and Jane Heap, who had spent a couple of days together in Paris, gave a party for the house. The next day, Edith moved into an apartment in the "Ritz," the second floor usually reserved for honored and first-time guests, and where Gurdjieff had his own rooms. Why she rated special treatment is difficult to say, since the total amount of money she lent Gurdjieff over the years amounted to less than $4500. Perhaps it had something to do with her automobile, for she doubled as Gurdjieff's chauffeur and delivery girl for local trips to Fontainebleau, as well as for trips to Paris and to Le Havre and Cherbourg to meet special guests. On the other hand, it may well be that Gurdjieff wanted her far away from Toomer's lodgings on the "monks' corridor" on the third floor. At this time, most of Gurdjieff's own family circle lived in the Paradou.

On 8 July, Gurdjieff led a small group on a trip to Orleans with Jessie, Orage, the Hartmanns, and Gurdjieff's younger brother, Dmitri. Jean and Edith were not invited, I suspect because Gurdjieff preferred not to speak to either Toomer or Orage when the other was present, and he was probably annoyed at the antics of Jessie and Edith when they were together. Besides the usual complaints about Gurdjieff's driving, many of the party complained of food poisoning. Orage was very ill in Biarritz and Vichy on the 13th and 14th of July, and when Gurdjieff was too drunk to drive outside Biarritz, he ordered Jessie to drive. Within minutes, she sideswiped a *fiacre*, a style of horse-drawn carriage, and the party was stranded for a day while the car was being repaired and while Gurdjieff was using his charms on the driver of the fiacre, whom he paid off with very little so they could get going again. They didn't arrive back at Avon until the 22nd, and Jessie was still upset about the accident, but more about the food poisoning. She

---

[59] Fritz Peters, *Boyhood*, p. 102, is certainly mistaken when he writes that Mme Ostrovsky died in the spring of 1927. He goes on to say (p. 116), that soon after her death, Gurdjieff lived with a married woman who became pregnant. I have not been able to identify her.

told Edith that Gurdjieff had "forced" Orage and others to eat spoiled caviar. It was not unusual for Gurdjieff to prove the digestive powers of his pupils, but Jessie's anger increased when, a couple of days later, Gurdjieff made fun of Orage's "American stomach" at the supper table. Jessie, furious and slightly drunk, went to her room [Orage did not share her elegant quarters, since Gurdjieff had strict moral standards along these lines!], took a pearl-handled Browning revolver that she had "borrowed" from Edith, and went down the corridor toward G's room to shoot him. Edith intercepted her and calmed her down, but Jessie, even after the effects of the drink had worn off, swore that she would get back at Gurdjieff for poisoning Orage. Orage took such incidents in his stride, saying once to his friend and biographer, Philip Mairet, that he had acquired a great deal of tolerance by having "been insulted by an expert."[60]

Edith had received a cable in the meantime that said that her mother was dying, and she left for the United States the next day. That evening, Jane Heap arrived with Margaret Anderson and Georgette LeBlanc, and moved into Edith's apartment in the "Ritz." On 1 August, Gurdjieff set out with Jessie, Orage, and a few of his close friends on an excursion to Sens, Auxerre, Geneva, and Chamonix, while Jean was left behind to work on the book. Gurdjieff discussed plans for the United States with Orage while Jessie acted as a mobile typist, typing book fragments in the back seat even while Gurdjieff drove and chatted with Orage beside him. In Chamonix on 5 August, Jessie wrote in her diary: "Rowed with A. R. last night because of his attitude towards G which strikes me awfully." Four days later, back at the Prieuré, she lamented that "Orage and I had a discussion and missed dinner," and her mood dipped further when, on the 12th, she found a love letter to Orage from an admirer "signed with kisses and endearments. I've never had such a feeling." Gurdjieff made trips to Bar-sur-Aube, Nevers, and Rouen, all without Toomer, but the tension between Gurdjieff, Orage, and Jessie was steadily increasing, and Jessie was beginning to feel that her anticipated marriage was being threatened by Orage's deference to Gurdjieff's whims. On 25 August in Nevers, Jessie wrote: "O and I quarrelled again," and the next day she said: "I wish I could feel it would be alright."

She cheered up in early September when Edith reappeared suddenly, saying she had returned on the same boat on which she sailed from France. From the pier in New York City, she had called her mother, spo-

[60] Cited by Philip Mairet, *A. R. Orage: A Memoir* (Hyde Park, NY: University Press, 1966), p. xxix. Peters, *Boyhood*, p. 31, records Gurdjieff's rage at Orage in his room in the summer of 1925. Orage looked surprised, but stood calm as Gurdjieff insulted him in most violent terms.

ken instead with her stepfather who insulted her, and so turned around and got back on the boat. To celebrate her return, Edith gave a party in the ironing room of the château for all the women, an event she noted hastily on the back of a handwritten recipe for "escalope de veau française": "Georgette Le Blanc's departure,[61] Thornton Wilder's parting-guest tirade. My banquet in ironing room, Madame Ouspensky came." Of the same event, Jessie wrote in her diary: "It was a great success, including the cocktails I mixed." Without her apartment available, Edith moved into her American friend's flat in Paris, though it might have been that she felt uneasy having an affair with Jean under Gurdjieff's roof.

She drove down to the Prieuré almost daily, and noted one day: "Mayor of Fontainebleau luncheon, wine served in ancient bottles, de Salzmann children, Sofia, Luba, Genia, Leda, Bousic [de Salzmann], Michel [de Salzmann], Nicholai, Dr. Sternval, Volia, Tom, Fritz, bicycle parade through Avon."[62] The bicycle parade was described with great humor by Jessie in her diary. It seems that Gurdjieff had bought bicycles for everyone at the Prieuré at a considerable cost, and instructed them on how to ride, his fashion. Then, to display his teaching, he led a long chain of bicycles through Avon and Fontainebleau. A week later, they were all gathering rust.

Through this brief period, Jean continued his private instruction. In early September, Edith cabled Jean from Paris, saying that she was about to leave again for Saratoga. Jean wrote to her from the Institute.

> As you now begin to read this, let your mask, its resistances and defenses, fall. Be what you are inwardly. Be this simply and honestly.
>
> Work upon and with oneself is its own reward, and no one external to oneself can either give or take away, increase or diminish this reward. Yet it is good now and again to receive a sort of confirmation from someone else. The efforts you have made this summer, and the results of them, are yours, independently. But I wish to give my note of recognition, to add my recognition and response to the totality of your experience during this phase.

---

[61] Georgette Le Blanc, star of French stage and mistress for many years of Maurice Maeterlinck, had arrived at the Prieuré with Margaret Anderson and Solita Solano in 1924. The three were inseparable friends until Georgette's death in 1941. Kathryn Hulme joined the group later, and after the war, Dorothy Caruso. The group was known by many as "the lesbian legion," but Gurdjieff called them "the rope" as a group. Margaret Anderson has written enthusiastically about her experience with Gurdjieff in *The Fiery Fountains* and in her account of his teachings, *The Unknowable Gurdjieff*.

[62] Luba, who died in 1995, became well-known in London as proprietor of "Luba's Bistro" on Yeoman's Row, and was author of a cookbook.

By your efforts you have placed in me the foundation and beginning of genuine respect. I mean that I now begin to respect you, not conventionally or because of personal motives, but really. Only conscious effort can win from me such respect. Just as I do not *respect* the growth of a tree, cellular division, or the movements of a cat, so I have no real respect for any sort of mechanical existence, whatever its qualities, from the ordinary viewpoint, may be. I may be interested, attracted, and so on, but I do not respect. Edith, I begin to respect you.

Your life here, and I mean now specifically your, or, better, *her* external behavior at le Prieuré, may be taken as a very vivid epitome or cross section, in detail, of how she has, and, if left to her own devices, of how she will always behave. All elements were of course intensified. But for this very reason they can be the better seen. Try to see them Edith, to see them as clearly and objectively as a second person might. Recall and work over all events and all behavior, candidly, before these things have time to sink back into the unconscious memory. Try to understand them. And then, above all, try to *realize* them, unforgettably.

There is one thing which, I might say above all else, I think you could do, and that is this: the twists, short circuits, doubts, fears, hatreds, and so on, in Edith, were all probably derived from a few outstanding and very painful experiences, which experiences, because of their pain and their painfulness in memory, have been driven deep within you and locked up. But as they were driven within they took much that was fine and splendid with them. And in locking them up, you have locked yourself. Unlock. Unlock by means of a deliberate recalling and rehearsing of these experiences in your consciousness. Non-identify and observe her, and, while continuing to do so, deliberately command the sea to give up its monsters. Try to recall the experiences completely and vividly in pictures. Try to *feel* to the full all that you recall and see, always observing and non-identifying from her. If you do this, you will free them and free yourself. They will pass, leave you forever, And I can think of no finer *exercise* for you for the next one or two months. But you must go at it regularly, consistently, and with complete determination, each day, skipping none, for a definite length of time and a definite hour.

Edith, watch your cleverness, as it may kill you. *She* is terribly clever, worldly-wise in getting what she wants. And yet, even so, her cleverness always falls short. It has never been and never will be enough to get her all she wants. But it can dictate the sacrifice of many things to itself. And it has too often commanded the sacrifice of essential honesty and simplicity.

But lets say that she is clever in controlling people for her ends. Do you become clever in controlling her for your ends. This will necessitate *real* cleverness. Let this challenge your genuine gift. Try to redirect your cleverness on *her*, and you will find all of her manipulations to have been meaningless child's play.

Always I will love what you are in essence. But Edith, do not allow that which has been violated in you to violate what I now tell you.

And always I will wish you a clean and honest life.

Mechanically, she can live cleverly. Now consciously try to let and make her live honestly.

Do not permit *her* to think and feel that she merits and deserves as a matter of course what *you* have received at le Prieuré.[63]

Edith drove down to the Prieuré the next day to say goodbye to Jean and her friends. When she left, she gave Jean a letter, and a day later, three days before she was to sail for New York, she received Jean's reply.

---

le Prieuré, 9 Sept 26

Your letter, which I have just read and which evokes in me the state of being that I had Tuesday, is from you. And again, as I did then, I feel, so wonderfully, that his is a holy place, and that you and I touched and now do touch and intermingle in what is sacred.

Let us call what happened the birth of essence in you. You being born into consciousness. For it was in truth, dear Edith, a moment when the consciousness of your essence manifested in

---

63 Edith Taylor Papers.

and almost completely dissolved your ordinary, acquired, and superficial consciousness. It was a moment foreshadowing the introduction of objective conscience into your usual awareness. During it—and you still experience it—you tasted, in actuality, the qualities which make up conscience: you felt faith, impartial love, the desire to make conscious effort, courage (contrasted with which your ordinary show of 'courage' was so false and shallow), and aspiration. But I had better say that you foretasted these things, for the full experience of them is a hundred times deeper and more intense. But the foretaste was real, actual, and deep. Doubt as to conscious possibilities, doubt concerning essence and being, were dissolved in it. You knew for certain that these things were so. And also you knew beyond all doubt that there are two of you, you really, and her, with whom you have been identified, whom you have been hypnotized to believe was you.

The experience still lasts. But, dear, my figure of a birth must be taken literally. All new born things must, by their nature, fall to sleep often. And the periods of sleep are always longer than the moments of waking. Before so very long, unless your own efforts combine with an exceptionally favorable set of circumstances to effect the contrary, you, the essence, will fall asleep, will retire into the subconsciousness. As a _real_ _state_ _of_ _being_, this experience will slip away from you. And what will then be you will only be able to recall it in memory. And you may even be led to doubt that it ever happened. But _it_ _did_ _occur_. _It did_ _occur_. And now there comes for you the long, slow perhaps, and perhaps painful—but consciously painful—task, no, not task but _duty_, of making it and other similar experiences occur again, and then again, and then again, by deliberate conscious effort, until the point of definite, final crystallization, until you have it as a state of being subject to your will, independent of external accidents.

In order to achieve this, three things are necessary, one of which is already provided, namely, Time. And the other two are: your own constant and ever increasing conscious efforts, and, external circumstances which are favorable to these efforts.

To make conscious effort, it is absolutely necessary to have _energy_ at one's disposal for this purpose. Nothing is possible without energy. And from one point of view, energy is the secret of it all. In general, each one of us has a definite, quite definite quantity of energy for use. It is possible to increase this amount.

It is also possible to increase the quality and intensity. But to begin with, we have just so much, which energy is derived from the mystery of existence, and which we also derive each day from the food we eat. But at the present time, with most of us, this energy serves our essence practically not at all. It comes into us. It is differentiated for various usages. And just at this moment, the machine, personality, and the consequences of Kundabuffer step up, and not only claim but suck up and carry off practically all of it.[64] The demands of the machine are much too large, because the machine leaks and is without a driver who can intelligently look after and control it. And the demands of personality and Kundabuffer are literally criminal, with the result that we, as beings with conscious possibilities, are, from the point of view of <u>contained</u> energy, bankrupt. More and more I come to see and realize that <u>he</u>, together with the consequences of Kundabuffer which are still in him, are like monstrous, blood sucking creatures whose enormous mouths are constantly sucking <u>my</u> substance, my energy into themselves. As long as I remained

---

[64] "Kundabuffer" is the Gurdjieffian term for the peculiar organ in Earthmen that blinds them to the providential design to which their existence contributes—to save them from destroying themselves in despair—and that heightens physical feelings of pleasure. See Gurdjieff, *All and Everything*, pp. 87–93, 1120. Later, in the chapter "The Holy Planet Purgatory," Beelzebub explains that kundabufffer is an organ at the base of the tail that functioned to prevent men from seeing reality, "never-allowing-one-to-sleep-in-peace." It makes the imaginary and the illusory seem real. Louise March, (McCorkle, *The Gurdjieff Years,* p. 39) says that kundabuffer is a name for Original Sin. The organ, more properly known as *kundalini*, is now lost, but its effects remain, so that we believe the world we see is real. We know external things, then, but not internal things. The world is real, but our seeing isn't. Orage says: "There must be something to explain why we are all such fools, why we are not self-conscious, why we treat ourselves with such care; this something we call kundabuffer" (C. Daly King, *The Oragean Version*, p. 259). Earlier Orage notes that "in reality Kundalini is the power of the imagination, the power of fantasy that takes place of a real function" (p. 220). It keeps man in his mental sleep. There are four states of being: sleep (lack of consciousness), waking (a hypnotic state, daydreaming), self-consciousness (awareness) and cosmic consciousness (one's self in its totality). Man has and needs many buffers. They protect him from unwanted outside influences, and they can be removed only with careful instruction. Others have seen kundabuffer as a term for original sin. The neurosurgeon Dr. Keith Buzzell has made an etiological scan of the concept in "Kundabuffer," *All & Everything '97*, eds. H. J. Sharp and Seymour Ginsburg (Bognor Regis: Privately published, 1997) pp. 80–103. Toomer is echoing Gurdjieffian terminology throughout this and the other letters. The "machine" that is man is his mechanical instinct.

unconscious, I could of course do nothing, but was helpless. And even now, owing to the relative smallness of my mouth, and to the fact that gravity, that is <u>habit</u> and all social influence, is in their direction, a constant vigilance is necessary if I am to get a bare minimum. And without this, nothing at all is possible.

And here we see the sheer chemical, that is, energy reason for a whole aspect of the Gurdjieff work. Gurdjieff says, no titillation. By titillation he means all the varieties of masturbation that the mechanical contemporary person is habitually engaged in: sex trifling, bodily inactivity and unproductiveness, all the types of emotionalism, romancing, dreaming, imagining, mental theorizing and so-called "thinking" on the basis of ideas which have no relation to the reality of man and the universe. God, how much of our energy is sucked up by these things. And it is only by closing their mouths and letting them die and finally casting them from us that we, as beings, will have the energy, which now goes to them, available for our purposes.

And it is the same in the case of our old, that is, acquired values. The other day at the café Gurdjieff said to me: Toomer, during my life I have had many aims, a different aim for each phase. Now I tell you what my aim is: to destroy, to kill all values.

The old <u>must</u> die, else we will have no energy, no wish for new, and for what every essence knows to be, real values.

Hartman [sic] told me of a simple but very wonderful thing Gurdjieff did during the last trip. Little Leda had somehow gotten possession of a cheap toy watch and had grown quite attached to it. One day while they were sitting at a café, Gurdjieff saw her kissing and fondling it. He reached over, snatched it from her hands, threw it on the sidewalk, and crushed it with his foot. Leda was heart-broken, went to her father and cried bitterly. All day she was inconsolable. Gurdjieff paid no attention to her. But the next day he bought and gave her a genuine watch.

This aspect of our work, this deliberate conscious attempt to redirect our energies, this deliberate killing and letting die old values, is the necessary complement of the aspect whose base lies in observation and non-identification. At first glance, the two aspects may seem to involve contradictory attitudes. Observation and non-identification imply an unconcern as to how these organisms behave. Whatever their behavior, it is enough to observe and non-identify. True. To redirect energy and kill old values imply a concern as to how organisms behave. We must make effort to do things with them. True also. And <u>both</u> must be included in one's work. For unless <u>she</u> dies and is re-directed, she will either make conscious work impossible, or, what is infinitely worse, <u>she will</u> grow and fatten on it, sucking the conscious energy which you generate, in addition to what she already sucks. This is the <u>great temptation</u>.

How these two attitudes alternate, complement each other, and blend, you will find out practically as you continue working.

About favorable conditions, I will write, or we will talk about them later. For the time being I think and feel that the course of your life will supply you with circumstances and problems and difficulties which are right and which will provide you with the opportunity for a direct continuation of what you began here. From your letter I get, in addition to the beauty of spiritual directness and essential response, a note of firmness, of resolution, and of clear direction. This is enough.

I am certain that you will have an unmistakable feeling as to your coming or not coming down for the bath. In either case, I will understand. And so also about writing me again before you go away. Things essential are not written easily, while it is most difficult if not impossible to write of other things while essence still lives in one. It was this letter, the one received this morning, that I wanted. I wanted it very very much.

We have, dear Edith, a deep, clean, rich, and somehow inexpressably sweet base, together. This is real. From it, all else will radiate, just as, from time to time, all else must return to it. Write when you can and feel to.

And too, if you feel to write about them, send me such notes as will let me see your practical problems and how you are handling them.

Within myself I feel that during the next two weeks, or, by the end of this month at most, my work and place of work will have been decided.

I have your New York address. Yesterday I looked in my address book and found, as I was sure I would, a whole page, my last entry, given to your addresses and telephones.

As I told you, I have already written Stieglitz to send the mss of my book to you at 747 Madison Ave.[65] I asked him to send it immediately, and it should be—as I wish—there awaiting your arrival. If it is not, and if it does not come soon, you might write him directly, asking for it, and saying that I wish you to have it, a letter having been sent by me to him to this effect.

So, dear.

Good by, and bless you.

Jean

And I am thankful, how deeply deeply thankful I am Edith that I did mean that [to?] you. Someday I will tell you, or you will see and understand what our experience till now has meant to me.

As you drove out and I took your hand there was that about you—I can find no words to tell it in—but it almost overwhelmed me. And then I listened to Mrs. Lithow enumerate all the Americans who had left le Prieuré!

J

Edith wrote back at once:

I read your message this morning and will read it again tomorrow morning, the next morning, in fact I will start each new day with it, and try to carry out its intent. I want this with all my being.

I am as much at a loss today to express my feelings as I was yesterday, in the concierge's loge, but I feel you know what was going on inside me, even better than I. Being away from Prieuré helps me so see more clearly all that happened to me there, nothing matters now but the work I have to do, all else I realize, as futile unless it can be used for this work.

Thank you for showing me truths, for showing me my direction, in helping me change my set of values—and for the richness of you. Good bye. God bless you to all eternity.

Edith[66]

The steamship was fully booked, however, and there was no cancelation to allow Edith aboard, so she stayed on in Paris until she could find a berth. Meanwhile, Orage was consulting with Gurdjieff concerning his return to

---

[65] The work was a draft of *From Exile Into Being*. It remains unpublished.

[66] Toomer Collection, Box 8, Folder. This is one of the two letters from Edith that is extant in his papers.

the United States to raise funds for the château and to prepare another visit for himself. Jessie was increasingly anxious about plans to return to America with Gurdjieff, and with some relief she wrote on 11 September that "Orage promised not to stay here more than two months and not to go back to New York if Gurdjieff goes." What Jessie did not know was that Gurdjieff was planning to keep Orage in France and to send Jean to take general control of the American operations outside of New York, where Gurdjieff himself thought of spending the winter and spring of each year. He knew well that the New York group was his major financial support, and he wanted to control the source.

At this time, Jean was writing out "Notes for a New Group," a sort of syllabus for a Toomer version of the work. He calls his terms "ordinary . . . but to these ordinary terms we give a new, exact and technical meaning. . . . Whatever contains, exists according to, and manifests the laws of 3 and 7 is a cosmos."[67] Then, in a lyrical outburst of extraordinary introspection, Jean wrote: "It was perhaps no accident that drove me to take me with the dust of earth which cannot leave this spatial sphere, and thus, obeying its own laws, binds me. It is as if there were one God in the universe who, at the moment of my birth, pinched my eyes to pinpoints and who now has touched them to become vague openings, saying, 'It is a matter of indifference to me whether you are more or not.'" [68]

While Orage and Jessie were off to London on the 13th to consult with his solicitor concerning his income and the sale of *The New Age*, Edith finally found passage for her own return to the United States on 17 September. When she told Jean, he wrote:

> le Prieuré, 14 Sept
>
> My darling
>
> Just after sending you the telegram I went with Gurdjieff to Fontainebleau and sat with him all morning while he wrote ten pages of the third descent.[69] He told me that he would go to Paris in the afternoon, and that we would not start off until sometime today.

---

[67] Toomer Collection, Box 46, Folder 956. Gurdjieff said frequently that deep thoughts must be disguised by ordinary expessions that appear emptied of meaning.

[68] Toomer Collection, Box 48, Folder 957. Toomer typed this out in an outline of a lecture to be given at the University of Michigan on 25 March 1927.

[69] Beelzebub's third sojourn on Earth in *All and Everything* during which he makes some telling observations on the vanity of contemporary earth societies, most particularly America.

After lunch, I suddenly realized that I had a twenty-four hour interval between two phases, one, completely ended and rounded off in all senses, the other, carrying unknown potentials, not to be begun for a whole day. And with this sense of interval there began to descend on me a weariness, a sort of accumulated fatigue that was so material that I could almost see it, like one can see chemicals precipitate in a test tube, or like one can see fog settling on a landscape. I knew immediately that I must either give in to it completely: loaf in the sunshine or go to sleep, or else I must make quick effort to drive through and pass beyond it. I decided upon the latter course, got into my work clothes, and went out into the garden to combine instructive work with mental effort. By tea time I had dug, raked, and prepared a bed, but all my functions moved sluggishly, and the fatigue continued to descend. After tea I went out to water—the hose seemed incredibly heavy. There was a touch of autumn in the air, but this only served to chill me, and despite my sweater and my quickened movements I grew colder and colder. Before long, I felt my throat getting sore, and the beginning of a head cold. And then there it was—the fatigue, the residue of four months' effort settled and fixed upon the body, causing it [to] feel, for the first time in months, downright wretched. I finished watering—by the way, our tomato plant is not only thriving, it is absolutely <u>husky</u>—and came in.

I came to my room right after dinner and laid down, giving up effort, simply relaxing and giving way to what I felt. The worker gave way to the man. Very much I wanted you. I wanted to rest in you. For once to rest in you. To have you take and hold me, all being you and I so living. I had an image of your eyes, direct, simple, inwardly glowing, and tender. They are very wonderful then. I saw the extra-ordinarily fine line of your face curving from neck to chin. I felt the play of your fingers and the exquisite yielding in giving which your body is capable of. And then my weariness began to lift, buoyed up by a stream of sheer playfulness. There is a fund of playfulness in me, and I want to play with those I like, though it is not frequent that I do so. I wanted to play with you. I went through capers and antics that even in pictures make me laugh. I saw you too <u>really</u> laughing. It was all so good that before I knew it I had bounced off the bed and was standing with open eyes looking—at the bare walls of this room.

They would have dashed my mood had I continued so. I went upstairs, found Gertrude, Ilonka,[70] and Liliane in their room and gave them what should have been lived with you. I played with them, told them stories, and made them laugh until 11:30.

Once back here, I found that I could again think to some purpose. And as usually happens, you came in for your full share of what concerned me. I shan't try to give you now all the pros and cons of my thinking; I'll simply tell you in brief what it was I saw really clearly for the first time. Your attraction towards, and external comfort with, a certain type of person has been a subject for my analysis during what seems to me a very long time. Certainly this attraction is not accidental, but has its source in what have been the necessities of your own nature as modified by social, that is, external influences. And these same necessities have, on the other hand, made you shun and feel uncomfortable with another type of person. You know what the two types are I refer to. Up till last night I had discovered several what seem to me basic and accurate explanations of this. And last night I added another, which is so interesting and may prove to be significant. It is this: it is a question of <u>articulateness</u>, of what things you can express, on what planes of experience and reality you are <u>articulate</u>. In all of us there is the wish to be articulate, and we will necessarily be drawn to deal with those things and those circumstances which are likely to provide us with the opportunity of being so. Early in your life, and over a prolonged period you were repeatedly and, I judge, rather forceably inhibited, not only from speaking sincerely, but also from speaking about those things which really interested you. And often, in any case, you had no one at all to speak to about anything. With this double result: because of lack of simple practice, the aspects of life which had real meaning for you became literally inexpressable, you became gradually inarticulate with respect to what <u>you</u> really thought, and questioned. And moreover, the time came when there grew up and crystalized in you, in sheer reaction, the attitude, as you once expressed it to me, that no one would get your response to anything without asking for it, and he would be damn lucky to get it even with the asking. And, secondly, there grew and accumulated in you, owing to the same cause, the need to speak to, communicate with, and contact

---

[70] Ilonka Karasz, later a noted illustrator for the *New Yorker*, married to Wim [Wilhelm] Nyland.

something, anything, anyone, selection in terms of real interest being no longer in question, the one desire being to break your mute loneliness by means of almost anyone or anything. Circumstances were such that you broke (in a sense) and became articulate on what you have always known to be a superficial plane. On it, you are now articulate. And this fact binds you to it.

But though the expression of essential things was difficult and came to be almost impossible, you did not cease to function inwardly in essential terms. Only, you have, as they say, kept your real thoughts and feelings to yourself. I think that you must now try more and more to develop an articulateness which will be commensurate with your real experiences. More and more seek people with whom you can express these things. And, once having found them, more and more talk to them, encouraging real exchanges and discussion rather than the opposite. I want you to become articulate with me. And to this end I want you to write me much more often than a certain part of you will be inclined to. I want you to write me of what you do, tell me your thoughts and feelings, what you discover in life and in yourself, your realizations, and all the various significances. Now I want to know what you have done in Paris, what inner experiences have run parallel with this, what Paris, your old life, your old grooves and pigeon-holes, your old acquaintances now mean to you. I will expect a letter, however brief, mailed before your boat sails. And then one about your passage over, written on the steamer, and mailed when you reach New York. And then one about your reestablishing contact in New York. And as many more as you like! Yes, Edith?

And Oh, I am to get a cable from New York. We will be back for the bath a week from Saturday, a day or so before the de Grasse reaches N.Y.

There can be no good by

but all my love

J-

When Edith arrived in New York, a letter in a "Grand Hôtel" envelope mailed from Briançon with an undecipherable postmark date, addressed to 747 Madison Ave., New York City, Etats-Unis was waiting for her.

Sunday

Darling

Just about the time your boat was leaving yesterday, I was ascending the Alpes toward the Col de Gabilier on foot, owing to the fact that the de Dion, crawling and sputtering and panting, could not stand my weight. What a day! We were up at 6 A.M., and I began the day with coffee and three marcs.[71] This was in Albertville. About 10 o'clock we reached St. Jean du Maurienne—the finest French town that I've seen—and there had, for us, a large breakfast, including eggs and cheese, and, of course, any number of marcs. Soon after leaving St. Jean, the ascent up and over the Col de Gabilier began. Gurdjieff bought no essence [sic], and, among other things, I expected it to give out before we were half way up. I can't begin to describe all that happened. We had to run in first speed. Every two hundred feet or so we'd carry water from some more or less accessible mountain stream, fill the radiator and move on. Picture this happening all the way up. And then, at times, the car simply could not pull all of us. Gurdjieff and Madam Hartman would remain in it, and the rest of us walk. Somehow, about 3 P.M. we reached the summit. The sight of earth from there was enormous, and I shall never in all my life forget the picture of Gurdjieff, standing on a promontory, looking over it all.

After passing through the tunnel to the other side, the car practically stopped dead. Not only had essence given out, but the gears and things were so swollen that there was no moving them. No essence to be had by ordinary means. Gurdjieff works manipulations on the driver of a sort of sight-seeing car, and manages to get a little. At the little summit house we drink coffee and five of the worse marcs I ever tasted. No food. Gurdjieff promises food at the first town we reach. At 4 we start down. Car cannot carry all of us—descent very steep and tortuous. Picture Hartman and myself, full of marc, running down the mountain short cuts in advance of the car, like a pair of mountain goats—I was never so sure-footed—Hartman telling me one Russian anecdote after another. After about 3/4 of an hour of this, the car picked us up, and on we went. I sat with Gurdjieff in the front seat. The fumes and finally the smoke of over heated oil began to trouble

---

[71] A potent aqua vita made from the grape skins left over from pressing for wine. It is a specialty of Bourgogne.

us. And the seats beneath got hot. The smoke, growing thicker and more stinging, soon became unbearable. We stopped, and we no sooner raised the seats and one floor board than flames shot up. There was a scurry to put the fire out, Gurdjieff raising hell, as he had been doing all day. When we next tried to start, it was almost impossible to shift the gears. And though we did manage first and second, high speed was impossible and remained so for the rest of the day. Essence was expected to give out. Somehow, on we rolled and jerked. We came to one town, a possible stop. G looked at it, and moved on. Still no food. In this way we passed three towns. In the third, we luckily got essence. By the grace of Beelzebub we finally arrived here and stopped, about 7:30. Now the car is in the garage. Today therefore we remain here, but, if possible, start off again before nightfall.

I enclose an Alps flower, It is very near your color, very near you, and so I saw, picked, and now send it.

love,

J-

He wrote again a day or so later in an envelope postmarked "AVON BAN-LIEU S.E 10^{30} 29.9.26."

le Prieuré, 27 Sept 26

Darling,

Our trip ended marvelously and quite in keeping with all that went before. On the last day we had two accidents, and the car, disabled beyond repair, had to be towed cross country to Dijon, there to await a new part, while five of us, leaving Gurdjieff and Madam Hartman in Dijon, took a train which finally landed us in Fontainebleau at 5 with the moon still shining.

Today I find myself in Samois, at the same hotel where the bicycle party had coffee. I went to Fontainebleau for my typewriter which also was in need of repairs, and, on the way back, saw the train for Samois and simply took it.

During the trip Gurdjieff and I talked "business." It was decided that I come to America to conduct the work there, while

Orage is to remain here for work with Gurdjieff on the book. So it was decided, and if this were not le Prieuré and if Gurdjieff were not Gurdjieff, I would say that it is definitely so. But there is still another trip to be gone through before I can possibly eliminate all alternatives by sailing for New York. Gurdjieff has already gone off again. Orage has not yet returned. He is expected today or tomorrow. When he does, then he and I are to set out to meet Gurdjieff wherever he may be then. And during this coming trip, the decisions of the previous trip may be blown into thin ribbons. At the present time, however, everything combines to confirm my coming to America. This is all I know.

"We shall return from the present trip within ten days, and soon thereafter, by all _normal_ calculations, and if the present plans hold, I should be sailing. And so, dear, within three, or, at most, four weeks, you may expect a phone from me. If you don't get it, then immediately know that the long arm of the Institute has cut the wires between this possible and its actualization.

my love

Jean

[At the bottom of this page, an additional note:]

29 Sept

I kept this letter a day or two, awaiting new developments. Orage has not yet returned and for the moment at least his whereabouts are unknown. Meanwhile, Hartman and myself are going ahead with the translation of the 3rd descent and, by Gurdjieff's orders, I am to devote all my time to this. And by the present plans, if Orage does not return before then, Hartman and I are to leave here Sunday to meet Gurdjieff in Briançon. So!

Your cable came last night and brought me joy and more than joy. But it gave me a sense of the distance between us, and this was cruel.

love, dear,

J-

The next letter was written in pencil:

Fontainebleau, 5 Oct

Edith my darling my dearest my very very dearest, all the while I was at work here in a café in Fontainebleau, something—I didn't at first clearly realize what—kept insisting on my recognizing it. First it was, I think, somehow just the place itself—and a great large something in me. And then the sound of French horns. And then the purring of a special motor which I have learned to know. And then the actual nameplate! Donnet Zedel. And then someone passing with a hat which reminded me of yours. And then finally I knew that the whole place was full of you. And then just the opposite—suddenly I realized that the whole town seemed to be taunting me with your absence. The feeling was so acute, my wishing for you, my wish to feel to see to hold, my feeling of a great vacancy at the side of me where my hand almost reached out for you, that I arose immediately and did what I could—sent you a cable. And since then I have been wandering about much much more than lonely,—I have been aching for you—

Today I practically finished my revision of the translation of the third descent. There are some extrordinary formulations in it concerning the genuine teachings of Saint Buddha, "Prana," and the most definite and detailed formulation of Kundabuffer yet given. And also some keen bits of comedy and satire. Hartman and I, even in the midst of driving work— which has sometimes lasted from 9:30 A.M. straight on to 2 in the morning—have had more than once to take time off to laugh or wince at them. Often I have wished that you were here to talk over passages with me and to help me with words and phrases—and to laugh! When and if I come over I'll bring the pages of the original translation with me so that you can see what Beelzebub reads like in the raw.

As for news at the end —
Gurdjieff is expected to return tomorrow or next day.
Orage is not yet here, and still no word of him. But within a week, whatever the case with him, I intend to have my own plans settled as to America or not.

Jane [Heap] is still here. And she still puffs out and has her fists up at me, but surely such regular attendance must win her objective merits.

However that may be, Metz is back and is out of sorts with me, not only because I am doing the translation, which he more than hoped to <u>fall</u> into, but also because he once saw Lillian and myself talking together.

And so it goes, merrily enough, but just a bit monotonous.

People are stupid not because they do a thing but because they repeat it.

Whenever will a letter come from you!!?

love

J-

How goes the reading of the manuscript?

And you, <u>You</u>? my darling.

The last letter in this series is postmarked "FONTAINEBLEAU 11 55 12 10 26" and was sent to the Madison Avenue address "par SS 'Paris' Oct 13th Havre":

Prieuré, 10 Oct

Dearest,

Today is Sunday and today your letter came—after what seems to me to have been long tedious ages.

It is a good letter. I wanted it. And now that I have it and just because it is a good letter it makes me want you more and it makes me miss you, you really, terribly.

I am very glad, deeply so, that you found out, without negative emotions and resentments and without imaginations, fancies, what Curtis means to you.[72] I am glad that he means just that. And it is a fine thing that you could have such a clean realization, and that you can tell me sincerely of it. I am glad for you,

---

[72] Curtis Moffat, the American photographer in Paris referred to earlier.

because I know by it that "something" which we'll go over together perhaps before so very long. Or perhaps we'll never need
to do so. For myself personally, as man, well of course you know.
Curtis cannot sincerely concern me since I do not know him,
save through you. But I think that this will be good for him also.

Your meeting with D. Watson must have been interesting in
more ways than one. That night when he got tipsy, and, for that
matter, all along, I am certain that you were more aware of his
manifestations than he himself was.

I hope that you have Donnet for use now.

About things here—

Translation has been going on at a furious pace. The third descent finished, and already the first part of the fourth. This work
has meant a very great deal to me. In addition to the effort and
intensity required, I have deepened my understanding as to ideas.
Gurdjieff's use of language, and the meaning of a number of
words and phrases which heretofore had never conveyed a pre-
cise idea to me. Gurdjieff's use of three little words, namely:
"there," "then," and "also" and too, "skill" and "already," is simply
miraculous from the point of view of psychological experience. I
told him this, and he replied that for a long time these words had
either been omitted entirely from the translation or rendered in-
exactly, and that he had only discovered this when this summer
he listened attentively to all that was read. And too, I have received from Gurdjieff personally what seems to be the only definitive formulation and explanation of "intentional suffering"
yet given. Always and all through the book one meets the phrase:
"conscious labors and intentional suffering." And no one seemed
to know what the last half meant. Well . . . so . . . but all of this
when I see you and in due time.[73]

It is strange that Alp flower did not reach you. When <u>dry</u>, it
was very fragile; but when it <u>lived</u>, it grew high high up on the
Alps.

But let me tell you something that will more than make up for
this. You know our tomato plant? Well, it has already given four
firm ripe tomatoes which I have eaten, right straight from the

---

[73] I have no idea what explanation Gurdjieff gave Jean here, but the sense Gurdjieff
seems to attach to the term in the chapter, entitled "The Holy Planet Purgatory," is the
pain of those trying to perfect themselves by purging "sin." In its more common and
banal use, "intentional suffering" designates the suffering caused by a self-observation
incited by another person's negative action.

plant. But this is only half of it. Something wholly unprecedented has happened. What do you think? You could never imagine it, and the thing has happened in fact. Beside our plant, in the same spot, <u>still</u> <u>another</u> <u>plant</u> <u>is</u> <u>already</u> <u>growing</u>, and it too now is having flowers!! Nowhere else in the garden are there <u>two</u> like this. In fact, a number of the supposedly hardy plants withered and died some time ago. But not only has our plant thrived, and, as I wrote you, become <u>husky</u>, and not only does it now give fruit, but already in the same soil <u>another</u> grows beside it! Even I, who often talk in symbols, would never have dreamed of such a thing!

Monday evening

I had to leave off writing yesterday—more work and to Fontainebleau with Gurdjieff. And now another day has passed, a day so packed full of things that I seem as though I would burst from sheer internal pressure.

As I write this, now, you in America already have my cable telling you that I come to America, and that I leave on the de Grasse this coming Saturday, that is, Oct 16th.

Orage has not returned yet. But as I wrote you, it was necessary for me to settle my own plans, if necessary, irrespective of him. Today I talked things over with Gurdjieff, and he again said that I go to America, while Orage remains here. So, after all, all plans have been arranged according to the decision reached during the trip to Briançon. And so my darling, a few very very necessary details concerning my arrival in New York.

The first, and the only first one I want to see when I arrive is—you. I leave France the 16th, and this means that I dock, in all probability, sometime on Monday the 25th. Whatever the case, I'll send you a radio the day before we land. Edith, for the sake of whatever you hold dear, <u>be</u> <u>in</u> <u>New</u> <u>York</u> <u>on</u> <u>that</u> <u>day</u> and Edith my dearest keep all that day and evening and the next morning and even the next day <u>free</u> <u>to</u> <u>be</u> <u>with</u> <u>me</u>. If I am not with you for the first day or so I shall be wrenched to pieces, I shall be twisted and torn more cruelly, so cruelly that I don't want to even foreshadow it as a possibly—so very much I want to see you. The first and only person I want to see on hand when I cross the gangplank is you, <u>you.</u> Can you feel how much I want this? If you can feel it with your whole being, darling, you will be there. I want you to meet the boat, and when I ask this I am aware that I am asking contrary to her wish not to be seen. I do it deliberately with reason as well as with wish. When you receive my radio, then reassure me by immediately sending me a radio telling me that you will be there.

For the first week I am in New York I'll stay at the Prince George, 28th St. and 5th Ave. We'll go directly there, and then, either remain there, or, if you'd rather, go up to your apartment, only, dearest Edith, we must not be bothered by anyone or anything. I shall arrange my own plans to fit in with this, and only on the second or third day will I begin what I have to do in New York generally.

I have not the slightest idea as to what my state will be just on arriving in New York. I may be feeling marvelous, joyous, full of power and energy. I may be tired and tense. My life here for the past few weeks has been really terrific. What the sudden change to an ocean trip will mean, I can't know. It may relax me, and land me in New York quite clear and calm. It may completely upset my rhythms and functions. God only knows. The one and only thing I do know is that whatever my state I shall want and need to see and be with you, immediately. And if I don't, I shall be unable to control the shock of it. Dearest, I write this to you with my whole heart.

Already it is very late, and I have had more than an ordinary day, having been to Paris to see about my ticket, talked with Gurdjieff, worked on a translation of the fourth descent—how apes came into existence, explained on the basis of cosmic laws—and I have had something like 8 marcs, 5 Quitches[sic], 10 Benedictines, 1 Armangyac [sic], 3 unknown drinks, one bottle of Médoc, 1 cognac, and innumerable coffees. And I have just come from G's room, after listening to some at once marvelous and terrible music. And I live—and indeed I am still sober. And indeed, dear— I must have several special names for you very soon. I have been clear and sober the whole day. The trouble is, that whereas 3 drinks before used to turn the trick, the devil only knows how many it would take now. And this is not only very very expensive! but the practice will have to be discarded the day before I reach New York, if not sooner. It is a special practice and belongs only to the special conditions under which I have been existing here.

> Or perhaps it is a good custom for everywhere under all conditions! You will have to decide that for me when I reach New York.
>
> Goodnight sweetheart
>
> J-[74]

The Orages returned to the Prieuré on 12 October, and decided that Jessie should sail to the United States before Orage. Jessie had passage on the MSS Majestic on 20 October, and her impending departure made the Prieuré seem all the more uncomfortable for her. She wrote in her diary that she was "most depressed to be back and hate the idea of going or staying." The next day, she wrote: "What a day! God how I hate this place." On 17 October, at lunch, Gurdjieff served Orage dogmeat, and Jessie was furious. The day after, Gurdjieff said goodbye to Jessie with the order: "You leave half of you here!"

She arrived in New York one day after Jean had arrived, and saw Edith, Gorham Munson, and Jane Heap the same afternoon to catch up on news of Orage's New York group. A day later, she had a long talk alone with Jean to give him Orage's news and to say that Gurdjieff was calling for the money held by the New York group. A week later, Orage wrote her from France saying: "By the way, the New York group is $650 short on its 1st quarterly payment! Toomer's doesn't count, of course." At the same time, he wrote Sherman Manchester, the new treasurer of the group: "You know from Toomer and Munson about the accounts of the $5000 fund; and Toomer's pluck and generosity in undertaking the repayment of the loan to your fund himself."[75] On 30 October, Jean visited Jessie to explain the account orally, and the next day he and Jessie met in Jane Heap's apartment to explain it for the New York group that she represented. Jessie noted laconically in her diary that "we thrashed things out." On All Hallows' Day at the Roma restaurant, Jean and Jessie lunched with other members of the New York group, including its temporary secretary, Rita Romilly, to repeat the accounting. In her diary, Jessie remarked: "Dreaded the meeting. I don't think it went off too well on my part. I guess I was too scared. Jean was awfully good."[76]

---

[74] Kerman and Eldridge, *The Lives of Jean Toomer*, p. 169, say only that my mother met Jean's boat, but I have no idea what their source was.

[75] Orage papers, courtesy of Mrs. Anne Orage.

[76] I can only speculate without any evidence on the animosity that seemed to exist between Rita and Jean. Jean never mentioned her name to me, but Rita spoke about Jean with consistent irritation. I would guess wildly that Rita had thoughts of being Orage's successor in New York or Gurdjieff's confidant in the United States, and that Jean was a threat to her ambitions.

On 4 November, a worried Orage wrote Jessie in New York, asking, "Have you heard from Toomer? He was to cable his Chicago address, but he hasn't so far." Three days later came another letter saying: "I_hope Toomer has left for Chicago"; then on the 9th: "Jean is probably in Chicago by now; and, in fact, G thought he was already there and half expecting a cheque from him. I didn't tell anyone that Jean was staying in N.Y. for some days, but I was mildly amused at the thought of it. As for any wrong impression he can produce—well, it's not so serious if he's not staying there. He'll learn a lot on his own in Chicago." Orage had no idea that Jean was lingering in New York because Edith was there, but assumed that Jean was helping Jessie with the financial accounts of the group. Consequently, on the 13th, Orage wrote: "It was quite a good idea to use Jean. You know I always did myself—and, of course, because I felt him to be really serious. He could always be counted on to be serious in a serious situation. I had written him re his gift to the Institute,"[77] a reference to Orage's explanation to Gurdjieff that Toomer was giving separately "for policy." On 12 November, Orage wrote Jean directly to say that Gurdjieff and Hartmann were still confused over the money sent. He assumed that Jean had authorized the use of the $2000 allocated to the publication fund for maintaining the château, and expected that Jean would replenish that fund out of his Chicago collections.

After Jessie wrote Orage about a luncheon and meeting at Edith's with Jean to discuss the status of contributions, since she and Jean were the parties through which groups' contributions were passing to Gurdjieff, Orage wrote back with little amusement:

> Jean's situation . . . is quite different. The Obermann business is nothing—I shouldn't find it so—he has a nucleus of people before him and a book behind him, Also, as you say, he should have gone [to Chicago] before his feet cooled. However, in criticising "Jean" in these days, I know I'm risking your reaction. I always said you were fond of him, you know! And I was not in the least surprised, except by your surprise, to hear you had rung him up from Edith's to come there, and take you home to talk or that your heart to heart talk left you liking him "immensely" and in relations you are sure Gurdjieff would like. In fact, my darling Jessie, if "Jean" were only white, I should consciously advise you to go to Chicago and cooperate with him there. You would be a thousand times happier in equal associaton with a being of your own age. . . . I have not the least suspicion, darling, that your

---

77 Orage papers.

frank and heart to heart talk with "Jean" travelled outside Institute business to your personal relations; but I merely take note of
the fact that in your desperation you <u>could</u> forget all about Edith
and "Jean" and time and place and so on. . . . Well, so much for
<u>one</u> unpleasant trifle. I shall only add that if "Jean" calls you
"Dwight" again, I shall take the occasion "to kavatar."[78]

Toomer's charm almost undid him on this occasion. A few days later, he
was off to Chicago with an Edith who also wondered about the sudden intensity of Jean's relations with Jessie. A few weeks later, Orage wrote to
Chicago in a cool tone to say that Gurdjieff expected money at any moment. Orage's earlier fears that Jean would be led by Gurdjieff into promising more than he could deliver seem to have been justified. Since his
return, Jean had been in contact with Mabel Dodge Luhan again, feeling
optimistic about the possibility of Taos for the work.[79] He probably mentioned this to Gurdjieff, who would have seized the occasion to ask for
more Luhan money that Jean assumed he could deliver.

At the end of November, Jean replied to Orage, assured him that the
accounts were straight, and appealed to Jessie's satisfaction with the bookkeeping in New York. He repeated that he had given Gurdjieff $500 when
he left France, but did not think he was expected to return the $1050 to
Orage's fund. Replacement of the money was a New York City debt, he
insisted, acknowledged by Gorham Munson and Sherman Manchester,
the new treasurer. Jean cited Jessie's understanding that the New York
group would send the money to Jean, implying that the money given Gurdjieff was his own $500, and that the New York group owed him $1000
once more. From "Château Gurdjieff," Orage responded stoically, saying:
"My dear Toomer . . . do with the money what you will," adding " I was
entirely under impression you had decided to present the whole $2000 to
G and to trust to your stars to recover it in time to meet the printing demand."[80] Orage continued to believe that Jean was going to send the New
York publication fund of $2000 for Gurdjieff's own use.

In December Jean and Edith returned to New York where, with Jessie, they together attended readings of Gurdjieff's work at the "66," but the
major event Edith recorded later was their seeing the Brancusi exhibit at
the Brummer Gallery on the 14th. A week later, Orage himself arrived in

---

[78] Orage papers.
[79] Rudnick, *Mabel Dodge Luhan*, p. 229.
[80] Toomer Collection, Box 6, Folder 205.

New York in the company of Margaret Naumberg, Jean's former lover. By this time, Jean was back with his group in Chicago, teaching out of the voluminous notes he had taken over the summer and drawing on the experience he had with instructing Edith in her harmonious development. He felt he had mastered both the Gurdjieff system, its esoteric authority, and himself.

Figure 1. Jean Toomer, 1923. Courtesy of Margot Latimer.

Figure 2. Edith Annesly Taylor, 1924. Taylor Papers.

Figure 3. Alfred R. Orage, 1929. Photo by Ansel Adams. Courtesy of Anne B. Orage.

Figure 4. Jessie Dwight Orage with son Richard, 1930. Taylor Papers.

Figure 5. Alfred R. Orage, 1934. Courtesy of Anne B. Orage.

Figure 6. Marjorie Content Toomer, ca. 1935. Courtesy of Susan Loeb Sandburg for the estate of Marjorie Content Toomer.

Figure 7. Jean Toomer, 1934 or 1935. Courtesy of the estate of Marjorie Content Toomer.

Figure 8. Jean Toomer, Taos 1935. Courtesy of the estate of Marjorie Content Toomer.

Figure 9. The Mill House and mill before renovations, 1935. Courtesy of the estate of Marjorie Content Toomer.

Figure 10. Marjorie Content, Donald Davenport, Jean Toomer. Croquet on the lawn, 1938. Taylor Papers.

Figure 11. Jean Toomer and Henry Poore, napping, 1939. Courtesy of Margot Latimer.

Figure 12. The Mill House, the kitchen in the 1940s. Left to right: Paul Winchester, Lin Davenport, Jean Toomer and Margot "Argie" Toomer. Courtesy of Margot Latimer.

Figure 13. G. I. Gurdjieff, spring 1949. Private collection. Used by permission.

Figure 14. Sophie (Dushka) Howarth and Dorothy Caruso with Margaret Anderson's Mercury on road to Dijon. Trip to Geneva, August 1949. Taylor Papers.

Figure 15. G. I. Gurdjieff and Jeanne de Salzmann on the road to Dijon. Trip to Geneva. Taylor Papers.

Figure 16. G. I. Gurdjieff on the road to Dijon. Taylor Papers.

Figure 17. Left to right, Cynthia Pearce, Tania Savitsky, Paul Beekman Taylor, and Dushka Howarth. Between Geneva and Chamonix, August 1949. Taylor Papers.

Figure 18. Tania Savitsky and "Petey" (Eve). Camonix. Taylor Papers.

Figure 19. G. I. Gurdjieff with Russell Page on the road from Chamonix to Nantua. Taylor Papers.

Figure 20. G. I. Gurdjieff, Paris, August 1949. Private collection. Used by permission.

The Descent: From Gurdjieff
1927–1939

A true individual belongs, on the one hand, to no less
than himself, and on the other, to no less than mankind
and the entire human world.
                                                    —*Essentials*

God wins either way.
   —G. I. Gurdjieff

Edith was in Chicago with Jean when he started his new group, and gave
his first lectures on Gurdjieff's cosmology and cosmogony, carefully explaining the function of the organ kundabuffer, but she was back to New
York in December and January to stay with the Orages. Throughout January 1927, Orage was reorganizing his group, while putting into publishable
form the material brought back from the Prieuré. He was still concerned,
however, about the financial accounts between Jean and Gurdjieff. After
conferring with Sherman Manchester and Jessie about the money, he
wrote Jean in Chicago, saying: "My dear Jean, Many thanks for your [last]
letter; it gives me just the facts I wished to have, & I think I now realize
yours and the situation in Chicago perfectly clearly."[1] Jean replied that he
was sure of raising large amounts of money in Chicago for Gurdjieff, but
Orage advised caution, and confided in Jessie that he was afraid that Jean
had become inextricably caught in what Gurdjieff called the "dirty dollar
question."

   Orage himself was trying to get a number of friends, including
Blanche Grant Rosette, Rita Romilly, Muriel Draper, Paul Robeson,
Lawrence Langner, and Glenway Westcott, interested in investing substan-
tially in Gurdjieff's work. Jessie resented Orage's putting his own reputation on the line in the interests of Gurdjieff, and they quarreled often, but
things appeared brighter when Orage's divorce from Jean Walker was pronounced on 22 January. After a six-month waiting period, Orage would be
free to marry Jessie.

---

[1]   Toomer Collection, Box 6, Folder 206.

In February 1927, Orage wrote Jean again to say that he had sent $500 to G, but "G says not enough." Orage fumed that Israel Solon had sent another $500 from the New York group unadvisedly, and laments that "G is really quite extraordinary about money, but not, unfortunately, unique. . . . Don't forget to keep me informed of anything you send; & by the way, as Mme. Hartmann is now . . . in Paris, sums should be checked to Miss Ethel Merston, on G's direction." Orage added that he was discouraged with the state of things in New York, as well as with Gurdjieff"'s way with money, and sent encouragement to Jean's reading group in Chicago before signing off: "Best of wishes, colleague!"[2]

Meanwhile Edith, in New York with the Orages, quietly made plans to return to France for another summer with Jean and Gurdjieff. Orage heard of their plans through Edith and wrote Jean in March to warn him that if he went to the Prieuré in the summer of 1927, more money would be expected to accompany him: "I should advise you . . . to save your resources to take with you, since you propose to go to the Prieuré this summer. . . . You might conceivably repay to yourself the sums you advanced from your trust-fund of $2000 without calling in the N.Y. group to repay you."[3] Orage predicted that many people from New York would have already made plans to go to France, but Orage said he was demanding assurance from the Prieuré that they would be admitted, recalling his bitterness when his good friend, Daly King, was refused admittance at the front gate the summer before, while Orage himself was on the premises.[4]

The warning came too late by all appearances, since Toomer had already responded to a letter from Olga de Hartmann earlier in the month which had asked: "Is there any possibility of sending us any money?" after describing Grudjieff's problem concentrating on his writing with money worries in his head. "Cable money to Barclay's," she pleads, "please raise something for a poor beggar!" Jean did so, and received a note from Olga a few days later saying that Gurdjieff was happy with Jean's letter and with the money he had raised. She quipped that Gurdjieff said: "Now Mr. Toomer already does things a half hour earlier and not a half hour later, as before," and concluded with a request that further money be sent in her name to Lloyds in Paris.[5]

In early April, Ethel Merston, now house manager as well as guardian of the children at the Prieuré, added her thanks to Toomer for $150 at the "right psychological moment" and "Mr. G was delighted." She continued:

2 Toomer Collection, Box 6, Folder 205.
3 Toomer Collection, Box 3, Folder 96.
4 C. Daly King, *The Oragean Version* (New York: Private Printing, 1951), p. 5.
5 Toomer Collection, Box 3, Folder 96.

"I told Mr. Gurdjieff your plan of preparing the groups first with the ideas and then only reading the book, and he said 'very good, necessary so!'" Then, reminding him of her role as head of the American pupils, she recalled the rules for new pupils to follow at the Prieuré: "You know—rules about hours and going out without first asking permission or not allowed to receive friends—etc., etc.[6] In other words anyone who comes must expect nothing from Mr. Gurdjieff and must be ready to join in the work of the place. Warn everyone won't you—paint it worse than it is because then all the oddments (like lack of hygiene and flies!!) which one can't paint in detail won't come as such a shock. . . . Terms $10 a week if willing to share any kind of room—otherwise $15 and upwards for single and better rooms." She asked for a list of those intending to enroll, and rooms required, and noted that the same had been asked of Orage. "Anyone very specially rich to be nursed; Mark too, will you?!" To help him, Merston listed prospective donors in Chicago, adding after one name that she herself was Jewish, then repeated the plea: "Can't you find someone interested 'uquocut' (= eedjot!) who would plank down a couple of thousand dollars to give Mr. Gurdjieff the necessary freedom for the writing?"[7]

In March, the Sunwise Turn bookshop was bought out by Doubleday, and Jessie sold her share, terminating her New York career. That spring, Frank Lloyd Wright came to New York to talk with Orage about the Gurdjieff work. He was living at Taliesin East, in Spring Green, WI with Olgivanna Hinzenberg, and was interested in Jean's Chicago group.[8] Wright wanted to know from Orage more about Toomer and the Gurdjieff work. Orage took him, with E. E. Cummings and John Dos Passos, to a demonstration of the dances by his group. Orage himself, however, was changing direction in his own teaching at this time, adding to his talks on Gurdjieff a series of "Psychological Exercises," a project that he had worked on even before his involvement with Gurdjieff. It consisted of mental exercises that called upon logic, mathematics and spatial perception (*Psychological Exercises* was first published in New York in 1930). When Gurdjieff heard this, he was furious, not only because of the departure from his own method, but because he feared that Orage would alienate a New York group that was still the major source of the funds that maintained the In-

---

[6] Nikolai de Stjernvall recalls that all the doors of the Prieuré, except the front door, were kept locked at night. A condition several complained of was that the writers of incoming mail had to be identified on a pad by the postal box, and outgoing mail had to be deposited in the same box for collection.

[7] Toomer Collection, Box 3, Folder 96.

[8] Their daughter, Iovanna, taught the dances in the Chicago area after Gurdjieff's death.

stitute. Orage had no such intentions, for his interest in Gurdjieff remained not so much with practical exercises such as the dances, but with the book that he was sure contained the code to secret knowledge that Gurdjieff possessed.

Sometime in February or March, Edith and Jean had broken up. The cause is not clear, though she may have thought that Jean's charm was too easily spread abroad. She was also sensitive to Jean's possessiveness. My sister told me after our mother's death that Edith had wanted a child and thought Jean couldn't give her one. At any rate, in early April, Jean was already involved in an affair with Clare McLure, one of his Chicago group,[9] and Edith was recoiling from a brief and intense lesbian affair.[10] In April, she returned to France and settled in Paris at 1 rue Git-le-Coeur on the Quai Augustin overlooking Notre Dame, in an apartment owned by Alice Delamar. Gurdjieff had foreseen that the summer of 1927 would be crucial for the continuation of the Institute, and he ordered Edith to play hostess for the Americans he expected to arrive from Orage's New York group and Toomer's Chicago group. He had her buy an automobile that would be worthy of her new assignment, saying that he would contribute to the cost.

In April, Orage told Jean that de Hartmann had promised that all American visitors would be welcomed, and commented laconically that "they will, in fact, be G's sole support until we are in harness again." Then he chided Jean again for sending advance money to Gurdjieff: "I still think you should have resisted the appeal. . . . After all, $1000 a month is not starvation. . . ." A few days later, Orage sent Jean the last section of the first book of "Beelzebub," with the comment that "you or I will have much to do at the Prieuré perhaps,—you rather than I." A week later, he wrote Jean of his own frustration at Gurdjieff's withholding the secret code for understanding the book, saying: "I hope you will spend some weeks with G as I did & do better than I in extracting light from his darkness." A third note followed fast to remark that the New York group had just sent Gurdjieff $2500 through him: "Now you see why I urged you not to send before." Obviously, Orage felt that Jean's eagerness to please Gurdjieff was causing undue competition with the New York group's funding.[11]

Jean was relieved when Gorham Munson wrote him to announce that, at the time when his term as treasurer for the New York Gurdjieff fund had come to an end, "Mr. Gurdjieff ha[d] been paid in full and the

[9] C. E. Kerman and Richard Eldridge, *The Lives of Jean Toomer* (Baton Rouge, LA: Louisiana State University, 1987), p. 183.

[10] Among her papers is a long love letter from "S," which may stand for Solita Solano. She refers to Edith's feeling of loss, particularly of her mother.

[11] Toomer Collection, Box 6, Folder 206.

enclosed cheque for five hundred and fifty dollars represents the balance on hand that is applied to the group's indebtedness to you for your advance from the book fund. The unpaid balance of five hundred dollars is distributed in pledges."[12] With the Luhan funds now fully accounted for, Jean must have sighed with relief as he made his plans to go to the Prieuré.

By June, pupils from Jean's Chicago group began showing up in New York on their way to the Prieuré, but Jean was hesitating whether or not to join them. They all arrived in New York with Jean's letters of recommendation and requests to Orage to arrange their reception in France. Though Gurdjieff had looked forward to the summer of 1927 as a crucial period for expanding the American presence and contributions, Orage disapproved of the general tendency among his own pupils, as well as among Jean's, to go to the "source" at the Prieuré. He told Jean that he asked his own pupils: "Why go to Tibet?" It wasn't that he worried about losing students to the Master, but he regretted having them go to Gurdjieff just out of curiosity, rather than for further instruction they really did not need.[13]

That summer, a group of young college students—including Payson Loomis, Philip Lasell, Nick Putnam, and Lincoln Kirstein—spent time at the Prieuré, but none enrolled immediately as regular pupils.[14] Edith became good friends with all of them. Jean arrived in France in July and, quite suddenly three weeks later, Orage decided he should go too—" if the

---

[12] Toomer Collection, Box 6, Folder 187.

[13] James Webb, *The Harmonious Circle : The Lives and Works of G.I. Gurdjieff, P. D. Ouspensky and Their Followers* (London: Thames and Hudson, 1980), p. 312, labels this formula "Orage's fallacy." I agree. In his *Life is Real*, Gurdjieff writes that on 6 November 1927, he was ready to die happily, but his writings to those "who did not know me personally could understand absolutely nothing" force a categorical decision "to mobilize all the capacities and possibilities in my common presence to discover some possible means of satisfactorily emerging from such a situation" (New York: Dutton for Triangle Edition, 1975), p. 33. That is, he had to find a way to have his book embody his person, for Gurdjieff was the only one who could teach his own system. In fact, the man *was* the system. No matter how much Ouspensky, Orage, or Toomer deferred to the "master," their own personalities, if not their own thoughts, were so distinct from his that their instruction lacked the force and efficacy of its source. On the other hand, to many, Gurdjieff, the man, overwhelmed his ideas.

[14] Lincoln Kirstein, who died in 1996, reported in his autobiography, *Mosiac* (New York: Farrar, Straus & Giroux, 1994), that his group were the only anglophones there that summer, with the exception of Metz. Nick, Payson, and Philip, according to my mother, had been at Hotchkiss together, Nick and Philip remained in the work until Gurdjieff's death and, according to Nick, Gurdjieff had assigned him the task of curing Philip's drug habit. Philip married Edith Taylor in 1958. In conversation in the last years of his life, Lincoln said that the three men who were the greatest influence in his life were Gurdjieff, Balanchine and Nick Putnam.

conditions are right," he wrote to Toomer. The news he was getting from the Prieuré about the slow progress of the book was disturbing him, and although the conditions were *not* right—Gurdjieff was not saying he would pay special attention to Orage's concerns—he decided to go anyway, foreseeing that, once married to Jessie, he would have to give up his group to concentrate on his marriage while finishing up Gurdjieff's book. Orage left on the 17th for England where, on 9 September, 1927, the divorce decree became final. Without going on to Fontainebleau, after barely two weeks abroad, Orage hurried back to New York where he and Jessie were married on the 24th. For the moment, he shelved all plans to return to the Prieuré.[15]

Meanwhile, Edith was waiting in vain for Orage at the Prieuré, yearning for some moral support in her uncomfortable situation with Gurdjieff, who seemed to have appropriated her for some design. Jean largely ignored her that summer, since he was still embroiled in an affair with Clare McLure,[16] but Gurdjieff, in turn, was ignoring Jean in anger over his amorous affairs at the Prieuré. Finally, after hearing that Orage had gone straight back to New York from London, Edith left, unable to bear the company of Gurdjieff alone. She took a temporary job in New York City with Buckwalter & Co. as a decorator, but came down with pneumonia a few weeks later, in October. Jean was back in town at that time and tried repeatedly to get together with her, perhaps as some sort of ploy to escape from Clare, but from her sickbed, Edith replied that she preferred to be left alone. The truth is, however, she had fallen in love with her doctor. On 13 October, she was well enough to go with the Orages to Rita Romilly's send-off party for Paul Robeson [en route to the Soviet Union]. Jacob Epstein, and Muriel Draper were also there, but the highlight of the evening was Robeson's singing.

Toomer went back to Chicago and began sending pupils on to Orage with the expectation that they would continue on to Fontainebleau.[17] Orage thought the exodus from Chicago and New York was unnecessary and told Toomer so, but he was having his own problems with Gurdjieff. In late October, he received an urgent letter from Mme de Hartmann re-

---

[15] Inexplicably, C. S. Nott, in his *Journey Through This World* (London: Routledge & Kegan Paul, 1969), describes Orage at the Prieuré that summer, adding that Gurdjieff was furious when Orage prepared to leave (pp. 118, 121–122).

[16] Kerman and Eldridge, *The Lives of Jean Toomer*, p. 183.

[17] Jean sent Jeremy Lane from Chicago through New York to study Gurdjieff's music with Hartmann, and wrote Gurdjieff that Lane was an emotional case: "Give him a task." Others sent to Gurdjieff from Chicago that fall included the poet Mark Turbyfill and Walter Lang, the youngest member of the Chicago group.

questing an instant return to the Institute. Gurdjieff was having serious doubts about the progress of the book and the money needed to support him until its conclusion. Jessie balked at the idea of going with the husband she had endured without for so long. "What is to happen now?" she wrote in her diary, and then, "[We] had a long argument concerning a return to the institute in two months." Three days later, they argued again from one to six in the morning. Edith was a faithful confident, but, finding it impossible to loosen her doctor from his unhappy marriage, she was making her own plans to return to the Prieuré for the summer. News from Gurdjieff stressed that only a more successful fund-raising in 1928 could save the château and allow him to finish the book. The "first series" was finished, but it still needed Orage's editing, and Gurdjieff had plans to use Edith to solicit funds from her Paris connections.

On 29 November, Miss Merston, now housekeeper at the Prieuré, arrived on the Mauretania from France to bring manuscripts to edit and to press for Orage's immediate return.[18] After a visit with Waldo Frank, who was entertaining Ford Madox Ford, the Orages sailed on New Year's Eve for France on the Mauretania, and arrived at Cherbourg on 6 January 1928. Edith, who had sailed a week earlier, met the boat train in Paris, where they all spent the night, before driving to the Prieuré the next day in her Delage. Edith was running from the disappointment of her affair with a married man who was willing to stay separated from his wife, but unwilling to marry again. In her vulnerable mood, she accepted Gurdjieff's personal attentions, which many of the residents took as a sign that Gurdjieff had personal designs on her.

Jessie found herself vulnerable as well when Gurdjieff kissed her in welcome, and told her that half of her [the Orage half] belonged to him now. The next morning, Gurdjieff invited all three to the Café Henri II, where he passed out portions of the last chapter that they were to read and comment upon. The next day, Edith drove Gurdjieff and the Orages to Paris, where they met Jane Heap at the Café de la Paix to discuss the chapter. Orage and Edith were guarded, but Jessie came right out and said she thought it was thoroughly bad, to which Gurdjieff replied that he pitied her. On the 13th, the Russian New Year and his birthday, Gurdjieff gave a formal dinner for over sixty guests in the main salon at the Prieuré. He ordered Edith and Jessie to organize the children's party for the next afternoon.

---

[18] Miss Merston was the early housekeeper, or administrator, of the Prieuré, succeeded later by Miss Gordon, the "old English spinster," as she was known. Miss Merston was severe with the children. Her name elicited fear in me. Once, in a rage at the antics of Nikolai and Michel, she tied them to a tree for an afternoon.

Auto trips followed in rapid succession. On 17 January, Edith drove Gurdjieff and the Orages to Rouen for a three-day visit that was marred by an argument between Jessie and Orage which Edith did her best to quiet. On 22 January, the same group went off to Auxerre, Autun, Bourg, Belle-garde, the Col de la Faucille (where they lunched), and then on to Geneva. Jessie wrote in her diary that night that "Edith wouldn't come to G's room [where music and readings were performed], because at lunch that was a picnic, he blew up about Americans, their filthy money, etc. etc, and at dinner he told her he meant it for her. He was superb during the outburst. I sat near him and stared. His eyes were never angry, obviously he was playing a role. Afterwards he came up to me and said he was sorry but he had drunk too much. I said, 'Don't apologise, you were delightful.'" Jessie could admire Gurdjieff's role-playing with her best friend, but she was soon to be the victim herself of a more sinister scenario.

Gurdjieff was obsessed with movement. One of Edith's fragmentary notes mentions a trip at this time to Vichy: "after dinner, a Belge, Orage, Olga [de Hartmann], transfer of money from stranger to Gurdjieff, name finding [Gurdjieff's game of finding the appropriate nickname for a new pupil]. To Chamonix: Nick [Putnam] and his cigar, Jeanne de Salzmann, Chartreuse used as anti-freeze."[19]

Another trip right away to Rouen, then Rennes, Chartres, and Or-léans. Gurdjieff was clearly agitated. On the one hand, he wanted Orage to stay with him until the book was shaped into final form, while Jean Toomer administered the New York group as Gurdjieff's agent, at the same time directing his own Chicago group. Then he discovered that Edith was pregnant with his child. A few days later, the same group was off again, this time to Cannes, via Vichy, where G had a particular liking for the waters. They drove by the Route du Napoléon over the mountains south of Grenoble, past Castellone, down to Cannes where Edith, Jessie, and Orage went to the Casino, leaving Gurdjieff drinking on the terrace of the hotel. At Nice, Gurdjieff had given each of the group 100 francs to play in the casino and, although Edith and Jessie lost their money, Orage was happy with the 150 francs he won. That evening, Jessie wrote in her diary, "as we left the dining room I heard an English woman say 'it's too good to be true,' and Edith said that the night before she heard someone remark 'Are those people ever going?' An amusing situation to be in. I can remem-ber saying things like that myself. G's loud talk about shit, etc. and eating with his hands—are not appreciated, it seems."[20]

[19] Edith Taylor papers.
[20] Jessie Orage Diary, 1928.

They drove back across the Massif Central, stopping at Thiers and Vichy again, where Edith argued with Gurdjieff and left the dinner table, sulking. Meanwhile, Jessie was feeling more and more uncomfortable with Orage's deference to whatever Gurdjieff decided to do with him. On the 19th, Jessie wrote: "I told G we were leaving next week. The atmosphere is sticky. Edith left for Paris perhaps never to return because G called her a harmful idiot." To make matters worse, back at the Prieuré, Jessie had a falling out with Mme de Hartmann over Gurdjieff's orders to all of them to plant melons in boxes about his room. Gurdjieff bragged that he expected to make thousands of francs from selling melons.

The final gesture that Jessie never forgot or forgave came in G's Paris apartment on 27 February, when "G took occasion at the table of telling me that I am squirming idiot, candidate for a harmful one, and if I kept O, his super-idiot, from being one of his inner circle because there must be one of each kind around him—the god of gods, then I would burn in Hell. I was so angry inside that I could scarcely breathe, but I looked him straight in the eye all through it and smiled."[21] The incident gave the Orages much to ponder. Jessie wrote the next day that she had "spent a very troubled night wondering about things. G seems to have challenged me as to that one of us shall have O. He is the biggest fool alive if he thinks he can make me do something by those methods. Also, I am sorry to leave with the feeling I have about him now. Yesterday I felt very friendly and quite sorry to leave him—now, I hope I never see him again. Spent the morning talking with O about the situation. G is finished for me inside absolutely and I am very sorry about it. I felt I wouldn't possibly go and eat at his flat. I never want to see him again. Finally I made myself go with O to the Café de la Paix. I had to finish out the two months even though it seemed impossible and then for O's sake I must. Edith joined us there and we stayed only thirty minutes. We had dinner at G's flat and it was an ordeal. Finally we said goodbye and got away. He would have kissed me but I drew away and his last words were 'bring a little one back with you next time.'"[22]

The Orages sailed from Cherbourg on 29 February and arrived in New York on 6 March, just in time to catch the evening performance of Gershwin's *Porgy and Bess*, starring Paul Robeson. In the days following,

---

[21] James Webb, *Harmonious Circle*, p. 363, who must have seen Jessie's diaries, gives the date here as 28 February and garbles the threat into: "If you keep my super-idiot from coming back to me you burn in boiling oil." He also mentions the caviar incident. James Moore, *Gurdjieff: The Anatomy of Myth*, (Rockhport, MA: Element, 1991), p. 223, cites mid-January 1928 as the moment Orage left the Prieuré, never to return.

[22] Jessie Orage Diary, 1928.

they spent a good deal of time with Zona Gale and Muriel Draper. Payson Loomis arrived with news from the Prieuré in late April to say things were going very badly there.[23] Many people were leaving, particularly those who had earlier been members of Orage's New York group. Orage decided to get as far away as possible to scan the chances of setting up groups for himself on the West Coast. He also had on his mind a message Gurdjieff had sent over with Loomis suggesting that Orage profit from Toomer's contacts with Mabel Dodge Luhan to find out if she was still willing to contribute money and her home to the Institute. Orage kept this from Jessie and, before leaving for California, wrote Edith on 4 May, from 28 East 28th Street, to her Paris address on the Rue de Grenelle:

> Dearest Edith, Thanks for your cable about Peggy [Matthews] and she certainly seemed highly pleased by whatever had occurred and is bent on returning to the Prieuré in June. I did not see her alone and have no other impressions than these. At any rate, she is all right. Mann is quiet and, in fact, also speaking of returning; she apparently doesn't guess how eager the French will be to see her. MC [McLure] has not turned up yet, but I've written Toomer to be prepared with cold water, and he tells me he has the hose ready. A letter from her gave him a warning, he says.[24]
>
> Mme H. [de Hartmann] wrote me a few weeks after my return here with the usual request. I replied that I'd given my share in anticipation, and could not send more. Over and above the $1000 I took from here, I gave Mme. H. $3000 between my arrival and departure and . . . told her that it was anticipatory. In my note I also said that my two former drawing-cards were now played out. G. was no longer ill, and the book [*All and Everything*] was now completed. Also, as I had no new chapters I couldn't "draw" any more on the book-reading. I've had no reply, and I'm wondering if any reached your ears. I'm really interested to know *what* the Prieuré will do. The American visitors will *not* be many; and unless your fund is freer or S [Israel Solon] has unexpected

---

[23] Jessie mentions Loomis's arrival, but Loomis was carrying the report of Edith, with whom he had become good friends that winter. At the time, Edith was feeling the first physical and moral pressure of carrying Gurdjieff's child, probably the last he fathered.

[24] Claire Edgar McLure wrote Jean a series of passionate love letters between 1928 and 1930 that embarrassed him. He did his best to restrain her, even to the point of ordering her not to see him (Toomer Collection, Box 5).

means, I don't clearly see what is to be done. Anyhow, it will be something; and I *do* hope you will keep me informed. If you reply to this, don't refer to the $3000 I gave Mme H. Jessie doesn't know and there is no reason to tell her now. She has been in bed with a grippe for a couple of weeks but is up today. We still plan to go to California in June—by car; and I am still uncertain whether we shall stay there for the winter. I'm leaving New York in such a way as to be free to return or not. I've been taking English Literature classes again this spring; and they are lots of fun and profit. Fancy $250 a lecture! And no complaint that they ought to be free! I wish I could have a class six nights a week for three months and loaf the rest of the year. How are you, Edith and Jean?[25] Are you staying the summer, going to M [word indistinct], or what? I should love to see you again before putting 5000 more miles between us. Also I feel sad with you left alone to carry the Prieuré!

Yours affectionately,

<u>ARO</u>[26]

Some time before she received this letter, Edith confronted Gurdjieff to ask him to assume some responsibility for his child in her womb, but he passed off the news with a wry smile and hardly a murmur. Of this incident, Gurdjieff wrote a few years later: "On this name day of mine [23 April], because of a certain action toward me on the part of one of the people near me, I decided to realize the following: "In the future, under the pretext of different worthy reasons, to remove from my eyesight all those who by this or that make my life uncomfortable."[27]

Edith felt Gurdjieff's "worthy reasons," but needed direction and insisted stubbornly that he assume some sort of paternal responsibility. She could only register her frustration at Gurdjieff's reaction, not only to her condition, but to his scolding her for defending Orage's and Toomer's insufficient fund-raising. To make his point, he released her from some of her more arduous physical tasks so that she could use her charms and contacts to raise money. He asked her to leave the Prieuré and contact friends in Paris like Gertrude Stein, Kiki Vanderbilt, Alice Delamar, and Natalie

[25] I don't know of any other "Jean" that Orage could be referring to. He may have made a simple Freudian slip.

[26] Edith Taylor papers.

[27] Gurdjieff, *Life is Real*, p. 45.

Barney for "double 0 donations." When Edith came up with nothing there, he sent her to see Lady Rothermere in Fribourg, Switzerland.

All this she wrote to Orage, who was doing his best for Gurdjieff in New York. Jean wrote from Chicago that Ethel Merston had written him for money, and acknowledged $250 sent, but reminded Orage that funds were very low because the New York group had canceled their plans to send $1000 per month. Orage wrote back that "G has called for $10,000. Can you give? This is SOS. You'd be useful at Prieuré if book decided to be printed in English, when do we meet?"[28]

Two days later, Orage replied to Edith's description of conditions at the Prieuré:

> "I'm so grateful for your letter, Edith. What would I do without you! However, it does seem that for the present you have done all that is possible. On getting G's cable re raising $10,000 here within three months, I did set to work, though not with much enthusiasm; and, marvellous to say, I got the money guaranteed in a couple of days, and called G to that effect. Jessie—as usual— knows nothing of this, though I shall probably tell her while we are on the trip and when she can do no harm. She is really at such odds with the Institute that she loses her head when money's mentioned in connection with it—and that is not very rarely! In addition to this guaranteed $10,000 (that, by the way, the people can well afford and are really enthusiastic about sending), the N.Y. group in honour of my leaving N.Y. sent G $1,000; so that what with this and what with that, I'm leaving for California without a scratch on my conscience. I've written Mme. H that I shall probably be in California until Xmas; and that she is not to expect anything from me until, at the earliest, in the New Year. I'm reckoning that something must happen at the Prieuré this summer. The $10,000 is, of course, just old debt; and I don't see enough visitors in sight to keep the Prieuré in bread. With you and me both exhausted, and no other millionaires at hand, surely G must do something novel. At any rate, I am at peace about it, and so too, can you be, Edith. Of course I don't altogether agree with your judgment—if it is final, that I doubt—that G is only a charlatan, or that that element outweighs or even affects the real factor in him. Ten million people may say the book [*All and Everything*] is nonsense; but I shall still say, because I cannot do oth-

---

[28] Toomer Collection, Box, Folder 205.

erwise, that it is the profoundest, most illuminating book that I have ever seen or can imagine. My only disgust with it, in fact, is not that nobody can understand it, but that I cannot; and I get so angry and desperate about it, just because I fail to grasp it, and G seems quite maliciously to have made it not difficult but impossible to understand. And what is worse, I cannot see him giving me any clues, except at a price I am not prepared to pay merely for the off-chance. I'm really very unhappily placed about it; and my only consolation is that I have done my best, and the rest I must leave. We'll see what G does next, but I think I can say that I'll not be at the institute again until G promises to make it really worth my while.

Affectionately,

Orage[29]

Orage had been taking driving lessons and, on June 15, he and Jessie drove south through Washington, on to Charlottesville, VA and Sparta, GA, then west to Greensville and Nashville, straight on to Forth Worth, Fort Sumner, and Santa Fe, where, at the end of June, they paused for a few weeks in a house Betty Hare had found for them. Throughout July, Orage and Jessie visited pueblos—Santo Domingo (that Jessie found unfriendly), Zia, and Taos (to stay with Tony and Mabel Dodge Luhan), where they found a letter from Edith that spoke of an urgent financial crisis and the defection of some pupils. Orage wrote back to Edith from Taos on 14 July in a long letter describing his trip west with Jessie, their stay with Mabel, and their plans to leave in a few days for the Grand Canyon, Los Angeles, and then San Francisco to teach the Method. After inviting Edith to join them there, the letter continued:

Edith! In your last but one letter, after your mission to Lady R [Lady Rothermere], you were fed up with the Prieuré; and I half expected your immediate return to America! But now you appear to be back there! Perhaps I'm glad, because I am exceedingly con-

---

[29] Edith Taylor papers. At one time or another, G had said to my mother that Orage "not like Toomer. He want learn from me what only *I* know, but Toomer want learn from me what only he already know but forget." To his dying day, Orage felt that Gurdjieff possessed a secret knowledge of the cosmos and of man's being. He finally succumbed to the despairing thought that Gurdjieff was purposely keeping it from him, as a sort of carrot to entice Orage's continued service. It must be said that few could read Gurdjieff as well as Orage, who perhaps saw signs in the book of his secret knowledge that others could not.

cerned with and about the whole place and person; but I'd like to know what happened between your two letters to change your mind. But probably you can't say . . . it is all too complex to be formulated? That I understand, because so often it is my own state. Merston writes that she was with you all in Geneva, and now she intends to live in Paris; but _her_ letter is dated early in May and I have only just got it. Probably she too is back at the Prieuré now! And where is Rita [Romilly]? She wrote one very intriguing letter after her first supper with G, and since then I have heard nothing. As for Stanley S [Spiedelberg], he is, of course, much too busy to write, and I excuse him—but; all the same, I feel awful gaps in my information! Well, with such as I have, my conclusion is for the present as follows; The crisis re Thompson [who held an outstanding debt on the Prieuré] has been got over, but the propects for the permanent maintenance of the Prieuré are extremely black, not to say quite hopeless. By September at latest G will find himself forced to make a new move of some kind, either to give up the Prieuré altogether _or_ to start something new there that shall be of a character to inspire fresh material support. One of these two things seems to me to be imminent in the absence of a miraculous draught of fishes. And I don't see what I can do about it one way or the other. I'm not disposed or able to maintain my former subscriptions to the Prieuré in the present circumstances; and I cannot forecast G's next move or my own reaction to it. So, altogether, I feel very much up in the air and anything but clear as to my own way. In fact, I'm really just filling in time, in hopes that something will emerge to make a decision possible. Theoretically, I'm even prepared to return to the Prieuré—but the "call" would have to be remarkably clear! Meanwhile we are bound, as you know, for San Francisco.[30]

At the end of July, the Orages drove west again through Flagstaff to the Grand Canyon, down to Phoenix and westward past Yuma to San Diego on August 2. Ten days later, they found a cottage to rent for two weeks in Carmel, giving them time to meet and talk with Lincoln Steffens and Robinson Jeffers. At the end of August, they took a flat in San Francisco, and Orage profited from his contacts with writers to gather a group. From there, Orage wrote Edith: "I'm intrigued to know that G continues to

---

[30] Edith Taylor papers.

spend money liberally. My suspicion is that he is spending the $10,000 collected here for the repayment of Thompson! Well, that's his affair—but a new 'crisis' will be again available—but, after all, who knows? I know that, short of a miracle, I personally shall not be able to send a penny. The summer has been a dead loss financially; and what with a new apartment etc my resources at best will be insufficient. So I shall watch the Prieuré's budget with a good conscience and some amusement."[31] The next day, Jessie noted in her diary: "A letter from Stanley [Nott] came this morning that upset us very much. It contained the news that E. T. was expecting a baby."[32]

Edith wrote news of her pregnancy to Jean, but he replied with a curt statement that the fact was of little interest to him at this time. He probably felt hurt and deceived by both Edith and Gurdjieff. From Fred Leighton's reponse to Jean's announcement in August of Edith's pregnancy, it seems that Edith had put some blame on Jean for her falling into Gurdjieff's bed: "I was glad to have your reaction to Edith Taylor's letter," he wrote. "I think it reveals a disappointing shallowness and spiteness of spirit and I do not think you have any cause of concern about the effects of her talk."[33] With neither Jean's moral support nor Orage's physical presence to strengthen her, Edith tried to get Gurdjieff to take some sort of responsibility for her state. Whether she asked him to marry her I cannot say, but he was in his late fifties and not inclined to marry anyone at this point in his life. He suggested that she marry Caesar Zwaska, Margaret Anderson's assistant at the *Little Review*, who had accompanied her to the Institute two years earlier and stayed on. Caesar, Caucasian in origin, was tall, muscular, with straight dark hair and dark complexion. His father had immigrated to Chicago at the turn of the century, where Caesar was born, probably in 1902, and grew up. There he joined the editorial staff of *The Little Review*, and wrote brief essays for it. When he arrived in Prieuré, however, he decided to turn his life over to Gurdjieff. Although Gurdjieff used him as a handyman and excluded him from most of the formal rituals of the Institute, Caesar was devoted to the "work," and did whatever Gurdjieff asked

---

[31] Edith Taylor papers.

[32] Jessie Orage Diary, 1928.

[33] Toomer Collection, Box 4, Folder 138. Margot Latimer (Toomer) had once entertained the idea that her father was also Petey's. Undoubtedly, Edith had approached Jean for some sort of support for her situation as a mother, but it is doubtful that he fathered her child. Someone in the Gurdjieff group once suggested to me that Gurdjieff was the father of Argie! In early 1933, Jessmin Howarth wrote to Toomer saying that "I was given to understand at the last New Year (1932) that G. was expecting a 'normal child from a normal mother'" (Toomer Collection, Box 3), but I know of no Gurdjieff offspring born this late in his life.

of him. Gurdjieff probably offered some tokens of security if Edith regularized her condition, and I suppose that Edith saw no other recourse. When Orage heard the news in September, he replied positively: ". . . As regards marriage, I think wise; and am pleased with you." In response, a letter arrived from Edith saying that she was through with Gurdjieff, and Orage answered in support of her decision to break with G, adding that he was leaving San Francisco to lecture in Los Angeles before returning to New York. By now, Jessie Orage was also pregnant, but under happier circumstances.

In early October, the Orages met Ansel Adams and Orage sat for a photographic portrait. A month later, pleased with having made many literary contacts but frustrated in his failure to assemble enough pupils for a group, Orage and Jessie set off by train for New York, stopping in Chicago to see Jean, who confirmed that Gurdjieff had announced plans to come to New York and Chicago. Orage asked Toomer's reaction, which was guardedly favorable. On 13 November, across the Atlantic in Rouen, Edith bore a daughter, far enough from the Prieuré not to cause a local uproar, though everyone there must have known what was going on. Zwaska wasn't with her and Gurdjieff was too occupied to show suitable appreciation for the gift of a girl, even though she bore the name he suggested, "Evdokia," shortened to Eve to accord with French name restrictions. Edith called her "Petey" from the very first, a short form, she told others, of Peterkins.[34] She confronted Gurdjieff with her baby ten days later, in hopes he would give at least token moral support, but none was forthcoming, and she left the Prieuré in a rage, not only because of Gurdjieff's muted reaction to her childbearing, but because of his anger at her defense of Orage's reply to Mme de Hartmann that he would not return until the future of the teaching was made clearer. Without mentioning the birth, she wrote to Orage in New York to report Gurdjieff's reaction to his refusal to return immediately to the Prieuré. Orage replied from Gramercy Park on 17 December 1928, mentioning that Rosemary Nott was also expecting a child, and that Jessie was pregnant and due in April. After reviewing the mood of the New York group, he gave her his reasons for staying put in new York:

---

[34] *Evdokia* (pronounced "Yevdokía) is the name of the beloved of the legendary Byzantine hero, Digenes Akrites. Closer to home, it was the name of the sister of one of Gurdjieff's early mistresses. Zwaska had inherited the rank of baron from his father, a fact that I learned during the Second World War, when someone on the phone asked to speak to Baroness Zwaska. My mother then showed me his signet seal, the only thing besides a heart-shaped photograph of her with Caesar on the beach at Biarritz with my sister that testified to their marriage. My mother divorced him in 1938. She received a letter from him during the war while he was serving on the USS Seattle during the Battle of Coral Sea. She had no further word from him.

I'm distressed beyond words by G's attitude, even though I understand the situation from his point of view very well. You are a darling to stand up for me, Edith; and I'm certain you have more influence over him than anyone living. My case is quite simple, as you see. I <u>have</u> to make money for the support of the family, and it is impossible at the Prieuré or anywhere within easy reach of it. So I <u>must</u> stay here where, at least, I can give lectures; and, at best and by luck, I <u>may</u> conceivably raise some money for the Prieuré over and above my own necessities. On the other hand I <u>do</u> realise the importance of the Book and of its English translation; but, as to this, I've suggested to G that he should send me the rough literal text over here and I will work on it like a dog. He can even, if he likes, send Hartmann over to work with me— or even Metz. I wouldn't waste their time. But come over there, in these circumstances, I cannot, and I will not. It's going to be difficult however, for you to defend me, Edith dear, because G literally will not see any of these things. No matter, however; things must be as they will be. I'm content to know that I'm doing my best."[35]

Edith was trying to do her best as a mother with support from neither her token husband nor the father of her child. After a while, Gurdjieff invited her to move into the Prieuré with Eve, but Edith preferred to rest in Paris. They argued and, after she left, he sent her an angry letter threatening to expose her to her friends. She replied at the end of the month with undisguised chill:

Monsieur, surely there remains nothing more to be said that you have not already communicated to me in one form or another, and although you may wish to continue writing, it does not necessarily imply that I need accept these writings of yours. Why trouble yourself further and so occupy your time?

I suppose that among our "common acquaintances" who are to receive copies of your letter to me, you include Orage; if this is so, I might mention also that he will as well receive a copy of my reply to that letter; as for others they are of no consequence to me.

Now then, do I understand I am expected to apologize:
For your beastly behavior and use of foul language?

---

[35] Edith Taylor papers.

> For your complete lack of self-discipline?
> For your physical abuse my third day out of the hospital?
> For your fiendish threats to me and those around me?
> For the plans it pleases your vanity to make regardless of what it may cause me?
> Can it be for these you demand an apology?
> You endeavor to make one helpless by first rendering him hopeless, and you refuse to credit my feelings as real, that are not complimentary to your pride, so it is useless for me to go on dodging. You have admitted I served a purpose for you; I will also admit that you have served a purpose for me, very well, then, it seems to me that on this score we are quits, so I can now tell you, in all seriousness, that I do not intend to be persecuted either by your letters or by any other means, without creating an obstacle and not the obstacle you propose, but another that will be extremely undesirable. Let this be the end.[36]

At this time, Orage and Jessie were visiting in Chicago, where things seemed to be going well for Jean, who was eagerly awaiting Gurdjieff's planned trip to the United States and Chicago in January. The Orages were back in New York when Gurdjieff arrived on 23 January. That night, Muriel Draper gave a party in his honor for over a hundred guests. The next day, Orage took him to talk with Mabel Dodge Luhan, but she was hesitant now to commit her property in Taos to a branch of the Institute. A few days later, in introducing the dances to an audience at Carnegie Hall, Gurdjieff gave a speech of thanks to Orage for seeing him through his financial crisis, and then embarassed both Orage and Jessie by saying: "Orage wish very much have baby. Now he very pleased. If boy I give him five books, if girl, nothing."

Orage understood that Gurdjieff was trying another strategy to squeeze money out of him and the New York group.[37] Orage was willing to do his best, and he wrote Toomer to come to New York with $5000. Jean was neither able nor willing to raise the money, and wired Orage a blunt negative response. On Saint Valentine's Day, Orage wrote Jean again that Gurdjieff intended to go to Chicago himself, adding that the "Chicago group should give $1000 thru you. After all it is *you* Chicago must look to." Instead, Jean came to New York in early March to confer with Gurdjieff

---

[36] Edith Taylor papers.

[37] In the Afterword of *All and Everything*, written perhaps a year later, Gurdjieff says that he came to New York at Orage's insistence.

and Orage. The three of them talked with Mabel and Tony Luhan, but failed to sway them into lending their ranch in Taos. At the time, Gurdjieff was thinking seriously of giving up the Prieuré and moving the Institute to the United States, but he needed strong financial support from Orage's and Toomer's groups. Near the end of March, Jean and Orage consulted for six days in a row with Gurdjieff who, disappointed in the failure to secure Taos, finally got Jean to promise to return to the Prieuré in the coming summer with a good number of pupils. From Orage, he got nothing but assurances of continued support, since the New York group had dwindled in number and he was too cautious to assume that he could raise very much. After this settlement, Jean returned to Chicago.

As Gurdjieff's stay in New York was extended, he seemed bent on disturbing the Orage marriage. He announced at one luncheon that Edith and Jessie were both sterile until he put a powder into their armagnac glasses. Then, Rita Romilly circulated the story that Gurdjieff had asked her to marry him, adding that he didn't marry Edith because she was having an affair with Rosemary Nott! Jessie was furious at both stories, but Edith wasn't around to respond with a story of her own. On 4 March, Gurdjieff invited the Orages to his farewell supper and, early in the morning of the 5th, Jessie wrote in her diary: "Orage danced a jig of delight when we got in because G has gone and he is free again. It has been getting pretty hard for us both," but she admits that "whether or not one likes or dislikes G he leaves an empty place." But, he didn't quite leave. The "Paris" ran aground off Brooklyn, and for two days Orage exchanged calls and cables with him, before the steamship floated free on 7 April 1929.

Not only did the New York meetings fail to persuade Mabel and Tony Luhan to lend Gurdjieff their Taos estate, they prompted Mabel to ask Jean for the return of all the money she had lent him. Jean replied with an account of his 1929 donations to the Prieuré, listing canceled checks for March totalling $1050 ($150, $850, and $50), and $200 for May. He summed up: $1050, $500, $850, $150, $200, $245 = $2995. Perhaps he intended to make a full accounting to Mabel, but didn't yet. Mabel let the matter ride for the time being.

From Paris, Edith, with a five-month old child in her arms and certain that Gurdjieff was on his way back from his trip on which she had refused to accompany him, left for the United States to look for some security. Jean did not volunteer to see her and Jessie had just given birth to her son, Richard. So Edith stayed most of the time with Peggy Matthews in Princeton while she investigated possibilities of living and working in New York. She had no success and in desperation decided to return to the Prieuré in August. She had heard that Jean would be there.

Throughout that spring, Metz was writing Toomer newsy letters about the renovation of the Prieuré, including the beginning of a swimming pool project (undoubtedly financed by Orage's hard-earned money), and other improvements he would see when he arrived. But when Jean crossed the Atlantic in September, he was more concerned with finding a publisher in Paris for the fictional account of his passage, titled "Transatlantic," than in courting Gurdjieff's favor or giving moral support to Edith. In the journal he kept of that trip, he records a number of frustrations during his stay, first among them the stereotyped black identity that prospective publishers wanted him to adopt. "The fact of *Cane*," he wrote, "once again coming upon me and forcing me to again realize the difficulty caused by my being associated with the Negro."[38] Other immediate problems included "again the problem of sex," regretting that his "chance affairs" were unsatisfying. On top of this, he was less than enthusiastically received at the Prieuré—bringing neither pupils nor money. Mme de Salzmann told him: "Once you were an eagle. Now you are a sheep."

Nonetheless, Jean continued working his charms on the Prieuré community. Luba Gurdjieff remembered one time when Jean was telling stories to a group of youngsters at the Paradou while Gurdjieff and others were in Paris. After a while, to a captivated audience including Luba and her sisters, Jean did imitations, mostly with gestures, and challenged the others to guess who he was mimicking. They recognized Metz's typical nervous strut around Gurdjieff, Hartmann's wringing his hands before playing the piano, Stjernvall scratching his head and stroking his beard as he thought over a problem, and Gurdjieff's directions for the dances. He concluded with an imitation of someone looking about as if lost, then moving hesitantly in one direction or another. His audience seemed puzzled, then someone shouted, "C'est toi, c'est toi!" [39]

Edith was there running errands for Gurdjieff most of the summer, but Jean's amatory attention was captured that season by affectionate letters from Bay Meyers in Toronto. It was at this time that he speculated in his journal that: "I will be interested to see what effect on my form results from having a wife and sufficient money." Meanwhile Gurdjieff seemed to ignore Jean's presence as a tactic to have Jean pay more attention to his "mission" in the work. As others as well as Jeanne de Salzmann noticed, he was paying too much attention to himself. By the end of October, he was on his way back to Chicago, where he reorganized his group with Gurdji-

---

[38] Toomer Collection, Box 61, Folder 1419. Kerman and Eldridge have him back in Fontainebleau in May.

[39] Luba couldn't remember the date of this performance, but she was twelve or thirteen at the time. She told this story to me and Metz in her bistro on Yeoman's Row in January, 1968. Metz confirmed Jean's antics with the children.

eff's blessing, had a brief romance with Emily Otis,[40] and began to compile a collection of aphorisms that he eventually published under the title *Essentials*.

Frustrated and feeling abandoned, Edith moved back to Paris after telling Gurdjieff that she was leaving the Prieuré for good. Gurdjieff wrote her there a few days later:

> Edith! Now, late at night. Sleep does not come to me. First of all because during the last few years, it has become habitual for me at this time of the year to suffer without sleep; and because during this present period I am working for the last time on one, in my opinion, serious chapter.
>
> Lying on my bed overwhelmed by every possible kind of thought relating to this above-mentioned serious chapter, I suddenly remembered, according to the information given me several days ago by someone, that you will soon leave for America; And, as I, also, will go from here, this time surely for a long time, then these two circumstances show without doubt that we, personally, will never see each other anymore.
>
> I do not know how these facts are cognised by your inner personality, but in my inner personality after such a constatation there arises sincere sorrow and anxiety about the future, in regard to the fact that I will often remember and will have remorse, that inwardly I parted as an enemy from that person who, owing to one thing in his manifestations concerning me, touched my soul so deeply, that in me there arose the wish, whatever it might cost, to make the continuation of his existence completely happy, but did not succeed only owing to his "inability" to be sincere, that was required thanks to his abnormal past existence.
>
> No! . . . Edith . . . I cannot continue to write; in me there is beginning that state, that during recent times has often recurred and that arises in me evidently from non-human inner exhaustion. Nevertheless, in spite of only this short writing of mine, I will give it to Metz in the morning to translate and send it to you,[41] also sending to you, à propos, one of those things that I

---

[40] Kerman and Eldridge, *The Lives of Jean Toomer*, pp. 185–86.

[41] It is perhaps characteristic of the man that he would speak to my mother more often in English, since he had, from the beginning, categorized her as "American." Actually, my mother had lived in France since 1914 and spoke fluent French. Gurdjieff's French, on the other hand, was as grammatically rough as his English. I have heard him in rapid succession make remarks in French, Italian, Greek, Russian, and Georgian.

> brought from America and that I prepared for you for your visit
> at Easter; but owing to your recent "putting me in goulash," it
> has remained and it seems has already begun to spoil.
>
> Yours affectionately, to whom you first ideally formulated the
> expression "fifty-fifty," but this time a whole hundred; this is,
> perhaps, because it might be the last.[42]

A few days later she accepted Gurdjieff's invitation to meet him at the
Café Henri II to say goodbye:

> "Miss, you have something to tell me?"
>
> "Yes, as per your instructions I am leaving at twelve o-clock, but
> would very much like you to wish me to [leave]."
>
> "I have not so much time, so short, you remember story I told you
> about rabbit and camel? I am rabbit, you camel, pulling together the
> wagon of life. You can see picture? It is better for you and for me that
> I don't see you again; you make me very angry and I angry, very much
> hinder. It is better for us. Last time I see you, all night I not sleep, re-
> sult next day, very bad. I not wish make you nervous, so not tell you
> what inside; I feel, this function very harmful for me, much better
> when I angry take it and speak, but with you I not speak and so suffer
> very much. Must be either I suffer or you suffer, so better my eyes
> not see you again. Long time ago I hear what you say you work for G.
> You know many times I say how I hate men who take money from
> women, like louse I make them feel, so you make me very angry in-
> side when you say you work to get money for G."
>
> "Who could have told you I ever made this remark?"
>
> "That is other question. Last trip when I go to Vichy, I go because
> necessary to go, but I go without money in pocket and some time I
> go. I tell Madame Hartmann ask Miss T bring 5000 francs, you know
> why I say 5000 no more no less. You remember one time I ask you
> how much it would cost to live few days at La Faucille and you say
> 5000 francs, so I tell Madame Hartmann ask you bring 5000 francs.
> She telephone me Vichy that I can be quite tranquille, Miss T bring
> money, so I tranquille wait, and you come and when I ask it you, you
> make so, so, so and say what you not have but what can find in Vichy.
> I told you what I ten times more can find, and so when time for go-
> ing, necessay pay. I order bill, go garage, put motorcar in street, but
> impossible start, because have no money, so I tell, 'put everything in

---

[42] Edith Taylor papers.

motorcar.' I go walk and return, and so I go you know where, where man drink water, I look in faces surrounding people. I find one more antipathetic than others, He go, I also go. He sit on seat, I sit like poor simple man and look at him. He take out all money he find in pockets and put on table, then he go away. I take money, return hotel and we start, true, true, this idiot he will never remember such power I have, but not often wish to use, and so we start. I not know if you get money or not get money. My principle, I not ask second time. Where you get money I very well know, but enough. Already I lose much time and you know what it is, my time. You are you, and nobody fault. Our relationship fortunate or unfortunate, I don't know, accidently receive it so. You were for me very good, help very much in my work, truth sometimes you very much help, but now you hinder and much better you go. Once I gave you my word what I will for you do everything necessary; and, for me my word is law. Madame Hartmann will do what I advise. You can see her when you wish, even after three months I can give you how much money you want."

"Goodbye."

"Come back one moment. I wish something more tell you. Order drink something, I already much time lost, can let work wait while I wish tell you very great secret."[43]

The great secret is not recorded. Edith left for New York City, where she arrived on 23 September 1929, went to work briefly for Fred Leighton, a close friend of Jean's who had set up a New York branch of his Chicago "Trading Post" for Pueblo and Navajo pottery, rugs, clothes, and toys. She consoled herself with Jessie and Orage, went to readings and participated in dances directed by Jessmin Howarth. Orage was still polishing up the prose of Gurdjieff's book, about which Jessie wrote in her diary at the end of August: "Orage tells me he has been depressed for two or three weeks at the insufficiency of his brain because he can't understand G's book. Poor darling. I wish I believed there was so much in it to understand!"[44]

A few weeks later, Metz arrived in New York to prepare Gurdjieff's winter visit.[45] He didn't extract any promises from Orage, but he wrote Jean to demand $4000 with Gurdjieff's threat that he would not see him in New York if this outstanding "dirty question is still not liquidated." Jean

[43] Edith Taylor papers.

[44] Jessie Orage Diary, 1929.

[45] In the epilogue to *Our Life with Gurdjieff* (London: Penguin, 1972) Olga de Hartmann says that Gurdjieff came at Orage's insistence, but says that Gurdjieff was in New York in October (pp. 129, 131).

remained silent. If money demands plagued Orage and Jean, tales of Gurdjieff's treatment of women were bothering Jessie and Edith. In November, Rita Romilly told them the story of Doris, an English girl who
committed suicide after Gurdjieff had seduced her. Gurdjieff said to Rita
that the incident is a lesson for those who make trouble for him. "They
will come to bad ends."[46]

In early December, Edith came down with appendicitis, offering an
occasion to renew her affair with the same doctor who had treated her for
pneumonia three years earlier. Ignorant of those events, Gurdjieff sent her
a note saying he would be in New York before the end of the year and ex-
claimed:

> Edith! Finished! Finished also is my inner "intentional suffering" that
> has all the time been for me the principal inspiring factor for the pos-
> sible actualization of my work during recent years.[47]
>
> As in several hours, the for me momentous day will arrive when a
> new and perhaps last era of my existence will begin, and as you were
> also during the last three years by the will of Fate, of course uncon-
> sciously, one of the sources of the engendering of the data for the pro-
> ceeding in me of this inevitably required inner suffering of mine, I
> therefore on the eve of the said era, also remembered you.
>
> And now, with this letter of mine wishing you a Happy New Year,
> I, à propos, take advantage of the opportunity, first of all to inform
> you that you can reckon on that perhaps at the present moment is
> even very necessary for you, and namely that in the very near future
> you will receive a notification that the remainder of my financial debt
> to you has been credited to your account in the bank Morgan & Co.[48]
>
> And the interest—that I have already long-ago decided and about
> that I have already, so to say "logically-hinted" to you last year on that
> day when the neck-cross of my last wife was handed you as a gift—
> will be her other cross set with a great number of precious jewels and

---

[46] This story circulated widely for a while as a sign of Gurdjieff's cruelty. Dushka
Howarth explained to me that the suicide occurred much later and was not related directly to anything Gurdjieff had done. Gurdjieff found it unprofitable to deny mis-
truths, but saw reason to shape them into parables readable as "truths."

[47] I understand two linked meanings of "intentional suffering": first is the suffering of
self-observation due to an unexpected outside influence such as criticism, accident,
business reversal, etc.; the second is the suffering involved in a self-imposed discipline
of work to perfect oneself. Intentional suffering is awareness that pain is the base of
comfort; that pleasure is an island within pain; and that deficiency and waste surround
pleasure.

[48] Gurdjieff's "debt" was $4,300 dollars. He deposited $2,000 at this time.

will be delivered to you at any time at the address you indicate to me to my new private secretary, Fraulein Göpfert, 32 Wielandstr., Charlottenburg, Berlin.[49]

And secondly, according to the totality of my principles constituting that individuality of mine that will soon be considered as ideal for all contemporary people without exception, I find it necessary to tell you, so that you should be aware of it, that even now after the lapse of a sufficiently long time, I cannot forget and cannot help expressing to you my essence-astonishment concerning that last manifestation of yours that took place in Rouen in relation to me, that is to a being, in a certain sense, similar to you.

In my opinion, all the other previous manifestations of you could still somehow be understood and justified by fully impartial logic, but this last manifestation of yours, even taking into consideration the degeneration of the contemporary American race and the results of abnormal education that you have also received, cannot be called otherwise than "absolutely-non-human."

> He who during the process of the whole of his
> existence has as yet never forgotten either any
> good or any evil done him by people he has met and
> with whom he has had dealings.[50]

Edith did not pursue whatever implications of this note she could glean. She felt she had succeeded in talking her current lover into divorcing his wife, and she felt comfortable living in Princeton with Peggy Matthews when she wasn't in New York with the Orages. After Jessie first saw Edith's child, she noted in her diary that "Eve is a perfect darling—very much like Gurdjieff."

Jessie told me forty-five years later that, when she had recounted to Orage Gurdjieff's outrageous story about the "love philtre" and the way he had treated Edith, Orage very patiently explained to her that Gurdjieff does not conceive of male-female relations in the same way most of the Western world does. He said that, as far as Gurdjieff was concerned, women are collaborators with men. They nourish men and bear their children, but no man should put his domestic relations before his work for self-ac-

---

[49] Louise Geopfert [March], arrived not long after at the Prieuré to take up her duties that included, Nikolai de Stjernvall told me, sleeping with Gurdjieff. There is nothing in her published recollection to suggest this, and nothing I knew of her would suggest the possibility. She moved to the United States before WWII, married and lived on a farm in New York State.

[50] Edith Taylor papers.

tualization. Some women, whose proper roles are collaboratively spiritual and moral, need not bear and raise children in the interests of men, but others should do so to provide Earth with more seekers for truth. Jessmin Howarth and Edith were chosen by Gurdjieff for this role, and Jessie to fulfill hers with Orage. Something had blocked Jessie's and Edith's bodies from the proper childbearing process. Since they did not realize this and did not know how to remedy the situation, Gurdjieff worked for them, not as a potential husband or father in the usual senses of those words, but as a guide. Edith had made the mistake of demanding husbandly affection and outward fatherly signs of care. By her demands, she had put into peril Gurdjieff's projects for his children. Jessie just shrugged her shoulders at this explanation, but Orage insisted that, in this, Gurdjieff was consistent with the implications of his teaching.

At the end of January 1930, Gurdjieff sent word to New York that he would arrive in a few days. Rita told Jessie and Edith that she received a call from G, who "brings you 1000 kilos disillusion, 100 kilos monetary happiness and 10 pounds of retribution, signed 'Ambassador from Hell.'" On the same day, Gurdjieff wired Orage to the effect that "if all his love for Gurdjieff had not been dissipated, he would arrange party and eats for Friday night, and apple pie after Childs, signed 'Grandson's phenomenal Grandmother.'" On 17 February, Jessie wrote in her diary that G was due to arrive the next day: "There is no need for diplomacy for Orage, as we are going away in May, and Orage says he doubts if he will ever hold groups again." Orage promptly contacted Toomer to warn him about imminent demands by Gurdjieff, and to assure him of his support.

Muriel Draper and Orage met Gurdjieff at the dock and brought him to 40th Street, where some sixty-five pupils of Orage waited to greet him.[51] Meanwhile, Metz wrote Jean in Chicago on Gurdjieff's behalf to demand $4000. Although Gurdjieff's right side wishes to see him, Metz put it, his left side refuses to meet Toomer if this outstanding "dirty question is still not liquidated." On 5 March, Jean replied lightheartedly that he was trying to get $4000, and he had Fred Leighton in Chicago looking for it. Jean's own left side hadn't the time to see Gurdjieff, since it was too busy looking for "zeros" (Gurdjieff's term for big dollar bills). Metz replied that he enjoyed the letter, but he said nothing of Gurdjieff's reaction. On the 18th, Metz cabled that Gurdjieff intended to go to Chicago, and that Jean should find two or three rooms near Bohms Dancing School.

Gurdjieff spent several days in Chicago, talking with Jean and observing the group at dances and readings. Once, fed up with the tastelessness

---

[51] James Moore, *Myth*, p. 235, says the large group met Gurdjieff in Orage's absence.

of Chicago food, Gurdjieff asked Jean to take him to an Armenian restaurant he had heard of. As he walked in the front door, the proprietor rushed up to him and said, "Come back in the kitchen and I'll serve you. Only whites can eat out here." Gurdjieff thought this very funny, waved the man off, and sat down. He couldn't be bothered to take such things seriously.[52]

Though Gurdjieff did not get the money he hoped for, he and Jean got along well. Gurdjieff flattered Jean by saying: "Toomer, you do not know how your subconscious is related to me,"[53] and Metz wrote later from New York: "G said very nice things about your group. He was impressed by their earnestness and general attitude. I'll tell you details when you arrive."[54] Jean stayed in Chicago, however, and for the rest of that spring he prepared and conducted his classes with scrupulous care, promising his pupils that each lecture would be an event.[55]

Gurdjieff's visit and his reaction to Jean's groups seems to have been a skillful ploy to put distance between Toomer and Orage in order to better control both. Perhaps he wanted to alienate each from the other, though I find no direct evidence of it. At any rate, Jean and Orage were unshakable in their high regard for each other. Further, Gurdjieff misjudged his Chicago deputy, for instead of holding closer to Gurdjieff's instructions for a new direction in teaching, Toomer took Gurdjieff's flattery as validatation of a feeling he could swerve away from the Gurdjieffian line, much as Orage had done with his psychological exercises in New York. In the spring, he went to consult Orage and observe the exercises in New York, but found them too intellectually rigorous and overreliant upon logic. Nevertheless, he was impressed by the emotional distance Orage was able to maintain from his pupils and, back in Chicago, he assumed the same posture with some success.[56]

---

[52] Incidentally, according to *All and Everything*, p. 50, "Darky" was the nickname given Gurdjieff by his playmates in Kars.

[53] Toomer's recollection in a letter to Mme Ouspensky, 18 January, 1953 (Toomer Collection, Box 6, Folder 202).

[54] Toomer Collection, Box 3, Folder 96. James Moore, *Myth*, p. 360, says that Toomer was teaching the dances before he knew them himself. This observation, probably taken from Fritz Peters' view of the Chicago group in 1931–1932, *Gurdjieff Remembered* (London: Victor Gollancz, 1969), p. 16–21, is uninformed. Toomer had worked hard with Jessmin Howarth, the premiere teacher of the dances in the United States, first in Paris and later with his own group in Chicago. On the other hand, from all reports, Jean was not a good dancer himself.

[55] Toomer Collection, Box 47, Folders 963–967.

[56] Kerman and Eldridge, *The Lives of Jean Toomer*, p. 173.

On 24 April the Orages had gone with Jean to a party for the New York group given by Blanche Grant.[57] Jean Toomer was there from Chicago and so was Edith, accompanied by her unmarried doctor friend whom she introduced to everyone as her fiancé. Jean took her aside and said that she was making a fool of herself. He was right, for two days later she discovered she was pregnant and, when the doctor heard the news, he refused to have anything to do with her until she rid herself of the child. Jessie talked her out of an abortion. Without telling the doctor of her change of mind, Edith sent him a note saying she needed a rest. Then she sailed for England, where Orage found a place for her to stay during her pregnancy. He warned against having a child in France, since all boys born in France would be automatically French and forced into military service. The Orages themselves arrived at the end of May and took a house at Petersfield. Edith came from Paris to stay with them and with the Notts nearby. While Orage went to the city to meet with the *New Age* people in view of resuming his editing career, Jessie, Rosemary, and Edith settled down to share motherhoods. Edith moved to Hampstead, where Orage had found a townhouse for her, and she awaited her second child.

Over the summer of 1930, Fred Leighton was at the Prieuré, from where he wrote Jean in the fall that "G says Chicago is a ball of shit and it's put him seriously in goloshes [in *All and Everything* (p. 163), Gurdjieff used the expression 'in American galoshes' for being deep in trouble, and in *Meetings* (p. 300), 'in deep galosh so high I can see hardly over the rim' describes a financial problem]—not simply because it did not send the $500 per month but because he says a sum was promised the second month that never came. [He] seems disinclined to admit publicly it was Orage's fault and seems to hint but does not say definitely it was your fault. At any rate, he says he needs 3000 to make up 18,000 he needed."[58] Toomer was tired of such demands. He was eager to put more energy into writing than into fund-raising. He had completed *Essentials*, *Transatlantic*, a number of poems and essays, and was working on an autobiography. When he started his fall program of teaching, he adopted a correspondingly looser attitude with his pupils.[59]

---

[57] Gurdjieff, alluding to Blanche Grant Rosette, was later to say: "And I possess such 'inner wealth' that in the objective sense it is worth many times more than all the money that can be imagined by the human brain, such as, for example, the whole estate which fell to the so-called 'New York five-and-ten heiress" (*Life is Real*, pp. 51–52).

[58] Toomer Collection, Box 4, Folder 138.

[59] Kerman and Eldridge, *The Lives of Jean Toomer*, pp. 189–190.

When he heard what was going on, Gurdjieff was furious and, from New York where he had arrived in mid-November, sent Toomer a demand in harsh terms:

> Perceive and transubstantiate in yourself what I am writing to you, not like a "half-baked" American, but like a being whose ancestors when they became responsible beings, also became at the same time, possessors of the spiritualized presences of three centred beings, and not possessor's only exclusively of the properties of the organ Kundabuffer.
>
> First of all, I inform you, that I am still continuing to labour upon my work, about which you also know a little, with the same intensity but only with this difference, that I myself already see the approach of its speedy completion, that is, I think I shall entirely finish all the books of Beelzebub in from four to six months.
>
> As you are partly the cause of the fact that I was compelled to come here to America just now at the period when my personal presence for the actualizing of my general task is particularly required there in Europe, that is why I propose also to you to do everything, even as Nassr Eddin says, "to jump-out-of-your-skin" in order to assist my speedy return home,[60] where under conditions which have become more or less habitual to me, and which consequently require from no less effort for the ableness of self-compulsion, I could finish this work, the unprecedentedness and the super-arch-magnificence of which on Earth is already understood by anybody, even by a psychopath who knows even a half of it.
>
> The fact is that during the last two or three years, owing to the impossibility for me of writing about such questions and at the same time of being occupied with dollar business, small debts in the connection with the Prieuré have little by little accumulated to about half a million francs, and the result of all this was that two weeks before my departure, information was received that on the following day the sheriff would arrive to take possession and put under seal all the goods and effects of the Prieuré in order to meet the sum total of these debts.
>
> Can you imagine my state when I was told about this! Maybe, you also know that during these four years, those around me, in

---

[60] Nassr Eddin is a well-known legendary sage whose aphorisms are popular where Gurdjieff grew up.

order not to disturb me, and by this not to disturb the productivity of my work, themselves tried to deal with all the questions arising in the Prieuré both concerning household affairs as well as ordinary existence; but, in the present case, as the prevention of the undesirable visit of the sheriff was beyond their powers, that is why they were just compelled to tell me about it all in detail.

In view of the fact that the delay before the beginning of the threatened catastrophe was very short, I went immediately first to Fontainebleau to power-possessing people, and when I learned from them that the prevention of the occurrence of the disaster was only possible if, before eleven o'clock of the following day, I paid off all the bills in ready money, I without losing a minute entered my car, and spent the whole night going to various acquaintances of mine from whom I borrowed as much money as was possible to be repaid in one week.

And I borrowed money for such a short term, firstly, in order to collect without fail the required amount, and secondly, in order to extend the period of the threatened catastrophe from one day to one week and to have the possibility in relative freedom of finding a way out of the situation which had arisen. That night, though with great difficulty, I collected the required sum of money and paid it the following morning at the required time.

Having in this way gained time, I began already in freedom, during the following week, to find money for a longer term and paid everything, but of course, meanwhile without gratitude.

In short, as a result of such an unexpectedly serious misfortune, such circumstances arose, that in order to avoid their repetition, I had, at the end of every one of the following three months, without fail, to dispose of not less than seven thousand dollars.

During this time I have already been able to meet the demands of the first month, and just tomorrow I shall meet those of the second month. And after that there will remain only the third month.

In addition, here in America, during the period I am here, I very much wish to arrange matters in order to have the possibility of finishing satisfactorily the mentioned three books, in the sense of a more or less tolerable material position, at least not worse than that which I, unfortunately for everybody, have had.

For this it is required that up to October [1931?] inclusively, I should be able to have at each month at my disposal 1500 dollars.

And as regards my expression at the beginning of this letter, namely, that you are also the cause of this present "Jericho" situation of mine, then the matter is, that when two years ago you categorically assured me that during such and such a period you would put at my disposal the amount 5000 dollars, and even during your return voyage you once more confirmed this by letter, I, believing it, gave the order to whom it was necessary to borrow wherever possible, 100,000 francs, and firstly with this money to improve. . . . [The rest of the letter is lost.][61]

Jean sent Orage a copy of the letter with a request for advice, and a prompt reply advised him not to commit himself to anything. In his anxiety over the control of Orage's New York group, Gurdjieff postponed his Chicago visit by having Mme de Salzmann cable Jean on the 21st to cancel the hotel reservations. A day or so later, however, Metz wrote Jean to advise him that Gurdjieff would arrive in Chicago on 30 December and needed lodgings for himself and two women, but "not same hotel as last year, wants the other $500." When Gurdjieff arrived in Chicago on the 29th,[62] Jean met him with an empty purse, but Gurdjieff sensed that the Midwest was still ripe for the picking and flattered Jean by attending his group meetings and making suggestions for reorganizing the Chicago group. He insisted that Jean train other group leaders for the greater Chicago area, as Orage had done for the New York and New Jersey area. Obviously, he was plotting a new role for Jean and the Chicago groups to play in a restructured American teaching. He was, in short, offering Jean overall charge of all operations in the United States outside of New York City, where Gurdjieff wanted to assume direct control himself. The reason for this was evident. New York and Chicago were financing the Institute. Without the flow of funds that Orage's and Toomer's groups could assure, the Gurdjieff work on a school basis was doomed.

As 1930 ended, the Orages were on the high seas bound for New York aboard the SS Washington. Orage had minimal interest in seeing Gurdjieff. He was, primarily, on business to terminate his obligations in the United States so that he could resume with a free conscience his abandoned career in England. Two days after the Orages left London, on 29

---

[61] The Orage Papers, Henley, Oxfordshire.
[62] Louise Goepfert March, Gurdjieff's administrative secretary, recalls in her memoirs that Gurdjieff left for Chicago on 28 December 1930, and returned to New York three days later. She adds that, on 11 November 1930, she heard an oath dictated to the New York group not to reveal anything of Gurdjieff's work or of his self, or of the Prieuré (Beth McCorkle, ed., *The Gurdjieff Years 1929–1949: Recollections of Louise [Goepfert] March* (Walworth, NY: The Work Study Association, Inc. 1990), p. 51.

December, Edith gave birth to a son, Paul, in Hampstead. She wrote a letter to the doctor announcing the news and received in turn his news that he was returning to his wife. She then wrote Jean, who regretted that he was busy in Chicago. So, she settled uneasily for a time in England, found a brief job in a decorating shop, then went to the Prieuré with her two children in the summer of 1931 .

Meanwhile, in New York, throughout the month of December 1930, Gurdjieff had been at work trying to wrest the allegiance of Orage's group away from him. Orage knew something of this from Sherman Manchester by post, and wrote to the New York group as a whole to say he welcomed a general reorganization that might make the material of the book clearer. On the day he arrived in New York, on 8 January 1931, Orage called Toomer in Chicago to ask what Gurdjieff had done there, and Toomer replied that he had made suggestions only about reorganizing his teaching into distinct groups based upon pupil development in the work.[63] Though Orage was reassured, he was not prepared for the public humiliation Gurdjieff subjected him to before his former group in the days that followed. To soothe the consternation of his friends and pupils, Orage told them that Gurdjieff was his brother who went to strange countries and learned strange ways—but they remain brothers.[64]

Orage publicly joined the newly formed group and, after Gurdjieff announced to all that he was going to instruct Orage anew as he had Toomer two weeks earlier, he and Orage spent time together almost every day until Gurdjieff sailed on 13 March. Orage reassumed direction of his group, and it seemed to many that Gurdjieff, despite his shock tactics, had solidified his hold on both Orage and Toomer. Later that spring, Fred Leighton wrote Jean: "There has been a great fight here over the question of Orage. Now I understand Orage has returned to the fold."[65] He hadn't, and apparently never intended to, though he resumed for the spring direc-

---

[63] James Webb, *Harmonious Circle*, p. 368, James Moore, *Myth*, p. 238, and William P. Patterson, *Struggle of the Magicians* (Fairfax, CA: Arete Communications, 1996), p. 136, following Gurdjieff's slanted record in *Life is Real*, p. 120, say that Orage arrived in early December. Gurdjieff writes that his public humiliation of Orage was on 12 December, though the Orages were, at this moment, happily in Hampstead. Gurdjieff's long account is all the more strange since Orage had decided several months earlier to abandon his work with Gurdjieff and return to his publishing career.

[64] Louise Welch, *Orage with Gurdjieff in America* (London: Routledge & Kegan Paul, 1982), p. 115. She also reports her own questioning of Gurdjieff to the effect that, if Orage had been teaching them wrong, he had, after all, been teaching them what Gurdjieff had taught him (pp. 110–111). On 23 January 1931, she says, Orage addressed his New York Group as "nearly [a] real brotherhood," and that in succeeding meetings with Gurdjieff, members of the New York group defended Orage fervently.

[65] 2 May 1931, Toomer Collection, Box 4, Folder 138.

tion of his groups. Just after Gurdjieff left, he wrote Jean in Chicago that he was looking for a publisher for *Beelzebub*. "Knopf turned it down," he said, "I sent it to Doubleday. . . . I share your opinion that no publisher will accept it." And he asked Jean "to dream dollars," noting that he himself was raising $5000 in subscriptions. "Mrs. [Betty] Hare promised $2000, and Orage $1000: Chicago for $2000? You and I have a job of *selling* a special edition. G says he talked it over with you, but he probably didn't!"[66]

The Orages sailed in June, never to return again. Back in England, it was reported a few months later that, although Orage once said that he would cross the Atlantic to see Gurdjieff, now he wouldn't cross the channel! So, Toomer was the only one left for Gurdjieff with the influence to keep money flowing. Unwittingly, Gurdjieff's treatment of Orage had turned many in the New York group cold to him.[67] Jean, on the other hand, knowing of Orage's decision, had decided that spring to go his own way. In the summer of 1931, in association with the brilliant young Wisconsin novelist, Margery Latimer, who secured an ideal country venue for him, Toomer conducted at Portage, WI, an experiment in communal living, ostensibly along the lines of the Prieuré; but, where Gurdjieff kept pupils occupied in individual and mostly unsupervised tasks during the day, Jean was the center of all activities at Portage; and, instead of readings from Gurdjieff's book, his lectures as well as the daily exercises consisted of interpretive applications of Gurdjieff's system. The Portage communal living has been described not inaccurately as "a laboratory of consciously controlled events."[68]

From there, Jean sent Orage in London a copy of *Essentials*. Orage wrote back praising the book, while wondering who his audience would be outside of people who knew him and the Gurdjieff work. Orage had already seen a very unfavorable review of the book in the *Milwaukee Journal* in mid-April. For Jean, the summer was a great success and he started writing an account of it, while planning to renew the experiment somewhere the following year. In the fall, instead of resuming his Chicago teaching, Jean married Margery Latimer,[69] and the two visited Santa Fe together to see about setting up a Toomer group there. From there, in December, they went on westward, following Orage's route to San Diego and

---

[66] Toomer Collection, Box 6, Folder 206.

[67] James Webb, *Harmonious Circle*, p. 412, considers that Toomer succeeded Orage as the number one in America.

[68] Kerman and Eldrige, *The Lives of Jean Toomer*, pp. 194–195.

[69] Among the many congratulations for his marriage came a brief note from Mabel Dodge Luhan on 19 November. Just before this, Jean had heard from Munson that Gurdjieff had decided to take up permanent residence in New York City (Toomer Collection, Box 6, Folder 188).

then northward to Carmel in the spring. There Jean duplicated the Portage experiment, but his candid views on racial identity led to unfortunate publicity, some of which his friends thought weakened Margery morally and physically throughout her pregnancy, which she discovered happily there. Local papers found grist in Toomer for their mill of sensationalism, but the chaff that broke the moral back of the couple was an interview with the Toomers which appeared in the RACES section of *Time,* March 28 1932, titled "Just Americans." It is worth reproducing here if only to recall the level of race-bigotry and cruel ridicule—not to speak of distortion of facts—of which the Toomers were victims and that the establishment press was capable of:

No Negro can legally marry a white woman in any Southern State. But Wisconsin does not mind, nor California. Last week at Carmel, Calif., "Provincetown of the Pacific Coast," there was an intellectual charivari. A parade of Carmel artists and authors marched to the cottage of Jean Toomer, 36, Negro philosopher (*Cane*), psychologist and lecturer, and Novelist Margery Bodine Latimer (*This Is My Body*), 33. It had just been revealed that they were married four months ago at Portage, Wis. Bridegroom Toomer, who has a small moustache and few Negroid characteristics, told the story of their romance.

One of Jean Toomer's grandfathers was Pinckney Benton Stewart Pinchback, a mulatto carpet-bagger who became Acting Governor of Louisiana but was refused a U.S. Senate seat in 1876. After attending the University of Wisconsin, Jean Toomer became an exponent of Georges Gurdjieff, the Armenian-Greek cultist who founded the Institute for the Harmonious Development of Man at Fontainebleau, France and whose most famed disciple was the late Katherine Mansfield (*Time*, March 24, 1930). Last autumn Disciple Toomer took a mixed party of eight, all white except himself, to a farmhouse outside Portage, birthplace of Novelist Latimer. She was one of the party. All slept in two rooms on cots, following the Gurdjieff method, made themselves uncomfortable to break down thought and body habits, sat around nights discussing their reactions.

"As a result of the experiment," said Toomer last week, "I am satisfied that it is entirely possible to eradicate the false veneer of civilization with its unnatural inhibitions, its selfishness, petty meanness and unnatural behavior. . . . Adults can be re-educated to become as natural little children, before civilization stamps out their true or subconscious instincts."

Early in the experiment, he added, he discovered that his own reaction drew him to Novelist Latimer, likewise a onetime Wisconsin student, who first heard of her future husband when she submitted articles to a magazine he edited. They were married. So re-educated had one member of the experimental houseparty become—Newspaper-woman Sara Roberts—that she neglected to report the nuptials.

"Americans probably do not realize it," Bridegroom Toomer told his callers last week, "but there are no racial barriers any more, because there are so many Americans with strains of Negro, Indian and Oriental blood. As I see America, it is like a great stomach into which are thrown the elements that make up the life blood. From this source is coming a distinct race of people. They will achieve tremendous works of art, literature and music. They will not be white, black or yellow—just Americans."[70]

"You do not protest against a person's religion," concluded his bride. "Why should you judge people by their color? I and hundreds of others have taken my husband for what he is—a brilliant man."[71]

The cruelty in this account is not so much in the misrepresentation of fact (there were five rooms in the farmhouse at Portage, and they did not become acquainted in this manner, they were married in October 1931, not December, etc.), or even in the unsubtle strategy of mockery. It lies in the denigration of a love between two people. Toomer conceived of love, as Orage and Gurdjieff had, as a force that can draw two parties into the same effort toward growth. Mutual love is a mutual exchange of positive energy in a fusion of a common consciousness. To love someone is to know that person even better than he or she knows his or her self. In this context, "mixed" marriage is a flat contradiction of terms.

---

[70] The more recent case of Anatole Broyard, as Henry Louis Gates, Jr. has exposed it in "White Like Me" (*The New Yorker* 17 June 1996, pp. 66–81), is tragically similar. As Gates points out, "society had decreed race to be a matter of natural law, but he [Broyard] wanted race to be an elective affinity, and it was never going to be a fair fight. . . . So here is a man who passed for white because he wanted to be a writer, and he did not want to be a Negro writer" (p. 66). There are pertinent differences, however. Gates says to the point in Broyard's case that "to pass is to sin against authenticity" (p. 78), but Toomer did not "pass" in Sparta, where he lived the black experience that generated *Cane*, but that experience was distinct from his more northern urban background. In other words, Toomer moved into authenticity in *Cane*, and believed he could do so with equal authenticity in his "white" experience in New York, Chicago, and Carmel.

[71] *Time*, March 28, 1932, p. 19.

Friends in New York heard of the interview and saw the advance text. Five days before publication date, Gorham Munson wrote Jean to say that Schuyler Jackson (husband of Laura Riding) had gone to the *Time* offices to try, unsuccessfully, to kill the story, then added his own late advice: "It all comes down to this. A. R. O. and G are right in never giving interviews to the press." Munson then advised Jean against trying to get *Portage Potential* published at this time: "This is no time to bring out anything but a very guarded book on G's ideas," he insisted. "One factor to be reckoned with is the impression Gurdjieff made on the thirty or forty publishers to whom he gave a luncheon [to publicize his book], and another is the harm caused by traitors from the Gurdjieff groups who have spread scandal."[72]

After the article appeared, Fred Leighton wrote an angry letter to *Time* correcting facts and attacking the slanted tone of the article,[73] but *Time* would not print it. Jean swallowed the bitter pill and tried to regain his composure by fictionalizing the Carmel experiment in a narrative he entitled "Caromb," but Margery took the attack on her husband badly. Later, a rueful Jean wrote a response to press attacks on his marriage in an essay entitled "Thus it may be said,"[74] but the damage had been done, in part because he had said too much honestly in public.

Nonetheless, they continued the Carmel work into the early summer, and returned to Chicago and Portage in August. There Jean and Margery recovered their almost ecstatic love for each other in joyful anticipation of the child she was about to bear. Holding her just-born daughter happily in her arms, she died of hemorrhaging.[75] Jean insisted on keeping something of her alive by naming his daughter after his wife.

Despite his own precarious position as a wifeless father without financial security, he refused to compromise his convictions. Shortly after his wife's death, he celebrated the ideals he and Margery had fought for, when he wrote to a consoling admirer: "You know that I am writing. That I am trying to win a certain strength and beauty from contact with American life. That I hope to see my efforts stimulate and contribute to the growth of an authentic culture here in America."[76]

---

[72] Toomer Collection, Box 6, Folder 188.
[73] Toomer Collection, Box 4, Folder 139.
[74] Toomer Collection, Box 51, Folder 1122.
[75] Inexplicably, Kerman and Eldridge, 205, have Margery's death on 16 September, and Byrd, 85, says she died two weeks before their first wedding anniversary, that would be about 16 October.
[76] Toomer Collection, Box 3, Folder 76. In *The Big Sea*, p. 243, Langston Hughes, in remarking on Toomer's stance toward race and marriage, remarks, "He was a fine American writer. But when we get as democratic as we pretend we are . . . nobody

To make matters worse, as well as the death of his wife and the necessity of having friends care for his daughter, and a general fall of morale in the Chicago group, Jean found himself still entangled in the question of the Luhan money. In May 1933, Jane Heap, acting as Gurdjieff's secretary, wrote an open letter from the Prieuré to Israel Solon for the New York group. A copy was sent to Toomer over the names of "Marvis McIntosh, Lawrence S. Morris, C. Daly King, Claire Mann, Willard Widney, and Jane Heap (chief)." It recalled that Orage held $3000 and Toomer $2000 for the *Beelzebub* publication fund, and demanded that the money should be sent to Jane Heap, that it was to be used *only* for publication costs and, finally, that the money should be placed in escrow. At the end, after noting that an identical letter was sent to Orage, it posed two questions: "Does money exist. Is it in Orage's name?"

In London, Orage ignored the letter, but from Portage, Toomer wrote on 26 May 1933 to the New York group as a whole to explain patiently that: his $2000 was the remainder of the sum given Gurdjieff by Mabel Dodge through him.[77] He recalled to them his pact with Orage in every detail, reminding the group that what he gave to Gurdjieff (the original $1000) was "to be repaid to me by the NY group." Some of it, he reminded them, was paid through Gorham Munson, but the remainder had been left unpaid. This seems to fit the facts, and since the $2000 was also turned over to Gurdjieff subsequently through New York in 1929, it appears that Jean was more owed than owing.

Gurdjieff was squeezing for all the money he could get because he had announced plans to open a new Institute with the Paradou as its center, insisting in his "supplementary announcement" to the *Herald of Coming Good*, on 7 March 1933, issued from Fontainebleau, that the Prieuré remained his permanent address. The pamphlet, which he asked Toomer to sell throughout America, was published in August 1933 in Paris and contained a detailed description of the new Institute in refurbished quarters which would house the same three separate groups of students he had dictated in New York and Chicago. Gurdjieff's saint's day, 23 April 1933, was announced as the date that the cornerstone of the new Institute would be placed.[78]

[76] (cont) will bother about anybody else's race anyway" (New York: Hill and Wang 1963). Henry Louis Gates, Jr., ("Introduction: 'Tell me, Sir, . . . What is "Black Literature?"' *PMLA* 105 (1990), p. 20) cites Richard Wright to the effect that "Black Literature exists only because of white racism; remove the latter and the former disappears."

[77] Toomer Collection, Box 6, Folder 96.

[78] G. I. Gurdjieff, *Herald of the Coming Good* (Edmonds, WA: Sure Fire Press, 1988), p. 88 (reprint of 1933 Paris edition).

Sales went badly and when Toomer arrived in New York from Chicago and Portage in October, he found awaiting him a copy of a wire sent to Rita Romilly from Fontainebleau, saying: "Gurdjieff absolutely destitute, Prieuré being sold. If you can arrange anything please cable funds writing Stanley [Speidelberg]." Added to the copy sent Jean is the plea: "We expect those who are willing and able will make their checks payable to Allan R. Brown, 11 Broadway. The Committee, Allan R. Brown, Muriel Draper, Fred Leighton, Rita Romilly, Israel Solon."

Then Fred Leighton wrote Jean on 21 December to tell him that Nick Putnam was bringing Gurdjieff to New York to straighten things out. To forestall further demands, Jean's Chicago group cabled Gurdjieff $150 a few weeks later and offered to pay his boat fare to the United States.[79] Notwithstanding his announcement, Gurdjieff surrendered his lease on the château and moved temporarily into a hotel above the Café de la Paix in Paris, so the Chicago money became nothing but pocket money. The last American residents at the Prieuré, Caesar Zwaska, Martin Benson, and Nick Putnam had already joined Toomer in late summer in Chicago, from where Nick wrote Edith on 1 October saying that they hoped that reports from Paris did not mean that Edith was now Gurdjieff's "number one adjutant." Then he closed, saying that Caesar had talked with a Chicago street singer, who said that he was also a former resident of the Prieuré.[80]

That winter, Jean was comforting an ill and depressed Georgia O'Keefe at Lake George and, in April of 1934, Fred Leighton introduced him to Marjorie Content, on Georgia's urging. In May, Gurdjieff returned to America and the Chicago group sent a note to Jean asking what the visit should mean to them, since they were at the point of disbanding. At the same time, Jean received an anonymous postcard, possibly from Metz in New York, saying that "Mr. Gurdjieff requests that you bring not only the money and subscription blank of any copy sold of *The Herald of Coming Good*, but any <u>unsold</u>." The Gurdjieff Committee of Washington DC wrote Jean at this time: "Dear and Esteemed Grandfather, We pledge to spread the word and buy *The Herald of Glad Tidings*." At the end of June, Fred Leighton wrote Jean saying that Gurdjieff was going to drive to Chicago with him to see Toomer and the World's Fair, or the World's Fair and

---

[79] Toomer Collection, Box 4, Folder 140. Fritz Peters, *Boyhood with Gurdjieff* (London: Victor Gollancz, 1964), p. 33, locates Gurdjieff in New York at the Henry Hudson Hotel in the fall of 1933. James Moore, *Myth*, pp. 249–250, has Gurdjieff there with Toomer and Munson at this time.

[80] Edith Taylor papers.

Jean.[81] When they arrived, by train instead of car, Jean was not on hand to greet them, but a large delegation of Jean's group was at the station.[82] Gurdjieff was anxious about the structure of the Chicago group, having seen the New York group diminish in number and interest after the break with Orage; and without Jean, the Chicago group would be useless to Gurdjieff unless there were others to take his place. He had doubts about Olgivanna Lloyd Wright in such a role, and Olgivanna had her own plans for a dance and theater group at Wright's Taliesin East.

When Metz asked Jean on Gurdjieff's behalf about the status of the Chicago group, Jean replied on 18 August directly to Gurdjieff from Espanola, New Mexico, announcing his forthcoming marriage and the personal obligations marriage would impose, before concluding: "At the same time I now, as always, want to do all I can to help spread the ideas that mean so much to me, that I believe the greatest ideas that contemporary man will be privileged to come in contact with."[83] On Gurdjieff's behalf, he asked Mabel Dodge Luhan again for support, but she declined giving any more money, saying, however, that there was local interest enough to carry a group on in Taos even after Jean left. A month later, Gurdjieff was again in Chicago and then at Taliesin East, where he talked with Frank Lloyd Wright who, in an interview published in the Madison, Wisconsin *Capitol Times* on 12 September 1934, declared that Gurdjieff's ideas were the most important in the world.[84] He had no intention, however, of having a Gurdjieff center on his property. Jean married Marjorie Content in September and began planning resumption of his own teaching on a new scale. The newly married couple moved into 39 West 10th Street; and, before long, Wharton Esherick had come upon an ideal location in Bucks County, PA, not far from Doylestown.

Mabel Dodge Luhan remained in the picture with a brief, final, and futile request on 26 November, 1934, for the money lent Gurdjieff. Jean replied gently with the simple figures: From the original $14,000, $12,000 went to Gurdjieff and $2000 was held by Toomer. Of the latter, he reminds her, $1050 was given to the Prieuré in an emergency, effectively breaking his agreement with Orage, but New York promised to repay him, and $500 went to the Prieuré for another emergency. Jean apologized at length for the situation, and he regretted the accusations of fraud implied by the New York group, but Fred Leighton and Gorham Munson had verified the ac-

---

[81] 30 June 1934, Toomer Collection, Box 4, Folders 138–141.
[82] Peters, *Gurdjieff Remembered*, p. 40.
[83] Toomer Collection, Box 3, Folder 96.
[84] Toomer Collection, Box 68, Folder 1548. Moore has Gurdjieff in Spring Green in June 1934.

counts. By return post, Mabel asked for the "lesser sum" borrowed in Taos (the $1000?), to which Jean replied that he considered that money lent as an investment in his own future. He said he would repay it when he could, but for the moment he was destitute. So the final tally had Mabel Dodge Luhan out $15,000, Toomer out $500, the New York Group out $2000 in their publication fund, and Gurdjieff, as he would say, *nalichie, nitchivo*—balance: nothing.[85] Notwithstanding the unsettled accounts, right up to her death in 1962, Mabel spoke with affection and concern for Jean.

Meanwhile in London, Orage gave a BBC talk on the evening of 5 November, felt some dizziness and pain, and died during the night of a blood clot on the wall of his left auricle. Jessie had Nott cable the news to Gurdjieff in New York. Louise Welch, who was with Gurdjieff when he heard of Orage's death, saw him "wiping the tears from his eyes with his fist, saying: 'This man, my brother.'"[86] Jessie Orage had Nott also contact Jean in New York, who cabled back the same day, saying: "Without Orage, there is no reason for me to stay in the work."[87]

At this moment, Jean was anticipating a new start in both New York and Doylestown, secured for the time being by his new wife's money and supported by her tight circle of good friends. Acutely conscious of what Gurdjieff had done to Orage in New York three years earlier, and suspecting that he might be Gurdjieff's next target for public humiliation[88]—if not worse—he decided to detach himself from Gurdjieff, the man, to concentrate on his independent course of teaching. Prompted by Fred Leighton, he had a series of brief meetings with Gurdjieff in January and February 1935, and handed over a final gift of enough money to cover Gurdjieff's boat ticket back to France. Gurdjieff wanted more, but Jean had too many scruples to apply to his wife, and so turned away. Gurdjieff visited Washington and Chicago to see what condition groups there were in, and whether they could raise money for him. After an anticipated meeting in early May 1935 with Senator Bronson Cutting of New Mexico failed to take place because of Cutting's tragic death in an air accident, a disappointed Gurdjieff returned to France, then disappeared from view

---

[85] If a finger of blame has to be pointed, I would point it at the treasurers of the New York group who, finally, wondered whether or not their missing money existed at all.

[86] Louise Welch, *Orage with Gurdjieff in America*, p. 137. C. S. Nott, *Orage*, p. 53, though he was not there, has Gurdjieff crying out: "I loved Orage as a brother." Gurdjieff's own account in *Life is Real*, p. 151, says a call came to Child's restaurant for him announcing that a telegram had been received from England shortly after 11 A.M. reporting the death of Orage, "my friend."

[87] According to Jessie Orage, 13 November, 1981.

[88] Kerman and Eldridge, *The Lives of Jean Toomer*, pp. 219–220.

until September, when he re-established his teaching on a more modest level in his brother Dimitri's apartment at 6, rue des Colonels Renard—near the Arc de Triomphe—where he was to reside for the rest of his life.[89] In Paris, meanwhile, Edith had been hoping still for some sort of security from Gurdjieff, but without any success. So, in the fall of 1935, she took her courage into her hands and sailed for New York, where Fred Leighton promised to find her a job. There she contacted Jean, who was living with his new wife in the same house he had visited more than a decade earlier to see Harold Loeb about publishing some stories. Edith and Jean renewed their friendship under conditions free of Gurdjieff's influence.

Two years later, although Edith had found a position with W. & J. Sloane, she was at the end of her resources and had exhausted her possibilities of finding help from old friends like Martin and Rita Benson in Washington, CT, and Thelma Wood in Sandy Hook. In May of 1937, she wrote Jean saying that she had a temporary job for the summer as part-time cook and acting coach in a summer camp in Harvard, MA. She was planning on returning to an acting career in the fall, but needed to place the children somewhere.[90] She consigned her daughter to a camp in New Milford, CT, and Jean and Marjorie took her son into their family in New York. Two men had deceived her and rejected the children she bore them. The man she herself had rejected welcomed her back. Jean Toomer never held a grudge long, except for the grudge he bore Gurdjieff.[91]

In his autobiographical record, *In Memory and a Devotion and a Hope*, Jean marks 1939 as the end of his involvement with Gurdjieff, though he hadn't seen him for over four years. The date, five years after his marriage to Marjorie Content, seven years after the death of Margery Latimer and the birth of his daughter, only marks Jean's *final* decision to abandon Gurdjieff's way. It came about in the conjunction of four interlaced causes. The first was the realization that his own ideas for a school at Mill House, based on Gurdjieffian methods, were no longer practicable, and had not been, really, since 1937, when the conversion of the mill into a large living unit was interrupted because of his wife's unwillingness to bear the huge cost involved, which

---

[89] The gap in records of Gurdjieff's life between May and September 1935, during which he may have traveled secretly to the Soviet Union to explore the possibilities of opening a new school there, is put into context by James Moore, *Myth*, pp. 254–257.

[90] 3 May 1937.

[91] In 1959, Edith married Philip Lasell in Nyon, Switzerland and Jessie, with her two children, Dick and Ann, and their families, came over for the event. Ann was eight months pregnant at the time, and the festivities brought on her labor, so she stayed a few days extra to give birth in the Geneva clinic. After a few weeks of marriage, Philip was put under medical care again, probably as a result of drug abuse, and spent the rest of his life in a succession of sanatoriums.

could only be covered by the generosity of her father, Harry Content.[92] The second was Jean's disappointment with Edith's and Fred Leighton's collaboration with Gurdjieff in the spring of 1939, when Gurdjieff made his last pre-war trip to New York. Though they had invited Jean to join them, he would have preferred that they renounce Gurdjieff in deference to his feelings; and so he escaped on a solitary holiday to Bermuda. Jean was not insensitive to Gurdjieff's anger ("disappointment" is perhaps too weak a word to describe his public posture) over Toomer's marriage, for, although Gurdjieff approved of marriage as a stage in man's "normal" life before moving on to the superior life of work on one's personal development which domestic concerns only hinder, he could not bear the idea of someone deserting the work for marriage. Jean knew at first hand of Gurdjieff's reaction to Orage's marriage with Jessie, recalled in *Life is Real* (pp. 92–95). Jean had heard from Edith some disparaging remarks Gurdjieff had made about his own marriage to Margery Latimer, and would rather avoid Gurdjieff than face him down as Orage had done bravely some seven years earlier.

A third reason was Gurdjieff's obstinate demands on Jean to raise money for the "work," while it seemed to Jean, as it had to Orage a decade earlier, that Gurdjieff was withholding secret knowledge from him. Finally, added to the feeling that Gurdjieff would not help him move himself up a level on the scale of consciousness, was his suspicion that some exterior force—possibly an emanation of Gurdjieff himself—was causing his physical problems. He had been contemplating a trip to India for some time and, after Gurdjieff arrived in New York, he decided upon it. When Susan Loeb questioned her mother concerning the reasons for the trip, Marjorie wrote: "Once before Jean was up against this situation—and Mr G helped him to pass a certain point—after that J. was enabled to proceed under his own steam for quite some time. It is for that J is eternally grateful to G no matter what may have happened since . . . Now, Jean seems to be up against something he can't negotiate. He is in some sort of condition that the doctors of the western world know nothing about. Jean feels something or someone is causing his physical problems. This condition has been in effect, in varying degrees, since February a year ago!"[93] It was in

---

[92] At this time, Jean tried to coerce Harry Content, with no success, by offering to found a university under his name. Content was more interested in a new woman in his life.
[93] Marjorie Content papers, Mechanicsville, courtesy of the estate of Marjorie Content. Kerman and Eldridge, *The Lives of Jean Toomer*, note that in New York, Gurdjieff was repudiating Toomer much in the same fashion he had repudiated Orage, and adding financial mismanagement to the charges. "This new series of accusations and events," they write, "broke Jean's last link to the official Gurdjieff movement" (p. 220). Added to this, in February 1938 Marjorie had lost their baby.

February 1938 that Marjorie lost her child with Jean; and, some years after his death, Marjorie told me that Jean had the illusion that Gurdjieff exercised powers over the physical well-being of certain people, including Orage and himself. The conjunction of his physical problems with the loss of a child may have had him believe somehow that Gurdjieff was responsible.

Gurdjieff had, in the meantime, returned in mid-May to a France tensed for war. As France was succumbing to the German army in 1940, Gurdjieff sent word to all his American followers to invite him to the United States.[94] After the fall of Paris, there was no word of Gurdjieff until the end of February 1942, when Jean received a circular letter from Donald Whitcomb, Israel Solon, and Fred Leighton, asking everyone to send money to Gurdjieff, explaining that $200 had already reached him, enough for a visa to Cuba, and that Gurdjieff approved. The letter suggested Mexico as an alternative, and estimated that $1000 would suffice to get him there. Jean did not respond and nothing came of the effort, perhaps because Gurdjieff had gathered together a French group before long, and the occupying German authorities were tolerating his activities. By this time, two other factors intervened to quiet Jean's interests in Gurdjieff. First, soon after the return from India, he had a kidney removed, but his intestinal disorders continued. Secondly, Harry Content died and left the bulk of his estate to his mistress. From then on, Jean and Marjorie were living off capital. The farm income could not even pay the wages of Ramsey and the Davenports.

In 1945, new attempts were made to interest Jean in the Gurdjieff work in connection with a new group being re-established by Orage's old pupils in New York. Toomer's reputation was still high in New York, and Edwin Wolfe invited Jean and Marjorie to dinner with Sherman Manchester in August of that year to talk over the re-establishment of New York groups in time for the expected return of Gurdjieff to New York, but Jean declined.[95]

In retrospect, Toomer seems to have gone to Gurdjieff not only to learn, but, in learning, to confirm certain ideas about himself. What Toomer digested of Gurdjieff's teaching did confirm much of his earlier thought; and, more importantly, it gave a structural framework and a vocabulary with which he could develop and transmit it. Toomer probably wanted, and even expected from Gurdjieff as well as from Orage, reciprocal respect and admiration as a partner in an adventure in ideas, but this he did not get in terms he could appreciate. It is obvious that Gurdjieff's per-

---

son and manner spellbound him, but by 1939, if not by the end of 1934, Toomer felt Gurdjieff was simply using him to raise money.[96]

I have always felt that, in view of the complexity of the relationship between them, it is curious that Toomer's name figures so little in the many recollections of Gurdjieff by pupils.[97] In my own conversations with many who were at the Prieuré during the time Jean visited—Fritz Peters, Bernard Metz, Jessie Orage, Philip Lasell, Nick Putnam, Lida Gurdjieff, Nikolai de Stjernvall—Jean was uncertainly remembered.[98] Some thought him a fake, others spoke of him as the Negro who passed as white. I overheard Stanley Nott wondering to my mother in 1940 why Gurdjieff had chosen Jean to be his American "steward," when Jean knew so little of Gurdjieff's teachings. When I spoke of Jean with Margaret Anderson in August, 1949, she said she admired him as a writer, but couldn't remember exactly what his role was with Gurdjieff.[99] Nikolai de Stjernvall, in conversation with me some time ago, recalled Toomer "as a shadow. Few people even noticed him; or, if they did, they didn't take notice or ask who he was. He didn't, as so many others did, draw attention openly to himself. He seemed to have a private and secret design."

---

[96] Kerman and Eldridge, *The Lives of Jean Toomer*, p. 235, say that Toomer rejected Gurdjieff the man by the summer of 1937. 1939 is the date he gives himself, and his feeling that he would prefer not to see Gurdjieff that spring made him realize that he had no further need for the man. They remark (p. 242) that Toomer's trip to Bermuda was a "kind of rest cure," and suggest that Bermuda had not done for him enough, so he decided to go to India. Actually, the India trip had been on Jean's mind for at least two years. In 1937, he had inquired about schools in India for Argie, saying that he expected to be there within a year.

[97] For example, de Hartmann, who recounts the events of 1924–26, (*Our Life*, pp. 197–209); Margaret Anderson, *The Unknowable Gurdjieff* (London: Routledge & Kegan Paul, 1962); Stanley Nott, *Teachings of Gurdjieff: Journal of a Pupil* (London: Routledge & Kegan Paul, 1961); and Fritz Peters, *Boyhood*. Besides the first, all of these works concentrate on the crucial years of the Institute, 1924–1926. The sole exception I can find to the scant notice of Toomer's presence at the Prieuré is in the privately printed memoirs of Louise Goepfert March edited by Beth McCorkle (*The Gurdjieff Years*, p. 20). In her description of the Prieuré in the summer of 1929, she mentions "Miss Taylor" and Jean Toomer, "the black author of *Cane*."

[98] Fritz Peters, *Gurdjieff*, pp. 16–21, 26–29, who joined the Chicago group for a while, without mentioning Jean's name, describes his teaching as being understood as license for "free love, adultery and radical social behavior." He accuses the group of reading Gurdjieff's book "allegorically." He brought these charges to Gurdjieff's attention, who thought this state of affairs amusing, but quite normal. The group leader, he says, in contrast to Gurdjieff, lacks humor! James Webb, *Harmonious Circle*, pp. 419–420, repeats this ridiculous assessment.

[99] Peter Washington, *Madame Blavatsky's Monkey* (London: Secker and Warburg, 1995), p. 257, calls Toomer at the Prieuré "a mixed-race misfit."

Recently, after rereading recollections of Gurdjieff, I realized the extent to which memories of the Prieuré are selective. The permanent residents—Gurdjieff's large family group and his permanent staff—are recalled easily, but the transient guests are as easily forgotten. Everyone remembers who Orage and Katherine Mansfield were, but few could tell me anything of what they did there. Toomer was less a "celebrity" to incite anecdotes, true or fabled. Luba Gurdjieff, who died in 1995 at the age of 81, and who had a more generous memory than most, did remember Jean. She told me how handsome he seemed to the young women and girls who gathered around him. She laughed, recalling his playfulness and Gurdjieff's good-natured joking about the attention Toomer got from his admirers. She added that it was commonly known what high hopes Gurdjieff had for Toomer in America.

Chapter Six

Beelzebub's Last Sojourn On Earth

Il devient une imitation monstreuse de lui même. Il semble que le péché de Gurdjieff est de ne s'être retiré à temps.
—Louis Pauwels

On one level Gurdjieff was a fraud, a liar, a cheat, and a scoundrel. He also possessed compensating qualities. . . . He attempted to use the friction generated by his negative qualities to strike fire.
—James Webb

As Jean was withdrawing from Gurdjieff's world between 1939 and 1949, I was moving steadily into it. After having heard stories of Gurdjieff throughout the war, I spent a good deal of time in my last year of high school and my first semester in college finding out as much "fact" about Gurdjieff as possible. I read Rom Landau's *God is My Adventure*, and I tried to verify his assertions that Gurdjieff was a certain Dordzeiff who served as a Russian agent in Tibet and zones of Russian influence in Asia at the end of the 19th century. In English archaeological and geographical journals of the time, I found mention of that name, and I found the name of an Ouspensky, P. D.'s father I assumed, who was an explorer in the region of southern Siberia at the time.[1] None of this information gave me much more than the same sense of mystery about the man that so many of his pupils relished. Though his works were not yet published, I had heard from Nick Putnam and my mother some of Gurdjieff's terminology, and I knew a great deal about his teaching from Jean's talks.

In December 1948, Gurdjieff arrived in New York and set up headquarters in the Wellington Hotel on 7th Avenue in an apartment on the 11th floor with as many pupils as the floor could accomodate.[2] Many other

---

[1] James Moore, in *Gurdjieff and Mansfield* (London: Routledge & Kegan Paul, 1980) carefully sifts the evidence concerning Gurdjieff's many identities.

[2] This chapter was read by Dushka Howarth, who has corrected some name-forms and reminded me of details I had misrepresented or forgotten. For example, I had assumed Gurdjieff had booked the entire floor, since there was so much traffic of his pupils in the hallways, but Dushka reminded me that two nuns remained next door and complained constantly about the hallway traffic and noise at night.

rooms in the Wellington, as well as in the Great Northern Hotel on 57th Street where Gurdjieff had stayed during pre-war visits, were occupied by the large number of visitors, new and curious as well as veteran and dubious. The principal reason for this trip, unlike his early pre-war visits, was not to raise money for his Institute, but for the publication and distribution of *All and Everything*. The voyage itself was financed largely by the English group and by Lord Pentland who had been living with his family at Mme Ouspensky's farm in New Jersey, but only a few of the English came over with G. One reason was England's draconian conditions for foreign travel which restricted the export of pounds to something like £15 per annum. At any rate, there was an abundance of Americans waiting, most of whom were eager to see the legendary master, and others hesitant before advance solicitations for contributions.

The huge crowds filing in and out of the Wellington were an organizer's nightmare. Jeanne de Salzmann had to establish a selection and priority for invitations, but unannounced arrivals were more the rule than exception. Furthermore, receiving scores of guests every day meant adapting to the circumstances the small living room and a small bathroom converted into a kitchen on one side of the large corner apartment G had taken for himself. It meant assigning certain new pupils, as well as older ones, the preparation of meals for between fifty and a hundred and fifty people almost every day for over two months, finding exotic foods in downtown 2nd Avenue shops and Fulton Street, and reserving tables at restaurants when G wished to eat out with a select entourage.

I came down from Providence in early December on a morning train and met my mother and sister in the lobby of the Wellington where they were talking with Nick Putnam. At one in the afternoon, we all went up to Gurdjieff's rooms, where Mme de Salzmann met us and said that Gurdjieff was resting and would be out soon. A half hour later he came out, saw Edith and smiled: "Ah, good you come." He gave my sister and me a warm handshake and sat down in an armchair stuffed with pillows. At two, lunch was announced and everyone already assembled was able to fit in the makeshift dining room. To my sister and me, the youngest among the crowd that day, he said: "Today you eat here, after at children's table."[3] As the meal began, Gurdjieff proposed the first toast, which I heard as "To Heometric Idiots." When I sipped my glass of cognac tentatively, he roared at me: "If you sit at man's table, you drink like man. Drink all!" The toasts

---

[3]   There was always a separate children's table at the Prieuré, and after meals the children could leave the dining area, while the adults talked. Most of the children were already in bed before Gurdjieff and the others moved to another place for readings and music.

continued throughout the meal, which was chicken and wild rice for us, but a sheep's head for Gurdjieff. The meal lasted about two hours, and then we went into a salon for coffee, while Gurdjieff went back to his room. Other people arrived until there were some fifty of us squeezed into the sitting room. G came back about an hour later, sat on the armchair set to face the crowd, picked up his *garmouchka*, a sort of harmonium which he held on his knees and played with one hand, while pumping the back bellows with the other. Someone, later identified as Donald Whitcomb, recorded the music on a wire-recorder, though it seemed to me that Gurdjieff was just playing around, improvising. "Enough," Gurdjieff said after a half hour or so, and then he left the room. As we started to leave, Mme de Salzmann stopped my mother and said Gurdjieff wanted to see her. When she reappeared, we left and took a taxi to Grand Central. On the train, she told us what had happened.[4]

"Gurdjieff wants us to move to the Wellington right away and stay there until he leaves in March, and he offers to take us all with him back to Paris." She paused for our reaction, but she knew the decision was really hers. I had my college studies to worry about, but I could take my exams in January and then come back down, though I couldn't afford to miss the entire second semester. I wasn't committed to Gurdjieff's teaching at the time, as some of the other young crowd were, but I was fascinated with the spectacle he orchestrated. Spending time with Gurdjieff was a distraction for me, a shift to a world far away from the sports and studies which had dominated my life for the past two years. I was also curious about my mother's relations with Gurdjieff and his crowd, and even more curious about what there was in Gurdjieff that had attracted and now repelled Jean Toomer. In short, I wanted to measure Gurdjieff against Toomer; and so, with enthusiasm for an adventure before me, I decided to go with the crowd to sit at Gurdjieff's feet for a while.

My mother called Jean later that evening to ask whether he would be coming up to New York to visit Gurdjieff. He replied that Fred Leighton

---

[4] Nick Putnam joked later that Gurdjieff had also spoken to him privately to order him not to use the Wellington as a stopover on his way to Lida Gurdjieff in Paris. Lida had been Gurdjieff's favorite niece, and he disapproved of Nick's commuting between wives in Los Angeles and Paris. Things became tense when Lida became pregnant with Nick's child in 1947. She had had the good fortune to be sheltered in a marriage with Russell Page, who not only adored her, but had become a trusted confidant of Gurdjieff. Nick did not respect either of his marriage bonds sufficiently for Gurdjieff's taste. Although I never heard from Nick or anyone else about an earlier marriage, according to a cable from Rita Romilly to Fred Leighton in December 1933, Nick had married someone then (Toomer Collection, The Beinecke Rare Book and Manuscript Library, Yale University, Box 4, Folder 139).

was keeping him in touch with things.[5] A day or so later, Gurdjieff commissioned her to persuade Jean to consult with him about his American group and to ask if Mill House could be used as a center, suggesting that Madame Ouspensky's Franklin Farms might be another. Jean was adamant in his refusal and Gurdjieff quipped to Edith with his inimitable smile that her powers of persuasion had not improved over the years. In mid-December, she and my sister moved into the Wellington, and a week later I deserted my studies to join them on the eighth floor and become one more anonymous figure in the huge crowd that filled his rooms. Except for a scant few days over the Christmas holidays, Edith and Petey were in New York. I was there until I returned to Providence in January for classes and exams, and then came back down for the rest of G's stay.

The frenzied pace about the Wellington was dizzying and touched the entire population of the hotel, especially the bellboys and porters who scrambled to serve Gurdjieff whenever he crossed the lobby, expecting and receiving large tips. I merged invisibly, it seemed to me, with the young group who sat for meals in the sitting room two or three meters from the long table at which Gurdjieff and his old pupils sat, and we were under the disciplinary charge of a stern brigade—Louise Welch, Edwin and Dorothy Wolfe, Wim Nyland, and Rita Benson, among others—whose job it was to hush the children in the other room so that all could hear the Master, or "the Old Man," as Nick and Philip Lasell called him, speak. Only Gurdjieff was expected to initiate dining table conversation and he would punctually order the toasts. Besides water, the only drink at the main table was either cognac or homemade vodka. The smell of exotic spices and herbs drifting from the converted kitchen was new to my senses, as were the heavy odors of unfamiliar and disguised meats which produced pungent odors that permeated the apartment and leaked out into the hotel corridors. The main fare was most often stewed lamb, but on occasion there was sheepshead, camel sausage, bear meat, and strange fish, such as fresh sturgeon. There were melons, halvah, turkish delight, and small candies after coffee.

I remember seeing Frank Lloyd Wright and his wife Olgivanna there. They kept rooms at the Plaza for their frequent New York visits. Olgivanna had become part of the Gurdjieff entourage in Constantinople and was at the Prieuré until 1926.[6] Other "celebrities" came to listen at the table to

---

[5]   William P. Patterson, *Struggle of the Magicians* (Fairfax, CA: Arete Communications, 1996), p. 186, says that Jean met Gurdjieff in New York in 1948, after which he confessed that he neither knew himself, his wife, his child, his friends, nor his aim in life.
[6]   In private conversation, Dushka Howarth speculated that Olgivanna's daughter, Svetlana, who died at an early age, was sired by Gurdjieff. One piece of circumstantial evidence was Svetlana's striking resemblance to my sister.

Gurdjieff's tossing of insults at middle-aged women and later to his post-prandial parables from the couch facing the sitting room where a few sat before him on chairs, but where most of us sat on the floor. At one time or another, my mother introduced me to Kathryn Hulme, Muriel Draper, Margaret Anderson, Dorothy Caruso, and Solita Solano. There were many young girls in attendance, including Patty, daughter of Louise and Bill Welch, and Carolla, daughter of Wim Nyland and Ilonka Karasz, a celebrated *New Yorker* illustrator. Five girls there—Marian Sutta, Iovanna Lloyd Wright, Tania Savitsky (recently married to Tom Forman and called by everyone there "Ouspensky," after her grandmother), Dushka Howarth, and my sister Eve—Gurdjieff had identified as "the calves," who would be trained to perform and teach the movements (a sixth, Lise Tracol, remained in Paris). My mother said that the older women—Jessmin Howarth, Rita Romilly, Solita Solano, Muriel Draper, Dorothy Caruso, Margaret Anderson, and herself, among others—were known familiarly as the "cows."[7]

After dinner, "honored" pupils like Stanley Spiegelberg, John Bennett, and Edwin Wolfe read from the manuscript of *All and Everything*, and Gurdjieff would interrupt occasionally and follow the reading with comments and answers to a few questions before concluding the late nights with his own music. When G had had enough in the evening, he would put aside the harmonium and announce that it was time for him to retire, then fumble in his pockets for fistfuls of wrapped candies which he threw in front of the children sitting up front; or he would ask me or someone else at the front of the room to pass them out. One evening, as I started handing out candies one by one, G bellowed "No! Like this!" And then he took and threw my handful across the room. Then everyone would line up to say goodbye. One evening when I said goodbye, I added "Thank you." "Thank for what?" he asked, and I said "for the education you are giving me." "How you know what I give you?" Without hesitating, I replied: "Jean Toomer taught me." "Ah," said he, lowering his glance. Then, reaching into a jacket pocket, he pulled out some bills and, without another word, thrust two one-hundred dollar bills into my hand. A few nights later, as I stopped before him to say goodnight, he asked me a few questions. When I replied in the affirmative to something he asked, he said sharply,

<hr>

[7] Dushka explained to me the origin of the terms "cow" and "calf" in this context. One of Gurdjieff's parables concerns the cow that looks at a newly painted barn door. She is confused about the change in her familar environment, knowing something about the function of the door, and eventually reconciles herself to it. The calf, who follows her mother, knows less and therefore follows her mother blindly. The "calves" Gurdjieff designated, Dushka adds, were chosen to be trained "as the first row for a future Movements Demonstration."

"Why you say 'yeah'? English 'yes.' If you remember this I give you Mercury car." I was elated with the prospect of an easy prize.[8] Another day, Gurdjieff gave me five hundred dollars and asked me to go to a bank and get five hundred silver dollars. When I went to a bank, the teller gave me a strange look in response to my request, went and talked with the manager, came back and asked me to sign my name on a piece of paper, and then gave me five sacks of coins. With three in one hand and two in the other, I trudged with difficulty back to the Wellington.

In the mornings, Gurdjieff set up his office as of old at Child's Restaurant on 56th Street, where petitioners could come, sit somewhere within his range of vision and wait for an audience. Some afternoons, the "movements" were practiced at Carnegie Hall under Madame de Salzmann's direction, and piano recitals of Gurdjieff's music, arranged by de Hartmann, were given by Carol Robinson.[9] Gurdjieff took me along with him and a dozen others to the Luxor Turkish baths under the Lenox Hotel on two Saturday evenings. Other "trips" included an excursion to Frank's, a steakhouse on 125th Street where, to Gurdjieff's dismay, there was neither vodka, cognac, nor armagnac for the ritual toasts to "idiots." After much persuasion by the headwaiter, he accepted applejack as a substitute, and Tania was given the rare honor as a woman of pronouncing the toasts. Gurdjieff ruled that the men must down all their drink in one swallow, while the women were allowed to finish theirs in the course of three toasts. After a few days, the regular young crowd was assigned tasks. It was a frenetic pace for a few weeks, and my studies paid a heavy toll.[10]

---

[8] My sister, who spent more time there than I did during those weeks, told me later that Gurdjieff had given her a thousand-dollar bill and told her to buy Christmas presents for everybody. It took her all day to find a bank that would give her change in small bills, and she proceeded to buy enough briefcases for everyone Gurdjieff felt like honoring. Beth McCorkle, ed., *The Gurdjieff Years 1929–1949: Recollections of Louise [Goepfert] March* (Walworth, NY: The Work Study Association, Inc., 1990), pp. 73–85, quotes Louise Goepfert March's accurate and vivid picture of the turmoil during this stay.
[9] The musical texts consist of thirty-nine movements (though there was to be a fortieth) and six obligatory exercises. See Thomas de Hartmann, *Musique pour les movements de G. I. Gurdjieff* (Paris: Janus, 1950).
[10] James Moore, *Gurdjieff: The Anatomy of a Myth* (Rockport, MA: Element, 1991), p. 354, lists twelve toasts, though the categories of individual idiots named can vary. These toasts—usually seven or eight were sufficient for a meal, though some have counted as many as twenty-one—are not so frivolous as the word "idiot" suggests. My own feeling is that the toasts, whose order constitutes a hierarchy, refer to the particular "idiosyncrasy" of a person which holds him back from "wholeness" of being and which chains him to mechanical behavior. Gurdjieff referred to himself as "Unique Idiot" and Orage as the "Super Idiot" (I have no information on what category of idiot Gurdjieff placed Toomer in). Gurdjieff's and Toomer's nicknames for his people

I was amazed, amused, and curiously impressed by this circus, particularly by the diffident comportment of those who had enjoyed circulating uncomplimentary stories about Gurdjieff years earlier. Now in his presence, they seemed absurdly solemn and reverent. I was also surprized that Gurdjieff seemed to take so much delight in humiliating women publicly, but rarely men. Curiously, those women he reduced to tears at the table were all the more reverent and deferent to him because of it. I expected him to talk seriously about his ideas and methods in the terms of academic discourse, but he simply made observations, invited and answered questions. Like Socrates, he could move dialogue to where he would have it go. What I heard did not seem entirely new to me. I had heard the vocabulary before, for Jean had often used the same terminology, but the readings from *All and Everything* were beyond me, and I was unable to ignore my aching knees and twitching muscles as I tried with less success than others to remain cross-legged and motionless on the floor. Near the end of his stay, he asked me one evening if I was satisfied with what I was hearing. I said "yeah" casually, and he smiled and said: "You lose Mercury car." I was hurt at first, but my mother told me outside in the corridor that one doesn't lose what one never had. That was scant consolation, but it didn't take much reflection to realize that I was never in for a Mercury and that, in "losing" it, I had become self-conscious about some of my speech habits. It was little consolation to learn years later that "yeah" is closer than "yes" to the earlier Old English form anyway.

At the end of January, Paul Anderson, acting as Lord Pentland's secretary, invited Jean to see Gurdjieff before he left. Three days before the scheduled departure—obviating a possible rejoinder—Jean wrote thanks for the enclosed publicity for Ouspensky's *In Search of the Miraculous*, said that he knew of no reason why he should go, and signed off with "Good greetings to you and to those others with whom the old ties endure."

Gurdjieff planned to return to France in March, but in February decided he had had enough. The subscriptions to his book, at $400 a copy, were disappointing. My mother had been assigned the task of soliciting or-

---

10 (cont) draw their attention to such idiosyncracies. The number of toasts reflects the Platonic scale, or chain of being between God and man, that is, the orbits of the seven visible planets and the musical proportions their distances from each other describe. Perhaps more to the point is the fact that drinking and eating were serious ritual occasions for Gurdjieff. What and how one ate and drank were important signs for him of human character. His meals were blends of aristocratic material and philosophical orders. Looking back on them now, I can see how much they resembled Plato's *Symposium*, in which the form and use of the drinking cup is a metaphysical bond with the transcendent. Gurdjieff, like Socrates, could drink enormous amounts without showing signs of drunkenness.

ders and her copy of the "book position" in June of 1949 had only twenty-nine names of those who had paid in full, eight partial payers, and 221 pledges for future purchase. She had contacted Jean, of course, but he only replied that he knew everything in the book and wasn't interested in giving to the Gurdjieff "factory." The amount of money collected was $13,145. The English total, with only six subscribers, came to nine hundred pounds.[11] Gurdjieff was disappointed, and also tired. He invited the "calves" to join him on the Queen Mary, and those who couldn't leave right away were to come to Paris as soon as possible. My sister and mother went together in March and stayed at the Hôtel Belfast on Avenue Carnot until their money ran short. When Edith returned to the United States, Petey moved into Ancy Duprés' house in the Square du Bois de Bologne, just off Avenue Foch, a few blocks from the Etoile, where other pupils were lodged. Gurdjieff spoke of the calves as his "American" group, future teachers of the method and the dances. To some of the older crowd, it seemed as if Gurdjieff was preparing for America what Orage and Toomer had failed to do. He commanded clearly now the vestiges of Orage's group, the Welchs, Muriel Draper, the Manchesters, Wolfes, Nylands, Spiegelbergs, and others, as well as Madame Ouspensky's people, for her husband had died two years earlier.

My mother returned from Paris in May and in June I flew over in a DC-4 from Bradley Field, CT, on a refugee transport plane, earning part of my passage as steward and handyman. We were scheduled to land at Gander for refueling, but weather forced us north to Goose Bay, where, in the early light of the morning, I saw a polar bear at the end of the airstrip. From there, we flew across the Atlantic toward Prestwick, but ended up landing in Shannon, Ireland in the late afternoon. Then on toward London, landing early in the morning at Bovingdon on a deserted RAF airstrip. I took a train into London, then a cab, and arrived at the Orage's on 60 Oakley Street in Chelsea at eight A.M., almost two days after leaving Connecticut. I stayed there for eight days, getting reacquainted after five years. The Notts occupied the top two floors of the house, but I saw only enough of them for polite chat. Instead, I was with Ann Orage constantly. Jessie was out almost every evening and did not cook meals. Although I

---

[11] When the book appeared several Gurdjieffites like Paul Anderson and Anne Fremantle wrote laudatory reviews. In an undated *New York Times* review (Toomer Collection, Box 69, Folder 1565), Gerald Sykes writes: "Mark Twain called 'The Book of Mormon chloroform in print.' We have much better anaesthetics now." Oscar Ichazo, "Letter to the Transpersonal Community," *The Arican*, 1991, p. 90, judges Gurdjieff "a very bad writer with no idea of composition or how to develop and present his themes."

pressed Jessie as often as I could about Gurdjieff and Jean over breakfast coffee, she was not in the mood to talk much about the old days. She did repeat the story of her attempt to murder Gurdjieff because of his poisoning Orage, but she had forgiven him and even visited him in Paris before his second automobile accident, finding him milder, kinder, even gentle. She remembered Jean best from New York and said that Orage was constantly worried over Jean's independent initiatives that nearly always put him in hot water financially with the New York group and Gurdjieff. She mentioned Orage's great admiration and affection for him, and thought that no one had come so rapidly and easily to an understanding of the work as Jean had, but that they did not always see eye to eye when it came to negotiating with Gurdjieff.

I joined Gurdjieff in Paris at the beginning of July in 1949, almost twenty-five years to the day after the automobile accident which changed the pace and direction of his life's work.[12] My sister, Iovanna Lloyd Wright, and Tania, now on a summer honeymoon without her husband, Tom Forman, were all staying in the townhouse of Ancy Dupré, whose husband Marcel, organist and composer, was also known for his stable of racing horses, and the George V and Plaza Athenée hotels in the center of Paris. Since I had a little room at the other end of Paris in a student residence near the Place des Nations, I spent my leisure time with the "calves," even spending the night on the floor occasionally when evenings at G's went past the time the Métro stopped. Evening meals started around 9:30, and with readings and talk, most evenings went on past midnight. The number of people rarely exceeded twenty in the small apartment, not counting the Gurdjieff girls and a helper or two in the kitchen.

G seemed pleased to see me, and invited me to join his table as often as I wished. He handed to my sister a roll of bills pinned together—twenty thousand francs—and told her to give it to me bit by bit for my summer use. The girls had settled into a routine: mornings free, performing the movements at the Salle Pleyel on the Avenue des Ternes in the afternoons, and then to G's at eight to help prepare the evening activities. The afternoon lunches were usually reserved for receiving honored guests, and they mirrored the meals at the Wellington—formal and ritual—whereas the evenings were more interesting for me because G talked more freely,

---

[12] See note 22, chapter 4 above, concerning the date. The period from 23 July until Gurdjieff's death on 29 October is detailed by the joint journal of Elizabeth and John G. Bennett. Our memories do not always accord. For example, Elizabeth Bennett, *Des Idiots á Paris* (Genève: Georg, 1991), p. 4, says that she joined Gurdjieff in Paris in January 1949, when I have him in New York until mid-February. (This book is also published in English as *Idiots in Paris* by Samuel Weiser, 1991.)

and his audience seemed to know more of what he spoke than the New York crowd. After supper and coffee, he would listen to a brief reading and then would often comment spontaneously on the reading or use it as a pretext for an illustrative story.

I wrote notes to the talks each evening—or rather, in the early hours of the morning—and joined them to my diary. This is not the place to reproduce them, but the topic that I remember most easily from those talks is self-remembering, not so much for self-reliance as for awareness of how to collaborate with others in waking up from "this sleep we call life" and keeping awake. Intentional suffering, both physical and moral, was only one way of making oneself sensitive to one's powers of self-observation and criticism. G continuously derided the "American" syndrome, the fascination of the West for technical gadgets that gave people an excuse not to think about self-control. "You must know how mechanism work to make it useful to yourself. Alarm clock useful, but not if you forget to wind up" was one of his themes. Every one, particularly wives, husbands, and lovers, are means of enhancing self-awareness, but the American program for progress is a program for sleep, not the sleep which revivifies, but the sleep of negligence. He insisted that one need not know the physics of an internal combustion engine to drive well, but one cannot drive well without understanding the rapport between man and his machine. To master a mechanical act such as driving, one must be able to coordinate it with another activity. It is not a matter of dreaming of one thing while working at another, but of doing two things simultaneously, each of which facilitates the other. In driving, you must feel and hear the motor, feel the gas pedal, smell the air, see the road ahead and behind, anticipate its obstacles, remember the condition of the motorcar when you started, hold an image in your mind of your destination, and plan your actions. None of these things should lessen another, but should be coordinated with them. This was one of the principles I could understand in the movements, where each dancer is expected to move different parts of his body to different rhythms simultaneously. Such exercises of mind and body reduce the chances of man being victim of accident. The movements also prepare the body to support the mind's wrestle with Gurdjieff's ideas. One thing that fascinated me in them was the conscious tracing in the mind of the body's movements, something which later seemed to me an aspect of the controlled movements of Oriental martial arts.

I recall that on 18 July, a woman whom the person next to me identified as Lawrence Olivier's sister was given the honor of sitting across from Gurdjieff, but she irritated him with her questions. He seemed to answer carefully, but she kept saying "certainement Monsieur Gurdjieff" with an inimitable English intonation. After a toast to the idiots, she asked Gurdjieff: "What idiot am I?" He replied without pause "Yes, eat!, No, better masturbate!" She was shocked into silence, but later in the course of the meal Gurdjieff asked her gently: "You understand what mean 'masturbate'? Think!" he urged, as if he hoped she would realize that he was asking her to observe herself, intimately.

On Friday, July 22, Gurdjieff gave me 7000 francs at the table, and then asked my sister why he had done so. I had no idea myself, but I suspected that he knew exactly how much he was apportioning to me. "Think how you spend money" is all he said. The next day, I joined Madame de Salzmann's dance group and spent the night on the floor near Petey, Iovanna, and Tania at Madame Duprés' so that I could be at G's at seven in the morning to help prepare food and supplies for a trip to Geneva and Chamonix. I was not included in the party, my sister told me later, but when she heard of my exclusion, she told Gurdjieff that if I didn't go, she wouldn't. With a cursory wave of his hand, he waved me in, and so I went along as the only young man in the caravan of three cars that started out a bit after seven on a Monday morning for Dijon. G drove the lead vehicle, his black, low-riding, front-wheel drive Citroën, with Iovanna Wright (who seemed always to be singing softly to herself), Madame Godet, Marian Sutta, and Dushka Howarth. Following was Cynthia Pearce in her Riley with Madame de Salzmann, Tania Forman, and a man whose name I have forgotten. My sister and I sat in the back seat of a black 1947 Mercury, driven by Dorothy Caruso, with Margaret Anderson and Elizabeth Bennett beside her. Peggy Matthews [Flinsch] promised to catch up to us in Dijon that night in her midget Simca 5 with Lady Pentland.

At two in the afternoon, we all pulled off the road after Sens and had a picnic on the grass shoulder. The food was typical fare: spicy salad with lots of cucumber, pâté de campagne, and to drink, of course, cognac. Right after lunch, Gurdjieff appointed me his "pick-upper," and I helped him to his feet, pulling too hard on his arms. "Not pull," he ordered with a grin, "hold arm, *I* pull!" The Mercury took second position and we took off for Dijon, but suddenly the Citroën before us sped up and started weaving all over the road. Margaret Anderson remarked that it must be time for G's nap, and, sure enough, his car swerved off onto a grassy verge, and G seemed to roll out onto the grass, where he lay still. The other cars pulled up behind and we all settled down to a ritual vigil which could last, as one person remarked, anywhere from ten minutes to two hours. I climbed down the slope toward the milky green water of a canal, stripped and dove in. Soon Marian, Iovanna, and Tania joined the swim, and we frolicked until we were startled by a sharp blast of a horn. G was up and ready to go, and scowled at those who were not ready as well.

Another hour down the road, we arrived at a railway crossing with the barriers down. After thirty seconds or so, with the offending train only a distant rumble, G made an abrupt U-turn and went off back up the road, saying that going any way was better than not going at all. Dorothy Caruso was very upset, afraid of getting lost on Gurdjieff's tail, and so we waited for a freight train to pass and then kept straight on for Dijon. At the entrance to the Grand Hôtel de la Clôche we waited an hour and a half before seeing G drive up with Mrs. Pearce behind. The hotel was not happy with the late arrival of thirteen people who had not reserved rooms, but Dorothy Caruso's name, impressive form, and charm helped find room. G dismissed us all and went to his room.

Early the next morning, Marian Sutta came around to wake everyone for breakfast. Only after we had finished our croissants and coffee did G arrive and announce that the bill had to be paid. Margaret Anderson and Dorothy Caruso took care of that detail discreetly, and we loaded up and left for Geneva in the same order we had quit Paris. By noon we were at Les Rousses, close to the Swiss border, but two of our cars were boiling over and we found ourselves stopping every few miles to fetch water for one car or another. We stopped for lunch on the French side, since no one had Swiss currency. My sister and I went with Dorothy and Margaret into one restaurant while the others went to another. The proprietor recognized Dorothy Caruso and, in honor of Enrico, he refused payment for the *truite bleu* he served us. Then all three cars passed the Col de Givrine and we coasted slowly down the winding road with the splendid view of Lac Léman before us all the way. After a brief delay on the Route Suisse due to a flat tire on Mrs. Pearce's Riley, we arrived about four in the afternoon in Geneva. Madame de Stjernvall had been called to arrange for rooms.

When we arrived, she was with G in front of the Hôtel Russie, and explained to us that there was no single hotel that had room for all of us. G turned his car over to Nikolai to be greased and have the oil changed, and he decided to stay in the Russie, while the rest of us were sent out to the Hôtel Angleterre and the Bristol. G took a nap in his room, the calves went looking for a Coca-Cola or ice cream, and Tania and I walked along the lake past the Jardin Anglais until dark, when we realized that neither of us knew where we were to meet for supper. Luckily the concierge at the Bristol recalled that a table had been reserved in the Buffet de la Gare for nine o'clock and we hurried to find everyone already at one long table upstairs in the station. Elizaveta de Stjernvall was the honored guest sitting at Gurdjieff's right, and her son Nikolai, now just 30, was down the table near two seats which awaited Tania and myself.

Gurdjieff was furious, stared hard at us as we sat down, finished a remark to Mme de Stjernvall, and then, looking down the table, said: "bad vibrations in room." Then he paused, his face softened into reflection and he started talking about time and clocks, noting that measuring time by clocks is not the same thing as measuring time by the accumulation of mental energy. There is donkey time and human time, he said. "The donkey senses time by the vibrations in his stomach, man by the vibrations in his head. It is better to be like donkey, who never forgets when to eat, than to be like the man whose mind is not connected to his stomach. This is the American man." I kept my mouth shut except for food.[13] When the meal was finished, Gurdjieff "discovered" that he had no money with him, and so he announced that everyone should contribute 2000 francs to the "pot." After supper, Nikolai de Stjernvall took the "calves" and myself to the Bar Roosevelt for a drink, then to the Picadilly Night Club, and finally to a café frequented by heavily made-up prostitutes. Nikolai suddenly disappeared and, after waiting some twenty minutes or more, we walked back to our hotels. It was after two in the morning.

We got a late start for Chamonix Wednesday morning.[14] G assigned me to Mrs. Pearce's car as her mechanic and water carrier, and we set out after noon for the French Alps. The radiator of the Riley boiled over constantly, and I spent a good deal of time looking for mountain streams for water. Worse, Tania had motion sickness and we had to stop a few times for her to leap from the car and find a convenient bush. Finally she felt better, but the road became worse as we passed construction sites for hydroelectric plants. When we hit one pothole, something cracked and then

---

[13] Moore, *Myth*, p. 309, has Mme de Stjernvall's version of this setting: "The meeting eventuated in a baroque station buffet, where a Swiss string ensemble, elbowing at full pelt, impeded conversation." He goes on to say that Gurdjieff called the headwaiter over to have this "masturbation" stopped. Tania and I arrived in the first class buffet, apparently, just after Russell Page had diplomatically convinced the orchestra to retire to the second class buffet. I can't remember anything "baroque" about the room. In his account of the visit to Geneva, *Daddy Gurdjieff* (Genève: Georg, 1997), Nikolai de Stjernvall gives quite a different picture of the dinner than I remember. I remember a U-shaped table for all twenty-five or so, while Nikolai recalls separate tables. He says Dorothy Caruso paid for the meal, and that Gurdjieff seemed eager to get back to Paris right away. The picture in Elizabeth Bennett's *Idiots*, pp. 14–15, is close to mine.

[14] Dorothy Caruso, cited by Margaret Anderson (*The Unknowable Gurdjieff* (London: Routledge & Kegan Paul, 1962), p. 189, gives another version of this portion of the trip. Bennett says the delay was caused by Tania's sickness.

dragged under the car. I crawled under the Riley to find a battery support rod broken, the battery itself cracked with half its cells exposed. I tied the support rod in place and, amazingly, the battery still worked. I was a dirty mess when we arrived, early in the afternoon, at the Hôtel des Alpes, where G had already lunched. Mrs. Pearce had the sandwiches for our planned picnic, which she had prepared early that morning. He dismissed us all to go our own ways for the afternoon.

Supper was very late that evening, and Gurdjieff uncharacteristically quiet, so we all went to bed after dessert. The next day was spent sightseeing. Tania, Dushka, my sister, and I went to the local swimming pool, whose freezing water was a run-off from a glacier. We had tea on a terrace where a singer with the three-man band was so happy to entertain Americans that he sang "I Love You for Sentimental Reasons" three times. We took the cable car to the top of Mont Tremblant in the afternoon, where I frightened the girls by leaning over a ledge to pick some edelweiss. When we got back down I saw the slopes full of them. The story got back to Gurdjieff and, as we went to our seats at supper, he laughed and said I was "real" American. "What you want flowers for, to cover the smell of American shit? Why risk self for thing you have no use for?"

Supper was at eight at a long table partitioned off from the rest of the dining room. There was both champagne and cognac on the table and, after the main course, we were served bowls of strawberries. Gurdjieff was in a playful mood, making jokes and laughing. He suddenly pointed to the large, full bowl in the middle of the table and said: "One thousand francs to person who eats *all* strawberries." Dushka and I reached but she beat me to it, cleaned out the bowl in a matter of two minutes and handed G the empty bowl. He gave her a wadded thousand-franc note.[15] We had cantaloupe melon for dessert, and then coffee and cognac. Gurdjieff pointed to a melon rind on my plate and said: "You eat to green, all green. For green skin I give 1000 francs." That was worth about two-and-one-half dollars, I reckoned with rapid expectation, and I volunteered quickly. I dug at the skin of the melon, but could not clean away everything to the green. The company got up and left the room while I remained behind digging with a spoon. Finally satisfied, I took the skin to where he was sitting in a small alcove drinking coffee with the others. He looked at the skin and said: "No, not all green."

Dushka saw my distress and, when I left the room, she led me upstairs to her room where she produced a bottle of green ink. Together we

---

[15] Bennett has the bowl full of raspberries, which is just as likely for the season in Haute Savoie, and she recalls that Dushka was one of four to share 2000 francs.

doctored the skin, and I returned downstairs to Gurdjieff and showed him the all-green rind. He smiled, pulled a crumpled bill from his pocket and gave it to me. Dushka and I went to our rooms laughing with our success. Before I got into bed, however, I sensed that G was laughing at me. I couldn't misread the first-rate-trickster look on his face when he smiled at a third-rate-trickster.[16]

Early Friday morning, I got into the lift on the second floor of the hotel to go down to breakfast, and found Gurdjieff there all alone. The lift descended only a foot or so when it stopped with a jerk. Gurdjieff looked at me with a half-smile, as if to reassure me, and then, as if nothing were more usual to the occasion, began to say that I had to learn how to tell stories. "Story pay for many things," he said. "I pay you last night, you pay me soon, but when you know how. You think you are clever, but you are what Americans call, yes, 'wiseacre.' Your Toomer was wiseacre, clever, but he wiseacre in a hurry, see fast, talk quick, think slow. Lunatic man lose way, forget to listen. Not remember self, forget others. You forget, and no Mercury car." The lift lurched back into its final three-meter descent, and the one-sided conversation had ended.

On Friday, we left Chamonix for Vichy around ten, and this time I was appointed G's mechanic and pick-upper. We stopped for lunch at a restaurant on the lake at Nantua for lunch. There was only one waitress to serve our table across the road on the terrace over the lake, and Gurdjieff told me to get up to help her carry the fish platters. The one I grabbed out of her hands was almost red hot and I raced to set it down. G was looking away from me toward the lake, but just as I reached forward with the fish, I heard him say "stop." I stopped, but the hand holding the platter was in excruciating pain. My sister and Tania looked at me as if I were crazy. Apparently they hadn't heard G. When I finally set it down, G said "What matter?" as I went to my place. "What's the matter?" echoed my sister. I had nothing to say. I wrapped my left hand in my napkin and ate with my right hand. An hour later, on the way to the cars, I looked at my hand, and it was only slightly red, and I felt no pain.

During G's after-lunch nap by the road an hour or so later, Tania and I went to look at some horses on the other side of a small marshy pond. By the time we returned, we faced an angry Margaret Anderson, who said that G had refused to wait for us. We got into her car, and after passing through Lyon and Clermont-Ferrand, we arrived at the Hôtel Albert Ire late in the

---

[16] Elizabeth Bennett, *Idiots*, p. 20, recalls that when I left the room after my initial failure, Gurdjieff referred to me as a perfect example of American education: good only for eating and shitting, but worthless for thinking. He said that his test would be a first occasion for me to work with my head.

afternoon. Gurdjieff had left a message for Tania and myself to see him where he was waiting in the lounge sitting room. He addressed us sternly, accusing us of acting improperly and creating bad vibrations. He ordered us to remain apart for the rest of the trip. Tania took this badly and went to her room for the rest of the evening.

G had supper alone and the next morning went out to take the waters. There were none. There had been a severe drought and Vichy was dry. G stormed back into hotel, ordered Marian Sutta to find everyone and round them up for an immediate departure. Then came a second explosion of rage when G learned that two of the girls, probably my sister and Dushka, had asked for orange juice at breakfast. He accused them of being frivolous, and threatened to force them to stay and wash dishes for the cost. He drove quickly, very quickly, back toward Paris, stopping briefly for a rest by the roadside and then for lunch near Pouilly, where he complained that we were all eating too much. He made a brief coffee stop before arriving at Colonels Renard, where he announced, after getting out of the car, that he would leave for Deauville the next morning, and that this trip would be different. It was. When we all gathered at the café the next morning, cars and all, he smiled and said, "no trip." The same thing happened two weeks later, when he canceled a trip to Dieppe, but that time without smiling. His car had broken down.

I was sent to help in the kitchen and to the movements "until," G admonished, " you learn eat and move feet." In August, I moved into the Rena hotel just a few meters from G's apartment and, except for a four-day trip back to London and Leicester with Tania and my sister, I was available as kitchen help, doing chores with the indefatigable Alfred Etievan, and sat on the floor in the evenings listening to readings. Gurdjieff told my sister when I was expected. The crowds at his apartment grew throughout the summer, and soon there wasn't room enough for all of the younger crowd. We all took time off to sightsee in Paris. Tania and I, and later Marian and I, went to the Bal Tabarin, where Petey knew an acrobat she had met on the boat coming over. We saw Roland Petit's spectacular ballet, "Carmen," at the Théâtre de Marignon and, with John Cage, we saw Tanaquil Leclerc dance at the Comédie Française.

In August, G seemed tired by the traffic in his small apartment and he was quieter in the evenings, assuming a humble posture as an Armenian rugmerchant. Bennett had arrived from England, and he and Gurdjieff talked a good deal together. I was conscientiously sensitive throughout that summer to the force of character which had so attracted Jean years earlier. I listened to Gurdjieff with an ear tuned to hear what I could relate to Jean's own "teaching." While much of the matter was the same, I sensed an enormous difference in voice, method, and apparent purpose. For one thing, Gurdjieff was more obviously intent on destabilizing, discouraging, and shocking his pupils, as if to turn them away from him as a means of turning them away from the "negative" of themselves; yet, despite the shocking language, the insults, and the haranguing, his "pupils," mostly middle-aged it seemed to me, not only seemed enchanted by him, but were flattered by and flattered the worst in him.

Another thing which "destabilized" his audience was his language. I've heard him speak many languages I could identify—Russian, French, German, English, and Italian—and others I could not, and he spoke these languages as if he understood their deep semantic underpinnings as well as their superficial rhythmic patterns, and yet he spoke each with a phonological, syntactical, and semantic bias—which included impromptu inventions of words and grammatical formations—that made comprehension extremely trying. I thought that he did this with the singular purpose of forcing his listener to concentrate his attention in order to get the meaning. One tired easily under such circumstances, and I always felt uneasy when someone asked him to repeat something he had said, for that seemed shameful admission of a lack of attention. Nonetheless, his speech commanded attention. His voice was low, but did not have the commanding resonance of Toomer's. He spoke slowly and carefully most of the time, and his phrases were rhythmically modulated, though fragmented and curt.[17] His questions and comments were strategically directed; he could move a discussion to whatever end he had plotted.

Not only his speech, but all of his personal habits on public display put others on the defensive. People found themselves forced to meet him strictly on *his* terms, whether it was the way he ate, dressed, moved, or drove an automobile; and yet he could reduce himself instantly to exaggerated humility and modesty. In the midst of almost any conversation, he would shift mood, look about him with those huge, dark, bear-like eyes of his, lower his head slightly and say: "After all, I just old rug merchant." To questions he deemed trivial or unprofitable, he preferred to remain silent rather than reply. When he shocked people, it was quite obviously to make them think of things they would prefer not to, and he set words in contexts that unsettled usual semantic expectations.

---

[17] Nikolai de Stjernvall, who lived with him for the first seventeen years of his life, said that the long conversations with pupils that Stanley Nott and Fritz Peters reported could not have taken place. First of all, Nikolai noted, G's English and French were not up to the kinds of conversations that Ouspensky recalled in Russian before the war. Gurdjieff himself said, after his 1924 trip to the United States, that he "knew not one word of the local language" (*Life is Real*, New York: Dutton for Triangle Editions, 1975, p. 30). Secondly, when G spoke in English or French, he spoke in brief segments. Only in Armenian and Russian did he speak in a smooth flow. This is also what his secretary, Louise Goepfert March, reports in her memoirs.

Furthermore, by his speech, dress, and postures, Gurdjieff seemed to do his utmost to maintain distance, as if he would encourage others to hear the teaching instead of seeing and sensing the man; and yet, when the performance grated, stung, or even soothed, one was attracted toward the spectacle of the man more often than to the sense in his message. I can appreciate that he would turn pupils back into themselves as a first and necessary step toward positioning themselves for his teaching, but if he was a mirror, the image in the glass was often distorted.

Consequently, life with Gurdjieff was like being somewhere in the midst of a three-ring circus, with too many things going on at once to know where one stood or what one was to see. No wonder so many people seemed unaware of the presence of anyone else in the group except themselves and Gurdjieff, who played clown and trickster. Everything he said could be taken as a joke, an absurdity, or a profound observation in disguise; and yet all the serious pupils were stone-faced and tense in his presence. They were either afraid or unsure of themselves, whether even to laugh at Gurdjieff's jokes; and, above all, Gurdjieff had an enormous sense of humor, an appreciation of the absurd he found and even incited all about him. As for myself, I little understood his method and faintly heard his message, but I was intrigued by both his performance and the different reactions of others to it.

I had only one other private conversation with him that summer, and that by accident, but it did give me a glimmer of something that I hadn't in the least perceived earlier. I was on my way down the Rue d'Armaille toward the Avenue des Ternes early the morning after Tania left, and noticed him sitting alone at a café by the corner. He saw me and beckoned me to sit down with him and have a coffee. He asked me softly if I had enjoyed my summer, and I replied with the usual banalities, but added, again, that I was learning a lot about life. He smiled and asked what I was learning. I said I couldn't really say, but I was seeing and hearing new things. Then I asked out loud what I had for some time been repeating to myself, assuming that Gurdjieff had the powers so many attributed to him, "How do you put up with so many people about you who seem so shallow?" Very slowly he lifted his head and looked at me with his deep eyes. No smile.

"These 'people' you call, 'idiots' you want say, you think they come only listen to me, hear what I know? No. *What* I know? I know how teach them listen to themselves. They listen radio, phonograph, love-song, typewriter, and forget listen to self. I not hear them, so I not tell them what in them they hear. I only teach them remember what they forget. I teach them hear the music in them. You Americans, you *like* noise. You jabber. You wiseacre. Like donkeys, you make noise and say nothing, because you listen to things outside, like own noise eating.

"You sit with me and eat, you sit and listen to readings, listen my music, do movements. Maybe you hear something, maybe not. All these people come listen. Some hear, some not. What is hear? I tell you. When you do movements, you listen to music. You move to music. You think about movements and you think about music. You do this every day. One day you do movements and *hear* music without listening. You hear it from inside when no music playing outside. This take a long time, hard work. You do same movement and listen to same music until you no longer hear or feel with body but with consciousness. Then, you on higher level. It is same with reading book. You understand *inside* only when you know *outside*. Outside is noise of world. Inside is music of self. Remember Mercury car? No, you not remember. You remember yourself, not *car*. You remember wish of getting car, but you forget self.

"Remember talk in Chamonix? Remember what I say about story? I tell you story now. A teacher say to someone who want to be pupil, 'Go away now and observe self. Come back after you try. If you remember self, I take you as pupil.' That person work hard, think hard, look in mirror, read books, then he come back. Teacher ask, 'Do you understand now what means to observe self, to remember self?' 'Yes,' say person. 'Wrong answer,' say teacher, and man go away. You see what story say? You like that person. You talk like Toomer talk, but what talk? You must not say thing unnecessary. That wiseacre talk. Think what you say? You say *what*, or *why*, or *how*? Come see me in New York, you pay me for summer here with story there, at Child's. Story is breath, life. Without story man have no self. Now we coffee drink. Good, eh?" He had touched the quick! As he fumbled in his deep pockets for coins to leave on the table, I floated down the street. When Gurdjieff had spoken to me directly with his intensive tone and look of care, he made me feel not only special, but unique. I was entranced, but also confused. I had been tricked somehow. In my confusion, I had refrained from saying a word in reply. I never heard his voice again. He had had the last word.

On August 17, preparations were made for G's trip to Cannes the next day. I could not go since I was leaving France on Saturday the 20th. I saw the group off in the morning, but before noon the next day they were all back, with no explanation of why G had turned around. I sailed from Le Havre the next afternoon on the Cunard White Star, Scythia. My sister returned a few weeks later.[18]

In early October, Paul Anderson, acting as Lord Pentland's secretary, invited Jean to lunch with them in New York to collaborate in the prepara-

---

[18] Petey returned to France two years later, became a fashion model, and married the photographer Jean Chevalier, one of the founders of *Elle* magazine. They have a son and two daughters.

tion of Gurdjieff's return in November. Jean replied on the 19th with regrets that he had not been able to accept, adding: "I wanted to convince you
that I have no interest in doing anything about either Ouspensky's or Gurdjieff's book at this time. . . . As you know, some drinks mix, some don't. I
must not mix what I am doing now with the world and works of Mr. Gurdjieff."[19] Meanwhile, Gurdjieff was ill, but kept to his plans, which were
canceled only by his death on the 29th from an abdominal edema associated with a nephritis he had contracted after his second automobile accident
a year earlier.[20] When Jean heard the news of Gurdjieff's death, he gave
shape to his feelings in a caustic threnody, titled "To Gurdjieff Dying":

> Thou Venerene ascending to desire,
> Knowing the Buddhic law but to pervert
> Its power of peace into dissevering fire,
> Coiled as a serpent round the phallic Tau
> And sacramental loaf, yet still alert
> To turn the nether astral light athwart
> The beam ethereal, wherefore art thou
> Snake and deceiver, Son of the Elder Liar?
> Thou hast deformed the birth-bringings of light
> Into lust-brats of black imaginings,
> Spilling Pan passions in the incarnate round
> Of hell and earth. Lords of the Shining Rings
> Skilled in white magic, may your skills abound!
> Save even Gurdjieff from his hell forthright.[21]

---

[19] Toomer Collection, Box 3, Folder 96.
[20] Oscar Ichazo, "Letter," pp. 99–100, says: "When his autopsy was performed, an extremely cirrhotic liver was found with terribly dilated, varicose gastroesophageal
veins. The stomach was grossly enlarged by the constant and abusive ingestions of
huge amounts of indigestible and lethal combinations of food and alcohol, which destroyed the functions of his pancreas and produced a calamitously constipated, expanded colon." He continues at great length and then concludes: "The operating
physicians said that it was strange that somebody could be alive with such an abused
and run-down organism. This was taken by the devoted Gurdjieffians as an unques-
tionable proof of their Master's realization. Ichazo does not say where he got this information, but it is unlikely he heard it from William Welch, Gurdjieff's American
doctor, who was at the scene.
[21] Jean Toomer, *The Collected Poems*, Robert B. Jones and Margery Latimer Toomer,
eds. (Chapel Hill, NC: University of North Carolina Press, 1988), p. 103.

Chapter Seven

Gurdjieff's Teaching Text

The harmonious development of man:
a man who is really in occupation of his house,
all three storeys of it.
—Orage

In Gurdjieff the ancient teachings of Lao Tse, Jesus and St. Augustine all have fresh import and find valid scientific support. The implications of this deeper science of Being no longer slumber in secret archives of the temples of the East. Sought by him they are made clearer to us in writing by one himself a seer.
—Frank Lloyd Wright

Paris had been a marvelous vacation for me, but the moment I moved off the quay in Quebec, loaded my baggage in the back of my mother's car, and settled in the front seat for the long drive down to Connecticut, I missed something, or rather, felt that I had missed something. Gurdjieff's presence—not only his words, but his voice and physical posture—would not leave my thoughts. On the one hand, I realized that he had showed me a way to take stock of my potentials, and I could strengthen my conscious thought to develop them. Without being aware of the implications, I had already been pushed one step forward to free myself from outer influences. Already, the previous spring when my mother was in Paris, I had received an appointment to the Military Academy at West Point, something she had planned for me all of my life. I turned it down, and my mother was very hurt. She brought the subject up again in the car as we drove across the border into Vermont toward St. Johnsbury. I told her simply that I didn't want to be a soldier, to which she responded in a tone that was almost a sneer: "What do you think you can be?" I said I didn't know yet, but that this would be a year to look at my possibilities.

I went back to school with the intent of investigating as much as I could in my studies. I jumbled up my planned program to include French as well as Russian. I enrolled in a Music History course and, much against my desire, my faculty counselor forced me to take economics to fill what was called a "distribution requirement in liberal arts." No sooner had I gotten settled down in Providence then my mother called me to say that

Gurdjieff had died. The words seemed detached from any meaning. I could not conceive of Gurdjieff *dead*, the body perhaps, but the *man*? Little by little, the consequences of his death for me became clear. First of all, it meant I would not see him in New York later in the year, and my vague plans to go back to Paris seemed compromised. My summer with him had made me feel my present course of studies was leading me nowhere and even my adjusted curriculum wasn't giving me the satisfaction I expected. So early in 1950, I went to Pat Kenny, the Dean of Men at Brown, and said I wanted to quit school. He advised me to finish my sophomore year first and then to withdraw rather than quit, so that, if I decided later to return, there would be no obstacles. Meanwhile, my mother had contacted her old love, Johnny, who said that he'd have a place for me in the cotton business in the summer. My own plans, which I kept to myself, were to return to Paris to study philosophy and work with the Paris Gurdjieff group. I had read through Ouspensky's recently published *In Search of the Miraculous*, which laid out systematically and clearly Gurdjieff's ideas. As soon as Gurdjieff's "First Series" was published that spring, I plunged into it, recognizing as I went along passages that I had heard at various readings in New York and Paris. I could hear not only Toomer's words in it, but his voice, and the connection between the ideas of each was obvious to me. I imagined I could read Gurdjieff through Toomer, while finding in Gurdjieff what had seized Toomer.

To me, *All and Everything; Beelzebub's Tales to His Grandson* was a tantalizing, teasing, and irritatingly difficult text whose vocabulary and structure deliberately obscured sense. After a short while, I found Gurdjieff's style obstructively dense and digressive, and his science obscure. I didn't have the patience to work through the book and I abandoned my vague project to make a systematic study of Jean's ideas along Gurdjieffian lines. Nonetheless, I knew well that in order to better appreciate Jean's ideas, I had to know more of their connection with Gurdjieff's. I wanted to have something of that relationship in mind when I next talked with Jean, so I worked up a sort of summary of ideas in the book and held it for some time before discarding it as unsatisfactory. My synthesis didn't make the text any clearer to me, but I have mulled over those ideas through the years, and the summary that follows could be considered a matrix for the teaching I received from Toomer and Gurdjieff.

It would be a thankless task to try to summarize the book as a whole, but I can locate many of the ideas in it that pervade Jean's teaching. To those who know the book well, I apologize for the narrow personal perspective that follows. I address it more to those readers, like myself years ago, who are unfamiliar with Gurdjieff's "system." In *The Herald of Coming*

Good (p. 45), Gurdjieff explains that he based his book on legends he had heard in his childhood, and he made Beelzebub his hero in order to expose "various facets of my ideas." The breadth of the book as a whole conjoins a psychological history of the world from its creation to 1921, with instruction for redressing the deteriorating condition of current human affairs. That deterioration is seen most clearly in the degeneration of man's moral and intellectual status in the modern world, particularly in the United States, which Gurdjieff saw as the emblem of a present and disastrous process of deterioration of personal and social values. The setting of the book is a spaceship in which Beelzebub, returning to his home planet Karatas (*Caritas*?) from an exile imposed upon him for questioning authority, lectures his grandson on the creation and maintenance of the Universe, including the history of our world's science and morality. His principle topic is why the people of the Earth have lost the facility to see the real, and why they flounder in unreality. The intent behind his account is a preparation of his grandson to redress the situation by teaching the esoteric lore of self-perfection no longer generally available to people of Earth.[1]

In his exposition to Hassein, Beelzebub finds it necessary, as a historical background for his psychological instruction, to recount the origin of all things, the principle of their maintenance in time, and the causes of their degeneration on Earth. This exposition, in the chapter titled "The Holy Planet Purgatory," contains the nucleus of Gurdjieff's complex philosophical system, *ein Weltsinn* that informs the entire book.[2] The planet Purgatory is the core of the universe through which the pulsations of everything in the cosmos pass. In the beginning, all beings were united with the Sun Absolute, creator of all life, but after a universal calamity, they could no longer blend with their primal source. So this planet was made for a certain number of them as a central receptor of concentrations of everything in the universe. Though it contains a bliss of vegetation and atmosphere, and although it is the favorite haunt of the Absolute, the inhabitants of Purgatory, who have earned their place there by perfection of their higher reason,

---

[1] According to the opening chapter of *Meetings with Remarkable Men*, A. R. Orage, trans. (London: Penguin, 1963), Gurdjieff's basic model for the seeker of hidden lore is Gilgamesh, whose trials and hardships to obtain the wisdom and prophetic lore of Utnapishtim were the topic of songs he heard his father sing in Kars.

[2] Orage claimed that he had read thousands of books on philosophy but that Gurdjieff's "The Holy Planet Purgatory" surpasses them all. By "Purgatory," Gurdjieff means the entire cosmos of ontological values. "Heaven" and "hell" are concepts he renounces as the "twaddle" (*All and Everything*, p. 803) of those who, in ignorance, supposed a binary opposition between things. In *Life Is Real* (New York: Dutton for Triangle Editions, 1975), p. 161, Gurdjieff recommends the chapter to those who would understand his ideas.

endure the most painful of torments. To explain this apparent paradox, Bee-lzebub then recounts the genesis and process of the universe.

Before the creation of life, there was nothing but empty space occupied by cosmic ether and the Sun Absolute that was the locus of the Endlessness, one of many epithets for that which others call "God." This residence of God and his agencies was held stable, without any influence from outside, by a principle of inner independent forces that consisted of two interlocking laws: the Law of Seven and the Law of Three. After a while, however, God realized that the Sun Absolute was diminishing by a flow of time, and so decided to create a universe whose operations would immunize the Sun Absolute from decomposition due to the effects of time.

The Law of Seven, also known as the Law of the Octave, describes seven centers, or concentrations of gravity, in a line of force, or "cosmic ray." The Law of Three describes a triad of three united forces—one positive, another negative, and a neutral third that reconciles them.[3] The one blends with the other to activate the middle, which itself becomes the positive in a higher triad or the negative in a lower, and so, between World Creation and World Maintenance, an intermediary force is set.

In order to have this structure of things move to his profit, God adjusted the two laws so that created things would flow into the presence of the Sun Absolute and maintain its existence through time. He did this by having the functions of these concentrations of energy, which operated independently, made dependent on outside forces so that the original independent maintenance of the Sun Absolute became altered into a mutual exchange of force with all created materials. The energy needed to effect this perpetual exchange was released by altering the distances between centers of gravity. The resulting asymmetry caused a compensatory flow of energy that produces new cycles of automatic effluences of energy from outside stimuli. The process of these new creations, depending upon the amount of external vibrations they absorb, produce further concentrations of different internal and external proportions of force.[4]

Then, after changing the function of the laws, God directed their actions from the Sun Absolute outward into the space of the universe by an

---

[3] Toomer quotes Gurdjieff's analogy: "We can have no bread without baking: Knowledge is the water, emotion the flour, and suffering the fire" (Toomer Collection, Box 68, Folder 1539).

[4] Russell Smith, *Cosmic Secrets* (Sanger, TX: Privately published, 1993), has exposed the entire mathematical system behind the Law of Seven and the Law of Three. There is a striking similarity in this released energy with Carnot's Physics of Entropy. For recent essays explicating aspects of *All and Everything*, see *All and Everything 96* and *All and Everything 97*, ed. Seymour B. Ginsburg *et al*, Proceedings of the First and Second International Humanities Conferences, Bognor Regis, 1996 and 1997. For earlier views of Gurdjieff's life and teachings, see Michel de Salzmann's entry in *The Encyclo*

emanation of his own force known as "Word-God,"[5] so that, in a chain of concentrations of energy, this emanation would flow back into the Absolute. Once this was accomplished, the effects of the changes in the laws carried on the processes of the universe automatically, and the effects of changes in the laws continue, so that each of the concentrations in the universe operates according to the altered laws of Three and Seven. For example, second-order suns, or cores of solar systems, become first elements in new formations generated by the Word-God, and so forth, in a chain of formations that fills the universe.

Each of these concentrations emits radiations, or emanations; and between each concentration of energy there is an intermediary force that balances the push and pull of masses; or, ultimately more important, mediates the exchange of energy between the seven largest "independent" concentrations of energy, and thus between all of them. The Emanation of the Absolute Sun, known as the Word-God, is the agency of cosmic operations. Then there are emanations from each second-order sun, planets, the microcosmos, the tetartocosmos, all planets, and, finally, the common radiations of all second-order suns. All these cosmic emanations constitute an issuing of everything from everything and an entering again into everything.[6]

In the created world, the lowest of animals, such as worms and insects, are "one-brained beings." Animals are "two-brained," or two-natured, when their physical or planetary body acquires sentiment or emotion. A human being, a microcosmic reflection of the universe as a whole, is capable of acquiring a third, or higher-being body: reason. When this body of reason succeeds in perfecting itself into Objective Reason, the

---

4 (cont) *pedia of Religion*. Colin Wilson, *The War Against Sleep: The Philosophy of Gurdjieff*, offers a synthesis of Gurdjieff's "system," but Wilson admitted relying heavily upon E. J. Gold, *People of the Secret: Secret Talks with Mr. G*, in which Gold's G is himself, and the system is Sufi. Philip Mairet describes Gurdjieff's system and his aim in his introduction to *A. R. Orage*, xxiii–xxiv. Webb closes *Harmonious Circle* with a brief look at the sources of Gurdjieff's theoretical ideas. Moore, who has lectured on Gurdjieff in university classrooms, gives a brief exposition of G's story of creation and of his entire "system" in *Myth*, pp. 40–62.

5 *Logos* in the Bible, and *spermatologoi* in the language of the Alexandrian philosophers.

6 In Gurdjieff"s "The Struggle of the Magicians," the Magician says to his pupils: "The chief idea of the exposition is as follows: that what is above is similar to what is below, and that what is below is similar to what is above. Every unity is a cosmos. The laws that govern the Megalocosmos also rule the Macrocosmos, the Ariocosmos (?), the Deutercosmos, the Mesocosmos, the Tritocosmos, and others, inclusively, down to the Microcosmos. Having exactly studied one cosmos you will know all the others . . . and for each one of us the nearest man of all is oneself. Knowing yourself completely you will know all, even God, since you are created in his likeness" (Toomer Collection, Box 69, Folder 1564).

triadic structure is capable of separating itself so that the higher-being part can leave physical mass and emotion and unify itself with the Creator in the Sun Absolute, thus fulfilling the divine purpose of Creation. Those higher-being bodies that fall short of completing their perfection and that do not unite with God, can join with other concentrations where their beings are needed in the cycle of evolution and involution; and, in successions of such cycles, they continue until they achieve perfection.

To perfect reason, a person must acquire a certain amount of independence from external cosmic causes by adhering to the operations of the Law of Seven; that is, through knowledge of his or her place in the totality of creation. Human reason is a positive or affirming force, the nervous system is a negative or denying force, and the thorax/heart, or breathing apparatus, is the neutralizing or reconciling force. Correspondingly, this triad is fed by three nourishments. Food and drink feed the body; air feeds the lungs and heart; and the cosmic substance in the air that perfects higher consciousness feeds the mind. Each person has an innate lamination of sense and reason, both of which can be nurtured to strengthen the collaboration between them. The perfection of reason constitutes Objective Consciousness, the hope and aim of Creation.

Only the person who has developed harmoniously can separate his or her centers to free thought from incitements of the body and the senses. The separation of Objective Reason is a result of freeing reason from subjective influences, and of locating one's essential ego—the proper "gravity center" or "I," if you will. This process leads to either a union with God, if completed, or to a union with other cosmic concentrations, if incomplete when one's planetary or natural body, dies.

So, there are three possible ends for single durations of life. The man who has not moved himself at all toward higher consciousness—toward acquiring a soul to move toward God—returns to the substance of the earth from which he came, for the body is time-bound and decomposes whether or not soul and Objective Reason conjoin with it. The one who has acquired a soul, but not attained the union with God, unites with other cosmic concentrations in a process known as *metempsychosis*, or rebirth in another form. Either he or she will fail to move in this new life toward separation and return to earthly substance in death, or he or she will continue to be reborn again and again until achieving the separation, for the soul cannot decompose, and it remains in the solar system unless and until it perfects itself in a reason which engenders "sacred" substance.[7] The Hindu might recognize this as a move from cycles of Karma to the otium of Nirvana.

---

[7] P. D. Ouspensky, *A New Model of the Universe* (London: Routledge & Kegan Paul, 1938), pp. 80–81 and *The Fourth Way* (London: Routledge & Kegan Paul, 1957), pp. 413–437, distinguish carefully between *recurrence* and *re-incarnation*. The first is mani

Those who succeed in attaining higher-being bodies—identified with Objective Consciousness—achieve union with the Absolute and immortality. In the process of metempsychosis, once the planetary body has died, a second-grade cosmic law governing gravitational attraction moves the soul, if it exists, to another center of gravity, or concentration of energy, while the body decomposes; and, by the same law, it rejoins its physical source in the earth. The astral body, however, formed of radiations from other planets and suns, decomposes and goes in different directions. The higher-being body cannot decompose and so exists until it perfects itself to Reason. While doing this, it is immune from harmful influences from external sources. The closer one moves toward Objective Reason and higher being, the more one is independent of these sources, or planetary forces, and the less, therefore, subject to accident, vagaries of physical and emotional incidents, unhealthful vibrations from others, and so forth. In other words, one can make oneself "relatively" immune from accident.

The modern-thinking person is caught, therefore, in "the terror of the situation," the terror of a soul, or Objective Reason, not yet achieved. One's time on earth is a period in which one must work toward achieving Objective Reason. One must, in brief, know oneself and know where one is. The process of self-discovery involves self-observation and self-remembering, and necessarily involves suffering, since one must first discover what one is *not* before discovering what one *can be*. "Intentional suffering" is, most generally, the pain of trying to perfect oneself by purging "sin"; and, more particularly, it is the suffering caused by a self-observation incited by another person's negative action.

---

7 (cont) fest in either absolute repetition of one's life, born on the same day, etc. (the agony of the hero of Ouspensky's *The Strange Life of Ivan Osokin*, recently staged as an opera in New York, is that he "thinks" that the chance to return to an earlier point in his own life will necessarily allow a positive chance to a higher form of consciousness. He only repeats his earlier errors with the added agony of knowing that he is trapped in an inevitability) or, a repetition in which one changes some things, but not the end, ascension or descent in process of life and, finally, a recurrence in which one ascends to escape the vicious cycle and move on to another plane of being. Re-incarnation is being born again into a different time and body. In Plato's *Meno* 81a–e, Socrates also speaks of recurrence and reincarnation, agreeing with Gurdjieff that in earlier existences, man had knowledge now lost, and that one can draw out what our souls knew in former lives. He explains that the soul is immortal, born many times, and that it contains the sum of the knowledge acquired in former lives so that all knowledge is recollection and remembering is recalling from previous existences what lies ahead in the soul. (*Plato: Collected Dialogues*, Edith Hamilton and Huntington Cains, eds. New York: Pantheon, 1961). The triadic spiritual geography of Christian dogma has Hell as the ultimate loss of substance. It is untouched and untouchable by God's bond of grace, since the cosmic reach of God extends no lower than Purgatory.

Beelzebub explains to Hassein the history of the falling off of our initial perfection on Earth in a number of crucial, or axial, events. The first was the disappearance of Atlantis, another was the rise and dominance of Babylonian civilization, the third was a moral decline brought about by Roman civilization, and the fourth is the technology and mechanization of thought in the present age. Before this catena of events, things proceeded as God had planned. Three-brained beings existed until they developed an astral body to mediate their reunion with God; but, this natural balance was upset by defection of the harmonizing vibrations necessary for humans to develop their astral body, and the flow of attractions and repulsions, normally activated by the difference in distances between the orbits of the planets and between the notes of the octave, was deflected so that people ceased to unite with God *automatically*. As a consequence, humans became subject to the same natural laws governing one- and two-brained beings; that is, to the inevitability of death. Furthermore, the duration of human life diminished progressively.

Thus the goal of human life is divided. Either we can complete the process of perfection in accordance with the Law of Seven in the time allotted us, or we can perpetuate the species before the physical body perishes. In order to accomplish the latter purpose, nature divided humans into two sexes to produce offspring.[8] Nonetheless, despite our intellectual degeneration, we have not lost *completely* the old knowledge of how to perfect Objective Reason. That is, we possess the information necessary to enrich the brain with higher-being affirmative force and to coordinate its functions with the negative force resident in the spinal column (mirroring the active relationship between secondary suns and Absolute Sun, or Protocosmos), and these two centers are able to work together as a harmonizing principle for everything existing and being born. The third being-center, the neutralizing force, is an independent center in the breast having to do with enriching the flow of blood in concert with both heart and lungs.

Over a period of time in the past, however, the collaboration of these centers deteriorated because the knowledge of the function of the spinal marrow diminished as grades of human denial outweighed shades of affirmation. Major natural catastrophes accelerated the disappearance of knowledge of these things. The destruction of Atlantis had already deci-

---

[8] Beelzebub digresses briefly at this point to describe a planet where there are three sexes which merge together by mutual attraction—almost growing into each other—to make a child who reflects his triadic source. In Plato's *Symposium,* 189d–191d, Aristophanes says that mankind once had three sexes—male, female, and hermaphrodite—and that Zeus, in fear of the power of the hermaphrodites, split them in two to isolate their sexual identity.

mated the number of those possessing "sacred knowledge"; and, though a small number of the former residents of Atlantis knew how to use the higher foods and knew the way to higher consciousness, the destruction of the continent led inexorably to our loss of higher-being sustenance. As a result, few were able to absorb higher-body food consciously. Some time later, we lost both the need for and knowledge of this food, and labored only to secure substantial food for the physical body. Consequently, striving for perfection all but disappeared in the helter-skelter of banal survival, and with it intentional thought and aims for life higher than physical and emotional gratification. At first, nature tried to compensate for this loss by causing intensive shocks, or calamities, to reactivate automatic assimilation of active elements in the cosmos, principally by dividing and localizing them in the vibrations of the seven independent classes of the Law of the Octave.[9] Though life expanded throughout the universe by cause of this general diffusion, centers of gravity became less independent, and flows of energy more weakly directed.

Unfortunately, a second catastrophic loss of knowledge occurred when Babylonian science structured the universe and its parts in dualistic terms.[10] From this came the error of binary oppositions such as good and

---

[9] Babylonian astrology, as it is later schematized by Ptolemy, contains the basis of this "law." That is, the distances between the orbits of the seven observable moving bodies in the heavens—Saturn, Jupiter, Mars, Sun, Venus, Mercury, and the Moon—are in harmonic proportion *do, si, la, sol, fa, mi, re*—and the *do* that begins a new octave can be associated with Earth. The scheme also defines the order of the hours of the day and the days of the week. This "sevenfoldness," as Gurdjieff called it, is but one small aspect of the Law of Seven. The important point here is that our tonic scale is not whole tone, and the differences in tonal distance reflects the alterations God had to make in order to incite compensatory flows of energy.

[10] Zoroastrian and Manichean doctrines are heavily dualistic, but the Western world has been most influenced along these lines by Gnosticism, which insists on the clear-cut division between flesh and spirit that pervades Christian thought. Like Gurdjieff's "system," Gnosticism contains notions of a suffering from which certain initiates could escape to a world of higher being; and it also makes heavy use of secret symbolism. The New Testament is especially full of secret symbolism. One could point to the obvious case of the Apocalypse, and Ouspensky, *The Fourth Way* (pp. 406–410), demonstrates neatly the esoteric code in the Lord's Prayer. There is considerable difference of opinion as to the source of Gurdjieff's "system." Some have found Sufi mysticism behind it, others Platonism, Hindu mysticism, Stoicism, Gnosticism, and Esoteric Christianity. In personal correspondence, William Patrick Patterson reminds me that Boris Mouravieff, *Ouspensky, Gurdjieff et les fragments d'un enseignement inconnu* (Bruxelles: Synthèse, 1957) p. 8, records a conversation with Gurdjieff in which he asked: "Is the system yours?" "No." . . . "From where did you take it?" Gurdjieff replied: "Perhaps I stole it." Oscar Ichazo, "Letter to the Transpersonal Community," *The Arican*, 1991, pp. 88–90, denies anything original in Gurdjieff's teaching.

evil, sin and grace, light and darkness, heaven and hell, strength and wisdom, thought and feeling, etc. So grew the notion that human moral tendencies gravitate toward either diabolical or divine states, an idea comparable in some respects to Augustine's description of the soul's natural gravitational pull toward its creator; but, out of this notion grew the conception of ourselves as images of a god whom we resemble and who resembles us. Such subjectivism prompted us to envision God in personalized terms rather than as a cosmic force, and it encouraged passivity and a despair that human will was not up to the task of self-perfection. Hence, we assumed that unifying with the Absolute requires a gift received from without, rather than from a task performed within. In effect, humans had lost mastery of themselves as independent forces.

Later in the Roman period, the conscious conjoining of the sexes to produce children was ignored in pursuit of empty pleasure and unconscious reproduction. Thus, not only did we lose knowledge of perfection of reason at this stage, but we lost something of the sense of purpose in using sexual energy to perpetuate the species in successive cycles of generation. The failure of collaboration of the two lower centers of being led to illness, or "sin"; that is, a defection of the process necessary for the task of perfection.[11] Put another way, when conjoining of sperm and egg is impeded by the negative vibrations of empty pleasure, or of interruption of pregnancy, then the power to use our biological potential in the service of Objective Reason and union with God is deflected.

Error, waste, and sin are the three coordinate destabilizers of the function of planets and, although many higher-being bodies had already assembled *about* God, the others who had completed the perfection of their reason were blocked and unable to unite *with* God, not out of fault in themselves, but because of impediments in the degenerated processes of cosmic laws. On the other hand, because their "soul bodies" had evolved out of the effects of laws of nature—death and decomposition—they could not remain on the surface of Earth. So God made and assigned them a place called Purgatory where they would have to suffer in a continuing effort to purify themselves of the effects of sin and disharmony that manifest

---

[11] P. D. Ouspensky, *In Search of the Miraculous* (New York: Harcourt Brace and World, 1949), p. 357, interprets *sin* in Gurdjieff's work as a designation for waste, something not necessary. "Sins," he says, "are what keep a man on one spot if he has decided to move and if he is able to move"; and, "sin is what puts man to sleep when he has decided to awaken." Therefore, one with no aim at all does not sin [Compare Saint Paul's letter to Romans (5:13–14) in which he declares that when there was no law there was no sin]. Sufi thought has man (humanity) responsible for the restoration of his soul to consciousness.

themselves in external emanations pervading the universe. In other words, they must keep themselves qualified and prepared for unification with their cosmic Source.[12] The universe knows of Purgatory, says Beelzebub, but few Earthmen know of what it consists; and Beelzebub knows of what he talks, for he himself is caught suspended in the efforts to perfect his being, though he knows of a line of teachers on Earth who still know the necessary method.

Gurdjieff's book as a whole looks to the present and its augury of the future caused by our falling off from our proper role to collaborate with the Sun Absolute. The predominant mortal illness that derived from Babylon still pervades the universe in the form of "wiseacring," (from a Dutch word meaning "soothsaying, prophesying") or erring due to an only *partial* knowledge of things.[13] What we know now is, at best, only partially authentic. Though pristine knowledge survives in transmission by a handful of genuine initiates, the new Babylon, figured by Western civilization's America, risks withering consciousness into a psychotic search for the *soul* and for identity with forms exterior to oneself, even though we no longer know if we possess a soul or if we are an entity in ourselves. What modern people lack is a capacity to absorb universal vibrations intentionally to perform the conscious labor and intentional suffering necessary to gain mastery over self and perfection of one's being. What we tend to call Paradise is but a reflection of the surface of Purgatory; what we call hell is a reflection of the anguish of our own inner states. "Wiseacring" is the increase and transmission of this error.

There are seven psychological signs of decline in knowledge of self in the present situation:[14]

1. Conscious and unconscious depravity.
2. Feelings of self-satisfaction from leading others astray.
3. Irresistible inclination to destroy the existence of other breathing creatures.
4. The urge to become free from the necessity of actualizing the being-efforts demanded by Nature.
5. The attempt by every kind of artificiality to conceal from others what in their opinion are one's physical defects.

---

[12] See Jacques LeGoff, *La Naissance de purgatoire* (Paris: Gallimard, 1981).

[13] In *Meetings with Remarkable Men*, p. 47, Gurdjieff recalls one of his father's aphorisms: "Unhappiness on earth is from the wiseacring of women."

[14] G. I. Gurdjieff, *All and Everything* (Routledge & Kegan Paul, 1950), p. 405. Beelzebub calls these the seven signs of "hasnamuss," a Turkish word designating unwholesome individual impulses.

6. Calm self-contentment in the use of what is not personally deserved.

7. The striving to be what one is not.

The greatest global destructive manifestation of all of these is war. In a smaller but equally telling manner, the taking of life in sacrificial rites and in blood sports are signs of depravity because, as Beelzebub insists, we should love everything that breathes. There is no hierarchy of life-value in the universe, even if there is a hierarchy of living forms. Sexual activity for pleasure instead of for either reproducing one's own kind or, on a higher level, as a means of strengthening one's "being-body," is wasteful, "mechanical suffering."

Beelzebub explains as well that the teaching of four great messengers from above—Buddha, Christ, Mohammed, and Lama—have been distorted, and that the secular structures of religious institutions on Earth at present debilitate rather than enhance the spirit.[15] The major distortion in the past was the conception of a binary opposition in religion between good and evil. Originally, good and evil were active and passive principles that were reconciled by a third principle that converted the tension between them into energy for self-development. A correlative error was the attribution of demonic character to visible beings who seemed to live longer than others, while giving angelic status to invisible forces which seemed to favor human beings.

In short, we are diverted from the proper role of self-perfection by false prophets, hasnamusses, wiseacres, the *kashireitleer* (Divine Book) of Lentrohamsanin (Lenin-Trotsky), etc. Earlier in his discourse to his grandson, Hassein, Beelzebub had rephrased the essence of the biblical dictum when he advised: "Do unto another as you would do unto your own." To illustrate the relative values of the functions of our three centers, Beelzebub explains that faith of *consciousness* is freedom; faith of *feeling* is weakness; faith of *body* is stupidity. Hope of *consciousness* is strength; hope of *feeling* is slavery; hope of *body* is disease. Love of *consciousness* evokes the same in response; love of *feeling* evokes the opposite; love of *body* depends on type and polarity.

Beelzebub recalls to Hassein his association on Earth with a certain Ashiata Shiamash, whose mission to Earth consisted of both defining the "terror of the situation" among mankind and of transmitting knowledge in a *Legominism*, or written code, in which he prescribed five "strivings:"

---

[15] To these, Beelzebub adds many others of secondary rank, such as "Saint Moses."

1. Striving to have in one's ordinary being-existence everything satisfying and really necessary for one's planetary body.
2. Striving to have a constant and unflagging instinctive need for self-perfection in the sense of being.
3. The conscious striving to know ever more and more concerning the laws of world creation and world maintenance.
4. The striving from the beginning of existence to pay for arising and individuality as quickly as possible, in order afterward to be free to lighten as much as possible the Sorrow of our Common Father.
5. The striving always to assist the most rapid perfecting of other beings, both those similar to oneself and those of other forms, up to the degree of self-individuality.

In all, the immediate goal of all positive striving is simply to live a happy life, a life in which unhappiness can be converted to service of an ultimate happiness. As Mullah Nassr Eddin, another of Beelzebub's friends, says, "Every real happiness for man can arise exclusively only from some unhappiness also real that he has already experienced." Suffering, then, is an essential step in our realization of self and in our work on self for perfection.

There is a considerable necessary component of suffering in Gurdjieff's method; but, whereas Gurdjieff rubbed raw the emotions as well as the physical senses of his pupils, Orage and Toomer sought to soothe the spirit while probing the intellect with the same message: We cannot speak the truth until we realize that we lie; we cannot awaken self-awareness until we understand that we are asleep; we cannot achieve individuality until we discover the extent to which we are mechanical; we cannot speak of self until we reconcile the various and contradictory "I"s in us; we cannot observe ourselves until we stumble in the dark of our own blindness. Even among Orage's and Toomer's pupils, it has occcasionally seemed that the insistence upon probing the negative aspects of oneself breaks down pride of self by an indulgence in masochistic exercises with only vague promise of restoration. Many would simply prefer to stop short of what the Apostles and the saints knew, that suffering is knowledge and knowledge suffering.

Gurdjieff's teaching technique was Socratic; he played gadfly and trickster, inviting doubt, skepticism, and self-reflection as purgatives for cosmic illness. Like Aristotle, who told people that they didn't know what they thought they knew, Gurdjieff would have his pupils doubt everything they did not know by personal experience. He was both Marysas and Apollo, witch and wizard, Juggler and Hanged Man, and teacher of dances upon the water.

Chapter Eight

Returning To Toomer

The Teacher is one who brings tools
and enables us to use them.
    —*The Wayward and the Seeking*

I'm leaving the shining ground, brothers,
I sing because I ache. . . .
            —"The Blue Meridian"

Poppy was much in my thoughts in the winter of 1949–1950 after my return from France, but I knew I just couldn't sit down with him and discuss Gurdjieff. I had to draw him out along Gurdjieffian lines. I stopped by once or twice after visits to Madame Ouspensky's farm in Mendham, NJ, where many of Gurdjieff's pupils congregated after Gurdjieff's death, but when I withdrew from college in June of 1950, instead of going to Paris (I didn't have the money anyway) I succumbed to my mother's wishes and went to work in Houston. I feared it would be some time before I could return to the Mill House. In Houston, while training to be a cotton merchant, I lived in a series of boarding houses before renting a house with a group of young Scandinavian apprentices in the cotton business.

A year later, in the summer of 1951, I returned east on vacation, bought a little car and drove down to Mill House. I was given my old room, now with a wall of bookcases filled with philosophical and psychological texts I couldn't remember ever having noticed before. I found Jean quieter and slower of movement than before. In the mornings, we took slow walks and some afternoons we sat in the kitchen, listening on the radio to Philadelphia Athletics baseball games, during which Jean would comment on players' styles. His favorite was the left-handed pitcher, Bobby Schantz.

We walked and talked about Mill House and the countryside. He told me that he and Marjorie had decided to sell the house eventually, but they would first give up the farm so that he could spend more time writing. In the front sitting room, he spoke to me about how the process of learning to love life and to love God starts even before birth, that an unborn child can feel and receive love as well as start a process of self-knowledge, but he didn't say much more. He seemed more tired and stooped in his posture than I had ever seen him and, after a few days, I decided to leave to have time on my way to Houston to see old friends. My first stop was Ocean City, NJ, where Margie was working in a refreshment stand with a friend. We had supper together and talked and laughed about old times. She was her old cheerful, carefree self, looking forward to college in a few weeks. I slept that night on the floor in her shared room, and drove the next day to Chapel Hill, NC to see an old high school friend. A day later I was in Panama City, FL visiting the mother of the poet Charles Henri Ford, whom I had seen much of in Westport in the company of Pavel Tchelitcheff who had lived in our little red house before us. From there, I drove nonstop to Houston.

I had no direct contacts with Jean between July and December, although my mother told me of several conversations with him, both on the telephone and during visits to New York. The principle topic, unfortunately, was my problems in Texas. I was ill-suited for the cotton business and had gotten myself involved with a girl from whom I found it difficult to escape. In his usual bemused tone, Jean told my mother not to let herself get overly concerned in a problem that was mine to work out. He gently upbraided her for having tried too often to direct me, and reminded her that she had persuaded me to go into the cotton business in the first place.

Finally, I made a cowardly retreat from Texas just before Christmas of 1951, leaving Houston at midnight and driving nonstop all the way to Sparta, GA, where, after twenty-four hours on the road without more than gasoline stops, I ran out of gas in the middle of a cold night. I slept fitfully and half-frozen in my car near a gas station. Waiting for it to open the next morning, I went into an old Inn where a huge woman was stirring a cauldron of hominy over an open fire. Fortified with hominy, toast, and bacon, and my car with gasoline, I drove to Virginia for a good night's sleep in a motel. In the cold morning after, my battery couldn't turn the motor over, and it was another hour before I could get someone to give me a push. It was late in the afternoon when I arrived at the Mill House. "Where were you?" Poppy asked. "We expected you last night." I told him that I had run out of gas in Sparta, GA, and had to spend the night in my car. He leaned back in his chair with a laugh and said: "Did you? Hmmm. Well, in that darkness I first felt myself black Ahab." I was confused by the riddle in his words, but let it pass. It was only sometime later that I realized what Sparta had meant for him thirty years earlier.

Jean seemed tired, and I was eager to get home again and prepare for readmission to Brown; but I needed some balm for my moral wounds. So, during a walk over the familiar fields south of the Mill House, I raised a question that had been on my mind since my brief summer with Gurdjieff. I asked Jean if he knew who my father was. He gave his deep and playfully mocking smile and said, "Should I? Isn't that a matter to raise with your mother?" I replied that she was suspicious of my resentment and evasive, saying things like, "You'd know him if you saw him." He asked me what I thought was my goal in wanting to know, and I replied that, first of all, I wanted to satisfy my curiosity and to have a firmer sense of my identity. At this, the smile straightened, and in a voice so stern that it stiffened my back, he said the following:

"Listen boy, are you looking for a name or for a person? If you are looking for a person you have to ask yourself whether the person wants to be found, and you have to respect the possible negative replies. Besides, what do you think that person has to do with *you?* Blood strain is an accident which binds people together long enough for them to decide whether they like each other or whether they've had enough of each other. This 'father' of yours is a ghost. Looking for the flesh only puts you in the position of wanting to get away from the ghost. The flesh only disappoints the thought. You have a father in you. Do you want to risk losing the father you have for the chance of finding a father whose person will not only destroy that image, but will lay a claim on your conception of fatherhood?

"But, maybe you are just looking for a name. You've changed yours already to your mother's, and the bond between that name and your mother is essential. Your father's name, no matter what it is, would just be another claim on your so-called identity. If you want to face someone in order to say, 'Okay, that's him,' then let's forget both image and person, and start to reformulate what a father means to you. Say that to your mother and you might get an answer. If you say, 'Gee, I'd like to know who my father is,' how is she to understand what is *really* on your mind? How is she to know you are after anything else except what is hidden in *her* mind?

"We have no choice in the name given us when we are born, but we have a choice of what value we can put into that name, or what names we can fit to our own conceptions of self. Before you can be what you want to be, you must want to be what you are. Names and the parents who use them are chains, identity bracelets worn on the spirit. Some people wear their names or their looks like ornaments, but the ornament is a gift from someone else. Feel your name, and feel yourself as a son, and then ask yourself what you *really* want to know, and why. If it is for a sense of identity, get this out of your mind. This is ego and vanity, for one thing. Worse, it is selling yourself short.

"Do not for any reason look for what is the same between your self and another. Look for what is different that can be drawn toward sameness. Names and family, like club memberships and school programs, are outward signs of this identity you mention. What I would have hoped you've learned from me is that being an *entity* is of greater value than joining an *identity*. Look for your difference, not sameness. Draw others to you rather than join them. The search for identity invites exclusion. An entity invites inclusion. You were born with a particular essence which has a particular place in the universe. Going about your job of living, you accumulate names and opinions of others like clothes. Take a good look at them, and then throw them away and make your own. For material, instead of a name and a person you would call 'father,' look for the place in this world you can operate as you, Polo, without labels like a can of soup. Use everything about you to find that place. Think of what I've told you for so long.

"Don't look for claims on yourself, and the worst to seek and hardest to quit is the claim of blood. Everything I've taught you is directed to free yourself from such claims so that you can reclaim yourself, for yourself. Go home tomorrow and look carefully at your mother, not at the outside you always see, but those things inside her which have held you together. Asking her to provide you with a father puts a claim on her. Forget that; you can find who your biological father is in a number of ways, if you insist, but don't do it in a way that gives another a claim on you."

I was back in Westport the next evening without questions for my mother. In January, I was readmitted to college and plunged into my studies with a commitment I had never been able to apply to anything before in my life, and things started to go very well. Early in the summer of 1952, I sailed to France with a trunk full of wedding presents for my sister's marriage to the French photographer and publisher, Jean Chevalier. The ship was a C-3 cargo ship converted to student dormitories; but, without the weight of a cargo for ballast, it rode high in the water and many were the students who suffered seasickness. Luckily, I had traveling companions. The son and daughter of Louise and Bill Welch were on board, and Patty and I sat late on deck talking about Gurdjieff. Her mother was training Gurdjieff group leaders in the New York City area, and Patty, who had only seen Gurdjeff briefly in 1948, wanted to know more about him. She was warm, attractive, and intelligent, and her questions, more incisive than my answers, gave me a hint of how people "outside" the work understood Gurdjieff's ideas.

In Paris, there was a joyful reunion with the Orages who had come over from London for the wedding, Dick with his finacée, Anne—slim, tall, and elegant Ann—and Jessie in extremely good form. They were staying in a family hotel in Montparnasse. My mother arrived by plane two days before the wedding and we moved into Alice Delamar's flat on Rue Git-le-Coeur, overlooking the Seine and Notre Dame. Every night was a late one with the Orages, who wanted to profit from the occasion, since there were still tight monetary restrictions for English traveling abroad. Ann, arguing that time was too precious even to sleep, kept me up two entire nights walking the left bank, watching the sun light up Notre Dame as we took coffee with workmen and prostitutes in cafés facing the river, before taking an early Métro to Montparnasse. The first morning, as we walked up the Métro steps close to her hotel, a passerby took one glance at her and at me and muttered "quelle jolie pute." Ann smiled.

One Friday, my mother took me to Natalie Barney's evening salon on the Rue Jacob and renewed past acquaintances. When Natalie asked my mother how she had reacted to Gurdjieff's death, she replied coolly that she didn't feel any particular emotion. Another day we had tea with Madame de Salzmann in her Rue du Bac apartment, where she explained the Rue Colonels Renard apartment would be preserved as a museum, and asked my mother if she would participate in the operation of the proposed Institute that was almost in place in New York City. From Madame de Salzmann's it was a short walk to Man Ray's apartment and studio on Rue Feron, where he was living with his young and attractive California wife.

At the civil ceremony at the Town Hall of the 7th arrondissement, Madame de Salzmann was a witness for the bride, and Ancy Dupré gave her away . The reception took place at the apartment of Alice Delamar, overlooking Notre Dame and the Seine, the same apartment my mother had lived in briefly almost thirty years earlier. The wedding guests included a broad spectrum of my mother's and sisters friends in Paris, from Man Ray and the actress Sophie Litvak to Hubert de Givenchy, who had designed Petey's wedding gown. My mother spent another afternoon with Madame de Salzmann, while I saw the Orages off from the Gare du Nord. The next morning, visibly upset about something, my mother said to me: "There's no reason to stay here any longer. I've booked passage for us on the Ile de France sailing in two days."[1]

It was only the beginning of July, and I found a job tending the beach bar at the Stamford Yacht Club to fill out the summer and earn some much-needed money. In the fall, because of my school record, I was able to persuade the Financial Aid Office to give me a full tuition scholarship. Meanwhile, Margie, now preferring to be called Margot, had graduated from Endicott College in Massachusetts and had taken a flat on East 52nd Street in New York City to study acting, modeling and sculpting. I visited her on occasion in New York for a movie and a meal, and kidded her re-

---

[1] Since she had met Solita Solano for tea, I can only surmise my mother's mood was a consequence.

lentlessly about her adoration for Marlon Brando, of whom she had even made a clay head. "That's about the consistency of his brain," quipped I. She, in turn, would kid me about my stuffy intellectual posture and my habit of inserting obscure words into my conversation. She always had a word ready to test me. Once it was "perspicacity," which I could define all right, but one evening she hit me with "eleemosynary" and I cringed. I met Jean sometimes in the city on late afternoons, when he was in New York for "meetings." During one supper together in the Oyster Bar, he told me that he worried about Argie's refusal to take her own potential seriously. I did not reply, because I knew Argie to be bright and vivacious, hesitant to display her thoughts before her father, where her words were susceptible to analysis. "When you consider who her father is, and her mother . . .," he said sadly, as if to himself. This was the first moment in my relations with Jean that I saw how emotionally vulnerable he was. The confidence made me feel closer to him, but it saddened me to feel that he was not completely free of the weaknesses he had worked to correct in me.

The meetings he was attending in New York were with the Gurdjieff group. He had accepted an invitation to Mme Ouspensky's in Mendham on 13 January 1953 to celebrate the Russian New Year and Gurdjieff's birthday. There he spoke with Madame de Salzmann. Five days later, he wrote Mme Ouspensky to say: "Mr. Gurdjieff once said to me, 'Toomer, you do not know how your subconscious is related to me.' I did not and do not yet know. But I feel, I have an idea, I have felt it ever since 1924. It has never left me. I don't think it ever will. He was and is the one being above all others whom I loved, in a way feared, and venerated. I cannot conceive of my life without him and his teaching, and the life he made possible."[2] A day later, he wrote John Bennett to recall the evening at Madame Ouspensky's and ask if they could talk.[3] Jean's own notes from this period reveal a heightened anxiety over the health of his mind and body which undoubtedly prompted him to re-enter the work.[4] To his subsequent request to assume the direction of a group, Mme de Salzmann put him in touch with Louise Welch, one of Orage's pupils from the twenties,

---

[2] Toomer Collection, The Beinecke Rare Book and Manuscript Library, Yale University, Box 6, Folder 202.

[3] Toomer Collection, Box 1, Folder 13.

[4] Toomer Collection, Box 64, Folders 1461–1477. In July 1953, Jean records that the Gurdjieff Foundation people—Edwin and Dorothy Wolfe, Bill and Louise Welch, and Rita Romilly, do not think "too well of Bennett. He's been out of the work too long." Actually, Bennett had been out of touch with Gurdjieff between 1923 and 1948, a period which he himself described as a "sleep," but he formed enthusiastic groups in southern England after Gurdjieff's death.

for retraining. He never mentioned this fact to me, and I personally did not notice any change in his public self, his humor and generosity of spirit during these years. Kerman and Eldridge, in their *Lives*, attribute his return to Gurdjieff in 1953 to the influence of John Bennett in New York, remarking that, in listening to Bennett speak, he felt that Gurdjieff had taught new things during and since the war, things that he had withheld from Orage and himself in the 1920s. In June 1953, Jean wrote a long letter to Mme Henri Tracol in Paris, asking her to explain how Gurdjieff trained her in the 1940s. After a few meetings in New York, Bennett invited him to join his group in England, but Jean didn't think his health was up to the move. More importantly, Argie had just come of age that summer and was exerting her independence in a way that Jean was not sure he could control with grace.[5]

Nonetheless, in July 1953, Jean was outlining new courses which would integrate Quaker ideas into his Gurdjieffian teaching. That same month, the Bucks County Workshop Associates invited Jean to participate in a lecture series. Stanley Kunitz was to give lectures on literature, Roger Marin on music, Dorothy Spaeth on dance, and Jean on philosophy. His bibliography ranged from C. S. Lewis to Ouspensky and Bennett. He was encouraged enough at the reception of his ideas that he thought they could be used as a core for a new Gurdjieff group teaching. As he explained to Fred Leighton: "You know, back there in 1924, and from then until I left the work—or it left me—I was continually in personal contact with people in the work, at Prieuré, in New York, in Chicago—Now no. . . . But now we read each other. . . . I knew this before. Now I know it as a fact.[6]

I let a year pass without seeing Jean, though I continued to write occasionally. My university work was going very well. Well, yes, things were going well on that level, but on 9 November 1953, my best friend swallowed potassium cyanide he had made himself in the chemistry lab. I fell into a deep depression, partly because I felt he had killed himself on a lark. He wanted to prove to himself, I thought, that he had the power to take his own life, and so did it without any good reason. I was tortured by the "why" of it all and, to get this out of my mind, I plunged into work harder than ever. I was a residence monitor in a freshman dormitory, head waiter in the Refectory, and had a history of music research grant. I wrote for essay prizes. I was president of a fraternity and member of the student governing board. I had no social life whatsoever. I wrote Poppy in late fall to ask him if I was doing the right thing in occupying myself outside in order

5   Letter to Marjorie Content, 25 August 1953. Toomer Collection, Box 8, Folder 245.
6   11 August 1953. Toomer Collection, Box 4, Folder 141.

to obscure thoughts of my friend. In a brief but strong note, he said that I should rather move him *inside* my mind instead of having his memory waver on the margins of my consciousness. "Write stories about your experience together. Observe yourselves together. His image bothers you now because you haven't given it a firm form to deal with. Do it, and you will be stronger by his presence in you. Let me see what you write, if you like." So I wrote, staying up late nights after completing my assigned study to write a series of poems and short stories about him. Immediately, it seemed, I felt at ease with thoughts of him, and even his presence in dreams joined my consciousness. He was no longer either "dead" or absent. I sent Poppy one short story. He didn't reply, but when I saw him the next time, he said, smiling, "So, you've started to observe yourself at last!"

After I graduated, in late January of 1954, to fill up the time until June graduation exercises, I drove to Florida where my mother's old friend, Alice Delamar, had offered me two months of sun and rest at her home in Palm Beach. I broke that stay with one trip north in the early spring for job interviews and to prepare a commencement address. On the way back, I stopped to see Jean. He looked fine and was full of energy. We took walks, now with Mickey's grandson, Smokey, a big shaggy police dog. Poppy tired quickly in the evening, but we sat as usual with a glass of ale mixed with stout before a television set in the kitchen, to watch the Yankees, to whom his baseball allegiance had shifted. Now his favorite player was Gene Woodling, the Yankee outfielder, because, as Jean said, "you can see how he watches the ball make contact with the bat."

I passed up job offers and joined the army in August with plans to enter the Armed Forces Language School in Monterey, CA. For basic training, I was sent to Fort Dix, NJ. Once I qualified for weekend passes, I took a bus Saturday afternoons or Friday evenings to Doylestown, where Jean would pick me up. For four consecutive weekends, I enjoyed the happiest times I can remember with Jean and Marjorie. Margot came down from New York a couple of times, and she had girl friends over Saturday afternoons to ride with. On one Saturday evening, Jean challenged me to concoct a cocktail in honor of Mill House. With what I was able to find in the pantry and cellar, I made a concoction of dark Jamaican and light Puerto Rican rum, shaken with lemon and lime juice and the white of an egg. Jean called it his "Rum-Yum."[7]

---

[7] Perhaps I overestimated my bar tending flair, or my drinks had too much punch. Since I wrote this, I have seen in Jean's papers a diary note to this weekend to the effect that Argie and I came down for the weekend, but that Jean regrets not remembering much of the evening.

In my old bedroom, now library, I read *Psychopathia Sexualis*, and was intrigued by the varieties of "searches for the possibilities of one's bodily mechanisms undertaken in desperation without being conscious of the 'sexual result'" "(as Jean phrased his reaction to my wonderment). He remarked that "in matters of sex as well as in matters of social behavior, there are those who will do everything they can to escape noticing themselves. The slave is he who would rather have decided for him what is too much trouble to learn how to do, and do better, by himself."

My affection for Jean those days was boundless, and we hugged each other hard before going to bed. After one Saturday evening beer and a hug goodnight, Jean said, "Goodnight, my son." I cannot remember a single instant of such happiness at any time earlier in my life. I felt that I had finally achieved a long-awaited potential, and had found my real father. He called me "son" two or three times more the next day, after which Marjorie remarked with obvious pleasure, "Did you hear what he called you?" I smiled and I told her that I had never realized before how much I loved Jean.

After I finished basic training, I was transferred to Fort Sam Houston in San Antonio, TX, for eight weeks, and then on to duty at Fort Lewis, near Tacoma, WA. The Armed Forces Language School was under congressional investigation, so I applied to the Counter Intelligence Corps, but five weeks later I received orders to report to the Army of Occupation in Germany. With a thirty-day leave at my disposal, I returned to the East Coast. After a few uncomfortable days with my mother, I decided to go to Washington to see if my Connecticut senator, Prescott Bush, would help me to have my orders changed so that the application I had put in at Fort Lewis for the Counter Intelligence Corps could be processed. Jean and Marjorie offered to let me stay with them as long as I wished before reporting to Camp Kilmer, my assigned port of embarkation. Jean told me that he had been amused to have been visited by the FBI in relation to my application to Intelligence. I had given, in typical political naiveté, the names of Jean Toomer and George Seldes as recommenders of my character and patriotism.

In Washington, I couldn't get to see either Bush or any of his aides. A secretary told me to leave a note with my complaint, and to go home and wait for news. I returned disconsolately to the Mill House. I was already extraordinarily depressed from the events of the months since my last stay. First of all, in San Antonio I had made contact with the girl I had run from two years earlier, and she had put pressure on me that I had not even half-heartedly resisted to take up where we had broken off. Then my duty, at sooty, dirty and wet Fort Lewis was a succession of kitchen police, guard duty, and nightime dispensary duty. All during this time, I was receiving calls from Texas asking for an invitation to join me; and one night she called to announce abruptly that she could wait no longer and was marrying someone else. I was both relieved and confused, not so much about her as about myself.

Relaxing at the Mill House, I went on a reading binge. I settled in the front sitting room to continue reading out of Jean's library. I absorbed myself in the *The Brothers Karamazov*, a book which only intensified my manic-depressive state, moved to Conrad's *Heart of Darkness* and *Victory*, and I sank deeper into depression. I took down the blue-bound *Cane* from the high shelf on the gallery by the upstairs study, and it hypnotized me. Dostoievski, Conrad, and Toomer suddenly blended themselves in my mind and I snapped suddenly into a manic state. I was indescribably high, and everything seemed so good about me that I floated completely clear of both the past and future. It seemed that for days I was alone with Jean and Marjorie in a private and privileged universe, and I felt a heightened sensitivity to everything they said and did.

All this time, Jean was soft and thoughtful in manner, and spent brief stretches reading in his chair next to mine; and while he napped on the couch across the room, I would go to my room to read. I even started to write a bit, so full was my mind of ideas I wanted to put into some order. We took short walks about the property with Smokey's son, Whitty, an old dog now who spent much of the day dozing fitfully on the scatter rug at Jean's feet in front of the fireplace, frequently jerking his legs and heaving his multicolored mane. Jean would look over his glasses at him and remark: "He's still chasing rabbits."

Marjorie often sent Jean and myself to the Farmer's Market to shop. Jean drove carefully and well, and we walked down long aisles of produce, looking, judging, comparing opinions on ripeness and freshness. He enjoyed listening to sales talk, often replying simply: "You don't say," before moving to another stall. He shopped thoughtfully and considerately, and with a twinkle in his eye, he would turn to me and say, "Let's get a bottle of rum." Jean seemed pensive, too. He and Marjorie were to move in a few months to the barn. There was a new road made of the old tractor path, so that they would not have to drive past the Mill House to get there. He talked optimistically about the new arrangments, how Marjorie would have her studio and he a work room. The old house and mill were too expensive to maintain, and there was no family to fill their spaces.

One afternoon, a radio crew came up from Philadelphia to interview him before camera in the front sitting room, with their equipment in front of the fireplace and Jean in his leather chair on the right. I sat and listened from the couch close to the entry, and I think Argie was there, too. This was the first time I had heard Jean speak "publicly," but the language was familiar, and he spoke with the soft but intense tone he had always used with me in serious moments. My mind was all over the place at the time, but I remember some of the things he said in the course of that afternoon. In general, he spoke of the moral condition of man and his future after the war. He talked of the need of man in general to develop a fresh and harmonious relationship with his environment and with his neighbors based upon self-awareness of the needs of his spiritual being. Someone asked him about the atom bomb, if it had marked a turn in history. Jean smiled and said that all tools were good when their potential was realized. "If man comes across something new, if he invents a new machine, it takes some time to explore the thing's potential. It is vital in any relationship between a man and the mechanisms about him that man never cease to increase his mastery—not over the *thing*, for that would be a collaboration on equal terms, but over *his own* activity with it. The ability to split the atom and harness its energy should incite us to split ourselves from spiritual poverty and engage ourselves directly with God. Unfortunately, we know more about the atom now than we know about the food we eat, more of the universe than of Him who created it. We risk accelerating this going at things backward, from the essential to the nonessential."[8]

During these days, Marjorie noticed my shifting moods and felt it necessary to engage me in social activities. We visited her daughter, Susan, a couple of times in Wycombe, where Susan, now married to "Sandy" Sandberg, invited me to a square dance as a diversion from my obvious worries. I played with her children, but my mind was everywhere at once. One afternoon while Marjorie was shopping at the Farmer's Market, I took the initiative and asked Jean, just after he had raised himself from his nap and settled into his chair, if I could talk with him. Again, his face shaped itself into that exquisite inviting smile of already knowing what was in the air, and he asked me with intended deliberation what I wanted to say. I related first my disappointment at the way my military career had gotten under way, and then told him briefly about my old problems in Texas that had resurfaced as a new problem. I explained to Jean that one of my anxieties concerned my inability to say "I love you" to a girl out of feelings alone, and now I felt guilty that I could not say what that girl told me she wanted more than anything else in the world to hear. I could not say it,

---

[8] Only recently, in reading papers in the Toomer Collection, have I found reference to this interview. "Operation Peace" enlisted several prominent citizens to record their impressions about the Cold War. On the 18th of April, Jean wrote thanks to the *Doylestown Daily Intelligencer* for having made his recording "readable" (Toomer Collection, Box 2, Folder 44).

I went on to explain without waiting for a reply, because I was afraid to commit my personal values—no matter what my physical desire—to a situation in which I could not "believe." I said that I couldn't say to the girl that I loved her because I didn't believe I *could* love her, since she wasn't the kind of girl I felt I should marry. This refusal to say "I love you" had hurt her, and she insisted that I couldn't be so affectionate with her and not love her. She wanted the words so much that I finally gave in and used them without any conviction. I felt I had blasphemed, entrapped myself with a lie. The phrase itself suddenly seemed dirty to me. Once I used it, she lost all of her physical attraction for me, and I felt even the more guilty for my change of heart.

The situation to which I was referring no longer existed, but I found myself caught between feeling guilty that I had not done the right thing by her, and feeling guilty for the strange exhilarating mood I found myself in for having escaped her. I ended my disjointed confession by saying that what was bothering me at the moment was my emotional "high." I felt wonderful, despite reason to feel terrible. Should I question happiness, or just enjoy it in ignorance of its causes or effects?

Jean never let on that he knew anything of my Texas adventure, nor of anything else I alluded to. He leaned back in his chair, took a deep breath, wrinkled his brow, and cocked his head, then spoke to me uninterruptedly for a longer stretch than he had ever done before. I have no idea how long his speech lasted, for I was hypnotized by the music of his voice, the intensity of its tone, and the penetration of his words.

"So you feel badly having told someone you love her? That is good, because shame of your weakness is a sign that there is strength somewhere. Don't worry about feeling weak in weak situations; but don't be weak twice in the same situation, and don't be weak in crucial circumstances. And where are you now? Well, you can't improve the past, but you *must* remember it in order to improve yourself.[9] If you feel happy now and don't know the reason, it is only because you are not in touch with your centers. One is sending you signals and at least you feel something is wrong, even if you can't read it, and you are doing something about it now.

"First of all, you feel ashamed about words because you do not know what they convey. You were trying to make a girl feel better by using them, but since you made *yourself* feel worse, *she* felt worse. What you had tried to

---

[9]   P. D. Ouspensky makes this point forcefully in *The Strange Life of Ivan Osokin* (London: Penguin, 1960), the story of a young man who is given the chance to correct past mistakes by returning to his boyhood, but over and over again, even with the knowledge of the future consequences of his acts, he repeats his same mistakes, simply because he cannot change his reaction to circumstances.

do, of course, is to move love from a physical to an emotional level. But in you, both of these levels are subjective. There is a third level which is objective and conscious, and that level contains the love which comes from thought. Conscious love controls the other two, just as emotional love gives value to physical sense.

"Loving at any level is an activity that cannot exist without return, for one loves for being loved and is loved for loving.[10] Actually, it is harder to receive than to give love, for the reception, more than the giving, sets the standards, shapes, and values of love. You could not *love* because you couldn't *receive* love, could not even recognize whether what you were called on to receive was love at all. Ideas—and love is an idea that functions like an organ in human beings—must be firmly attached to values. You must move the lesser to the greater value when you exercise love. You must look into yourself as receiver before you look into the other as giver. You must have self-control—awareness of that value of love in you—and then concentrate on transmitting or attaching it to the value of the other. You cannot really love until you are sure of that bond, and that its value is part of both of you. So that, whatever awareness you bring to the other, the other will bring it to you. To point out faults in the other will lead the other to see and point out faults in you, and your 'love' will exist on the level of fault instead of value.

"You must not reduce love to this. Tension in love is fine if it is productive; conflict is destructive. Love is precisely a force to neutralize conflict. Tension, however, is the symptom of an inner yearning for a lost balance. It is the occasion to look carefully at oneself, at the balance of one's centers. Love can only exist in essence once there is a balance of sense, feeling, and reason. So, if you do not see reason when you sense and feel, you are not in balance. What then? You can exercise self-discipline and renounce the love; or, you can look for the reason. It is never absent; it is simply hidden, too small to be noticed; or it is disguised right in front of you. It is the size of the reason which counts, for it must be large enough to contain the size of the sense which is contained in feeling. Looking within yourself for reasons is to scan the limitations of your reason, but this is good. To see a wall is to realize there is a way around or over it.

---

[10] I have since seen notes my mother took at a Gurdjieff talk on 24 May 1923 at the Prieuré that contained the following: "Every life represents God. Who loves the represented also loves the representer. Every life is receptive to love, feels it, is sensitive to it. Even a dead picked flower understands whether it is loved or not. Even unconscious life reacts to love and this love is reflected in many ways."

"Or, look at it this way, tension is the process of any art, and there is an art in loving as much as a loving in art. That tension, for example, is like the tension between the sculptor's idea and the shapeless block of stone before him. He has to turn the potential of this relationship into an actuality by his art, and art requires consciousness as well as passion. The sculptor ends up by selling his art, in other words, by renouncing his physical possession of it, but holding on to his conscious posession of it.

"So with love for a person. If you love only physically, you are actually loving your own body in its particular circumstances. The woman does not really matter to you, possession of her does. This love is merely the body's desire for a thing, whether food, drink, activity, or a woman's body. This is animal love. Fine, as long as possessing, like eating food, serves *all* of your centers, *all* of your being. There is food that is poison and food that merely passes through you without nourishing the body. Physical love is caused by two things, one exterior and one interior. The exterior is circumstance, the conjunction of two bodies in space and time, and the circumstance of seeing and desiring what is seen. The inner cause is a complicated chemical process over which few have control.

"Emotional love is a desire to possess another person's feelings, if not his body as well. This is what most people are thinking of when they use the word 'love.' It is sentiment, but it is not really thought of the other person. It is thought of the other person's feelings toward *you*. It is selfish love, because the concern of emotional love is *being loved* rather than loving. It is a love manifested by self-expression, like saying 'I love you,' and writing romantic poetry. You have to ask yourself in these cases: What of myself is worth expressing? What does it do for the other? Emotional love incites doubt, fear, and often hate in the other.

"The love which joins body and feelings with thought, the love which joins love of person, love of life, and love of God is conscious and objective. It is a concern more for the other than for the self. This is Christian love, and it joins the experience of the one loved with the experience of the lover, so that both become one essence. To love objectively, one must give up oneself. Who loves life loves its creator. All life is receptive to love, even a picked flower feels whether it is loved or not. Even unconscious life reacts to love. Good and bad feelings toward another reflect the good and bad feelings coming *from* the other.

"Like everything else essential, love is something that must be learned. Unless it is learned, it is passive, the love of one enslaved to circumstance. The love that is learned, that which is an expression of objective thought, is active. Passive love has no value, because it never leaves the person loving.[11] Active love touches the essence of the one loved, and therefore returns as a value to the lover. This is what Christian love is, and it is the love at the basis of most religious systems. If you love only when 'it' (the other) loves, the love does not come from you, but you only mirror 'its love.' This passive love is mechanical and will attach itself to almost anyone, even to those you *think* you shouldn't love. One must be trained for real, or Christian, love. One is not born with it. There is no best or only time for training. If someone shows real love, he has acquired it. But it is difficult to learn, and impossible to learn in the process of loving directly 'in the raw,' for the other 'it' will block learning.

"Remember, you learn to love someone by stages. You have to learn to love *things* first, and you will then learn to love life. You cannot love a person without loving life, without loving God. Life and God are everywhere, even among plants and animals—for where there is life, there is love. All life is a representation of God, and so is all love. He who receives love, receives its giver. Even flowers, which have no consciousness, feel the love you are able to give them.

"How, then, does one love? If different people sow the same seeds in the same soil, the results will be different. Man is like soil, but unconsciously much more sensitive to what is sown in him. Even animals are sensitive. They thrive or wither depending on the person tending them. Some become ill and die, hens lay fewer eggs, cows give less milk. Even a cow will give more milk when loved. You are more sensitive than that cow, but *unconsciously*, and so if you feel love toward another it is only because something in that other has reminded you of something in yourself that you love, and you lack the consciousness necessary to either reject or develop the feeling toward conscious reason. You can't do this without practice, and you should not, as you have done, try to love before learning to love. You learn to live before learning to love, and you learn to love life before you can love other persons and God. A plant will receive love, and an animal will dumbly resign himself to it, but a person will not be able to participate in its essence until he has learned how to transmit love.

"So, then, *what* to love? You must begin by changing your attitude to the outside world, to learn what should be loved and what should be avoided. This learned, you will be able to love 'objectively.' So, it is better

---

[11] Gurdjieff regularly spoke of self-love—distinct from "conscious egotism"—as "titillation" and "masturbation," and called it an impediment to his own teaching. True to his methods, he recommended "masturbation" to those he felt were not aware of the commitment of self necessary to enter a course of study with him.

to forget about the good and bad and begin to choose for yourself. One way to learn this is to acquire and explore different attitudes toward things and toward yourself. If you like something, find reasons to dislike it, and vice versa. But, what are you observing in another with feeling of good or ill? You should observe in others precisely those things you observe in yourself in the process of acquiring consciousness: posture, gesture, movement, expression, and voice. These things are the outward representations of hidden sense, emotion, and thought. Once you learn to control these, you will control their inner manifestations. So, observe these in things around you. Start with plants you like or dislike, then with animals, and then with people you do not yet know. You will be surprised at what you discover to like in one thing but not in another, because what you will be liking is not one thing, but the harmony of many things. Do this seriously and you will see many new things—discover many Americas, as the French say. Plants and animals have similar emotional bonds between themselves, but you can make your human relationships conscious only by training.

"You must learn to observe 'her.' You could not love that which was not receptive to love, and your feelings for her could not make her receptive. Your *thought* might have . . ."

I remember that he paused here, and I waited for him to continue. I heard Marjorie arranging things in the kitchen after a while, and I looked over at Jean to see that he had sunk back in his chair, his head back and eyes closed as if in deep thought. After a minute or so, I was sure he had dozed off. Perhaps he had finished what he had to say; perhaps he had lost the thread of his thought. After a minute or two, I left the room without a word and went up the front stairs to my room, where I wrote out a sketch of what he had said because I wanted to find in my notes the conclusion I did not yet hear. I recall how calm and alert to his voice I was up in my room. There was something in the music of his voice that kept the words alive and, as I wrote them down, I began to understand what they meant, or at least to think so.

I said nothing to him the next morning, though I had questions to ask. After breakfast, he said he was going to take a walk with Witty and asked if I wanted to come along. We strolled the old paths. Little had changed, and he seemed to be in a good mood. It was a brief walk, ten or fifteen minutes at best down around the mill to the stream, across it on rocks placed carefully years earlier, along its banks to the bridge, and back along the drive. We didn't say much, though he would call out to Witty now and then to stop him from romping out of sight over the ridges. He pointed out some changes I hadn't noticed, spoke about the widening and paving of the road that he thought a mistake. Back at the house, after he hung up his thick jacket in the front hallway, and went into the living-room, he turned to me with a a broad grin and said: "Well, you skipped away yesterday. Perhaps you had heard enough, but we haven't finished yet. Sit down, we have yet to get to the heart of the matter.

"You've been having trouble observing others, observing yourself, but particularly remembering yourself. It is only a beginning to step back to look at your relationship with your mother and and now with a girl. By the way, you remember Fritz? He had some problems just like these once, and he came to me for advice. I worked hard with him on them, but," he laughed, "oh my goodness, nothing came of it, and he almost had me think his problems after that were my fault.[12] Put that aside; your problem hasn't really changed since you were a boy. You simply can't free your *thought* from the weight of your emotions. You've been able, I think, to separate your emotions from your bodily needs, but you still react to outward in-fluences in ways that hold you back from realizing yourself. You worried about your father even though you didn't know who he was. Now you worry about a girl even though you have no more to do with her. You have still to learn how to forget. I don't mean how to lose something from your memory, but how to get unprofitable things out of the way when they bother you, or how to convert them to useful things.

"Let me tell you a story. There was a man and a woman who truly loved each other. I mean *truly*; that is, they each evoked the best of the oth-er in their love. It was a love that contained both of them together. You see what I mean? They did not love *from* each of themselves alone, but *to* the totality of them together. She died. What could the other do? What did he *have* to do? He really didn't have to do very much, you see, because all of his thoughts of her, his love for her, were still intact in the totality of their mutual love. He had only to hold on to that. Well, that is not so very easy, but they had a child together, and he brought the child into that love, and he brought that child up to love herself within the totality of a love that still included the mother, and that love can expand to include others."

"Yes, but how can somebody forget the pain of losing something loved," I asked.

---

[12] Fritz Peters was left by his mother in the care of her sister, Margaret Anderson, who, in turn, left him with Gurdjieff for short periods between 1924 and 1926. After Fritz returned to his mother in Chicago, he had several amatory adventures that turned out badly for him, of which my mother knew because Fritz confided in her during his stays with us during the war. The one Jean referred to concerned a young girl whose father suggested that Fritz marry. He finally did, and then had an automo-bile accident shortly after.

"There is no true happiness that is not based upon an unhappiness experienced and converted to use. Unhappiness is like pain. You make a friend of it by using it, and letting it use you. You must learn to trust pain. It is the same with what you feel is *pleasure*. There is positive pleasure, and that is the pleasure that becomes part of your knowledge of self. This makes the best of sexual relationships. But, there is, more often, negative pleasure, the pleasure that weakens knowledge of self, detracts thought, binds reason to feeling and physical sensation. This kind of relationship makes you forget your self, your 'I.' When you feel pain in remembering something in the past, even past pleasure, you have to erase the past."

"How can I erase the past without erasing what I learned in it?"

"You don't understand yet, do you? Observing the past is like observing someone else, or even yourself. You separate yourself from it, measure your distance from it, look at it objectively as long as it is necessary to see what is *not* you in it. Only then, when you see difference clearly, can you move it into you. You transform things past into your present self. That is what my story meant. You can only make unhappiness into happiness by bringing it into yourself. This is what the word *remember* really means. By the way, have you seen China yet?"

"No."

"Well, walking to China is the same exercise. You observe, then bring what you've observed into yourself. Then you can find the profit in the enterprise, any enterprise. You know why, in all my life, no one has ever really hurt me? Simply because how I receive their thoughts and acts outweighs whatever they intend with them. You don't have to convert *people*. You have to convert their physical, emotional, and rational impulsions in you. This is what reciprocal relationships are all about. It doesn't matter if she or another has more weight of morality or thought. Everything merges together when you actualize a relationship with another, or even with things. You, and others with you, will be able to transfer energy, make your experience part of theirs, and make theirs yours. This is what I am doing now."

"What you are doing now," I quipped, " is reading me better than I can read myself."

"Yes, yes, boy, exactly, and now we really understand each other. A cause for celebration. How about a Rum-Yum?"

I felt much better, now, and worries over my Army career and my woman problems faded in the glow of good feelings. Marjorie felt them as well.

The next afternoon, Jean and I left together on the train to New York City. He was going to see his doctor and then Fred Leighton before going to a meeting, and I was going on to Connecticut to say goodbye to my mother before reporting to Camp Kilmer for transport to Germany. Jean was in a suit and tie, as he always was when he went to the city from Doylestown, though he looked too small in the suit and his shirt neck was far too large. We made small talk during the brief trip, and I hugged him goodbye in the grand hall of Grand Central Station.

Two years later, in the summer of 1957, I was mustered out of the army at Fort Riley, KS. I drove east with my mother and we stopped at The Barn, Jean's and Marjorie's apartment in the old hayloft. We had tea with them, but there was no conversation and Marjorie seemed uneasy with my mother. Jean looked extremely tired, his body physically wasted, but his eyes still bright and his broad smile intact. A summer later, on my honeymoon in the midst of my graduate school studies, I bumped into Marge quite by accident at the Salzburg Festival, and we all took rooms in the same country inn. She was full of good spirits and I noticed how much she had grown into a mirror of her father. Her humor, her laugh, her deep eyes, and especially her warm smile were replicas of his.

On a hot summer afternoon a year later, I stopped at The Barn on the way to Chicago. Jean was asleep on his couch when I arrived. His body looked emaciated, like nothing more than a loose arrangement of bones. Marjorie chatted with me over a cup of tea, but her hearing had deteriorated and I feared speaking too loudly, so after a while we sat silently waiting for Jean to wake up. He stirred finally, but continued lying on the couch, turned his head and smiled. "Ah Polo, it is good to see you," he said, and then turned his head and stared at the ceiling for some time. With obvious effort, he finally got to his feet, came to the kitchen-dining area, sat in his chair, and asked me for my news. He was nothing more than eye, smile, and voice now, but these were still magical in their charm. He went back to bed almost immediately after supper and, after chatting about family matters with Marjorie, I went to bed, too. In the morning, I left before Jean rose from bed. I had seen him for the last time.

I continued to write sporadically to Jean and Marge after my move to Switzerland, but each letter to Poppy was answered with a brief note from Marjorie saying that Jean appreciated hearing from me, but could not re-ply personally. In early April 1967, my mother called to say that he had died on 30 March 1967. The fact seemed unreal to me. I wrote a long letter to Marjorie whose reply mentioned that *Cane* was reprinted, and that his papers were at Fisk University. Little by little over the months that followed, the bare fact of Poppy's death imposed itself on me, and I fell into a depression that I tried to hold within myself. I even took down from my shelves Ouspenksy's *The Fourth Way* to see what Gurdjieff said about death.

I found finally that I could put Jean Toomer out of my mind by making what I remembered of him part of my own consciousness, my remembrance of self. He visited me often in dreams, usually with a broad smile, shining eyes, a faint odor of shaving soap on his rough unshaven chin, and a voice full of life, consoling my wonder at his presence in a short phrase like, "You see, Polo, you and me, we know what love is." The past few years he is speechless in my dreams, communicating in a language of touch, once even through his moustache. Curiously, when we are together he is a head taller than I am, though I am well over six foot. One April, several years after his death, I returned to the United States on sabbatical leave. My mother had died in late January, and I was putting her affairs in order in the house that she had lived in, and that I now rented and lived in for a few months, when the phone rang. The caller asked for Edith, and when I reported her death, Susan Sandberg identified herself, explaining that she was in Westport to attend to some of her father's affairs. Harold Loeb, with whom my mother had played bridge several times over the previous few years, had also died.

A few weeks later, I drove down to Margot's house in Pineville, PA, for a sort of "family" reunion. Marjorie was there in very good spirits, along with Margot's children, Michelle and Philip. I made rounds of Rum-Yums, and Marjorie and I talked more openly and less self-consciously than we had ever done before. She was feeling nostalgic, but did not mention either my mother or Harold Loeb. She preferred to talk about my time at Mill House. She said, with her typical pixyish smile, that I must have thought her something of a witch then, and I replied that she had good reason to think of me as a brat.[13] Then she became very serious and said that she was very pleased that I had turned out well, and that Jean had been

---

[13] It is not an altogether flattering portrait of myself as a young boy that Marjorie sketches in her correspondence with her daughter Susan, and two excerpts from among many indicate well enough the trials I caused Marjorie. For example, 11 Dec. 1938. "Polo has no trouble with his studies as far as I know. . . . In other ways—at home here—he's absolutely maddening—not really bad—but careless literally and to a high degree. By literally I mean care-less without care for anything or anybody except one Polo. I don't believe I've ever met such a complete egoist of that age. Also he won't stand up and confess to anything—lies like a trouper about such matters. He says yes to everything and hasn't even listened to what you said! He loses something almost every day, but he'll never tell you until you discover it yourself. His clothes and other things are all over the floor. If you don't police his bath, he doesn't wash at all, etc. Every adult in this household is occasionally driven mad by him—yet he continues to look like a perfect angel, and impresses every new person that way—and at the same time he's not really a bad boy, nor mean. He's quite a case. Edith sees so little of

pleased with me as well. She confided in me that those first years in Mill House had been very hard for her. She had foreseen things very differently from what they turned out to be. She and Jean had had such a good chance to form a colony of artists there, but he had insisted on his teaching. "I disliked all of those Gurdjieff types," she said, shaking her head, "parasites, making meaningless pronouncements, so full of themselves, but without anything to give others. Jean wasted his time with them. I never understood what he was trying to do. There were so many other things we might have done together."[14]

In my silent confusion, I felt suddenly very sad. The sadness was not just in the realization that Jean and Marjorie had had different hopes for the Mill House, but that somehow I had not wanted to sense that difference.

[13 (cont)] him that she, of course, likes to make her short visits pleasant. Therefore she corrects nothing, beams at him, and all is beatific. However I remember times last winter when she was almost out of her mind with him. Maybe this is better—now he can think of his mother as someone who is always sweet, loving and never cross." Later, 6 Feb. 1939. "My chief trial is Polo. He really is a most difficult case. I haven't yet reached the point when I can thank fate for providing such an occasion for me to contend with myself—but I recognize that there is the opportunity. . . . It is really sad—he has the potential of being a swell kid . . . And yet, everybody that meets him (exclusive of those that have lived with him) exclaim about how affectionate he is (. . . without a bit of affection except possibly for his mother and especially when they don't live together)" (Marjorie Content Papers, Doylestown).

[14] In 1995, I read in the brief summary of her life by Ben Lifon and Richard Eldridge excerpts from Marjorie Content's journals in which she vented anger against his treatment of her in front of his "students" from Wisconsin (p. 35).

Chapter Nine

Shadowing Gurdjieff And Toomer

I felt certain I had brought
The gods to earth and men to heaven
—"The Blue Meridian"

. . . what if Earth
Be but the shadow of Heav'n, and things therein
Each to other like, more than on Earth is Thought
—John Milton

My feelings about Gurdjieff have remained mixed since my earliest memory of him. First of all, in my imaginative memory, he played a different role with everyone, and his various guises before me concealed his "real" self, if he had a single one. I understand what Orage meant when he insisted repeatedly that he did not regard Gurdjieff as a man. Even though I knew him best in his old age, I sensed reserves of mind and body in him lying under his many disguises and the trickster roles he played. I saw him several times in baths in the last year of his life, and he had a powerful frame that belied 83 years and questionable health. His muscle tone was not slack, but prominent. He was heavy, but not flabby or soft, except under the eyes and jowls. In speech, despite the agony of comprehension he caused in his auditors, he displayed no gestures before me that bespoke of a slipping of verbal control, a loosening of memory or dislocation of ideas. He was easily able to recapture stray thoughts, images and words by a concentration of mental will.

As a person, he was as unreadable to me as his book. Even the linear narrative of his *Meetings With Remarkable Men* hides layers of deeper texts. Nonetheless, Gurdjieff didn't seem to concern himself with what others read of him, and it even seemed to me at times that Gurdjieff went out of his way to dissociate his teaching and his writing from his own person. Toomer, on the other hand, as *Essentials* and *A Fiction and Some Facts* demonstrate, labored patiently to have himself understood as a person, and to align the person with his teaching and writing. Jean was never a mystery to me. I have never known anyone who opened himself up to others as honestly as he did.

Since I had not gone to Gurdjieff specifically for the "Work," I was open perhaps more to the man than to his teaching. Through Jean, I understood his basic premise about harmony of being, but was not sensitive to a disharmony in myself that required personal attention at the time I went to him. On the other hand, I never understood what my mother wanted from him. It is clear that she, like Jessie Orage, was fascinated by Gurdjieff. I am sure she quite consciously intended to have a child by him, but I can't for the life of me guess why. What Orage wanted from him was a formulation of the secret knowledge about man's original and ultimate place in the universe that he was persuaded Gurdjieff possessed. Jean Toomer sought confirmation, appreciation, and reinforcement of what he sensed of himself and his relation with the world. He drew people to himself, and even Gurdjieff was drawn to him. Gurdjieff would rather repulse people, and yet something in him attracted almost everyone in his presence. Even after Jessie repudiated him in her strongest terms, she felt a strange attraction to him. Despite the pain my mother suffered from his apparent indifference to his fathering a daughter, she would not, or could not, hold herself from returning to him.

Gurdjieff had reason to dislike me, but he didn't express a dislike, and I'm not sure Gurdjieff expressed liking or disliking of people in any conventional fashion. I even entertained the thought at times that he liked me, simply because he saw so well into me. His chastizing me for thoughtlessness cleared the air. Nothing more was ever said, even if the cause for his disapproval had not been redressed by me. From my point of view, I found no compelling reason to dislike him as a person, though I understood my mother's reasons for saying "he was not a nice man." He often "acted" slovenly and rude, and, though he looked elegant in his well-tailored suit and camel hair coat, he didn't seem to pay attention to his image, whether in appearance or voice, nor was there ever anything aloof or arrogant about him. He displayed himself as humble and self-effacing at times; and his expressed humilty—"I only a poor rug merchant," and "I only a teacher of dances" (this is the final epithet he mentions for himself in the foreword to *All and Everything*, p. 50)—seemed both sincere and self-effacing. He acted many roles, but he never "put on airs."

When he bullied people, it seemed obvious to many witnesses what he was doing, but it might not have seemed so obvious to his victims. I felt uncomfortable as a witness to his reducing someone to tears and his twisting the point of his insults to the quick, though I could reflect later on his therapeutic purpose. What continued to bother me the most, however, was his apparent patience with and tolerance of so many people of little understanding who wanted to hear his "wisdom" and experience his "magic" of being. It seemed to me in his presence that he was forced into being something of a personal counselor. People besieged him at his café-offices in hopes of hearing solutions to their psychological problems. In 1949, when I heard of his death, Nick Carroway's summing up at the beginning of Fitzgerald's *The Great Gatsby* came immediately to mind: "Gatsby turned out all right at the end; [but] it was what preyed on Gatsby, what foul dust floated in the wake of his dreams."[1]

Many people deserted him, the way people drifted from Gatsby. It is ironic that, in the last fifteen years of his life, when Gurdjieff attracted the greatest number of followers, the Prieuré had been lost, the Institute dissolved, and almost all of his closest followers and the most talented pupils who had followed Gurdjieff to discover answers to larger issues—the place of man in the time, space, and material of the universe—had left. Ouspensky says that he left Gurdjieff because he was being led to a religious abnegation of the world.[2] The de Hartmanns left because the Work interfered with their marriage; and, while Orage bore his wife's discomfort, he could not bear being denied the knowledge he felt Gurdjieff had promised. Toomer's final renunciation was incited largely by a feeling that Gurdjieff was affecting his mind and body negatively.

Despite the proliferation of teaching groups and instruction in the dances, no one of the post-war groups appeared to me to have the authoritative knowledge, influence, and gift to carry things further. Even when he was alive, I felt that Gurdjieff was to many a topic more than a teacher. Forty years after his death, his place in New Age thought has brought his name and certain aspects of his teaching to a broad public, but perhaps too much in the inappropriate context of extraterrestrial wisdom and cosmological therapy, and not enough in the categories of psychology and theology that his teachings touch directly.

My summer with Gurdjieff allowed me to understand and appreciate more of my relationship with Toomer, if not something more of Toomer himself. What I had found, I admit, surprised me, for in many essential respects, the men were very much alike. For one thing, while Ouspensky and Orage developed their own teaching on Gurdjieff's system, they reduced his emphasis on practical activities, while Toomer, in his emphasis on physical activities in tandem with mental concentration, *did* reproduce in Bucks County something of Gurdjieff's insistence on harmonious de-

---

[1] F. Scott Fitzgerald, *The Great Gatsby* (Harmondsworth: Penguin, 1963), p. 8.
[2] P. D. Ouspensky, *In Search of the Miraculous* (Harcourt Brace and World, 1949), 375.

velopment.[3] Having been touched by both of them, however, my impressions are affectively slanted. In retrospect, I feel that Toomer placed a higher value on a personal and even intimate relationship between teacher and pupil. In my case, he strove to make me sensitive to the good, and the good was associated closely with the delightful. Like Gurdjieff, he savored life in its variegated forms. Like Gurdjieff and Orage, he was a sensual as well as sensuous man. He trained the mind to sensitize the body's participation in the possibilities of life, and he trained the body to heighten the mind's appreciation of the beautiful and pleasurable. Like Gurdjieff, but unlike Orage, he stressed physical labor to push the body toward its limits in order to sensitize and bring it into closer collaboration with the mind.[4]

He was not, as Gurdjieff was, thought to either hold back a "secret" knowledge or concern himself with extensive preparation of his audience to make them ready to receive his wisdom. He wanted to share instantly and fully everything he knew. Where Gurdjieff and Orage alike thought that the work of self-development was easily blocked by the distracting presence of women and sexual activities, Toomer gloried in combining them. For Gurdjieff, untutored woman is "man's handkerchief," but in "conscious" collaboration with man she mediates growth of both into wholeness. Orage put more emphasis in his teaching on sex as a function of will than did Gurdjieff, who spoke about sex independently of the "sex result," which is both children and a bond between man and woman. Gurdjieff taught and practiced sexual relations free of both sense and reason, and, therefore, free of moral commitment. For Toomer, on the other hand, love for a woman shapes energy into a collaborative joy of commitment. So do sports, talking, eating, and drinking, though these are as fully intransitive, or reciprocal, as love for and of another person. So, he invited personal interactions as a way of enriching himself in league with his pupils, and he reached to others with a respect, admiration, and love that he expected to receive in return. He was as giving and receiving with men as with women.[5] From both, he sought admiration and the occasion to admire others.

---

[3] Rudolph Byrd, *Toomer's Years with Gurdjieff* (Athens, GA: University of Georgia Press, 1989), compares carefully the teaching methods of the two, and points out significant similarities.

[4] After his kidney operation in 1940 and the slow but inexorable decline of his health, which caused him almost pathological distress in the early 1950s, he spoke less of the physical development of the body.

[5] Gurdjieff, in an interview with the Madison, Wisconsin *Capitol Times*, 12 September 1934, explained that there are three classes of men: "Those who take what they can get, those who get what they can take, those who get what they can get" (Toomer Collection, The Beinecke Rare Book and Manuscript Library, Yale University, Box 68, Folder 1544).

Orage, it is said, was like Ouspensky in stressing the role of mental exercises to control senses and the body in service, rather than in mastery, of the mind in a collaborative quest for a higher consciousness. It was Orage's "mentalism" and lack of "doing" that Gurdjieff denounced. Orage believed less than Toomer that teaching could function as personal discourse or interaction, but rather stressed, as Ouspensky had, the formation of a group working together as a brotherhood for a common goal from which each participant could profit according to his needs and abilities. He believed in collective intellectual exchange in order to make, secure, and enrich individual human relations. The group was a stepping-stone to a school, and the school a whetstone for a culture.

In his later years, if not before, Gurdjieff disdained a teacher's insistence upon reciprocity, perhaps because he preferred in his teaching not to expose or feature "himself." He and Toomer alike relished playing roles, and both were master tricksters and shape-shifters. Both could be visibly absent and invisibly present, but Gurdjieff could be more easily blind, deaf, and insensitive when it served his purpose, and more piercing with his vision into the life core of others if the occasion called for it. Toomer was, perhaps to a fault, sensitive to everything in the space between himself and others. No matter the shallowness of any thought I expressed before him, he would listen, and then slide me toward understanding with the oil of persuasion rather than the rasp of contention.[6] I never for an instant in Jean's company thought I was being "tested" or "examined." He made me feel worthy of being noticed, and I was always flattered to be felt within his gaze. He made me aware of the importance of observing myself from *his* privileged perspective.

Toomer, like Ouspensky and Orage, developed a system of thought based upon Gurdjieff's teaching and, although he made voluminous notes and delivered hundreds of lectures, he did not publish his methods.[7] I am tantalized by the question: To what extent did others, besides Gurdjieff, show in their person and in actions with others the profit of their knowl-

---

[6] This is, of course, my own experience. Kerman and Eldridge, *The Lives of Jean Toomer* (Baton Rouge, LA: Louisiana State University Press, 1987), cite Jean's shocking of his wife, Marjorie, in an attempt to change the direction of her thought. In his review of *Lives*, Rampersad remarks that when Marjorie opposed him once, "he slugged her" (New York Times Book Review, 30 Aug. 1987, pp. 7–9). It is as hard for me as it is for others who knew him well to conceive of Toomer "slugging" anybody, no matter the provocation. Violence was simply not in his nature.

[7] Many others have developed different schools incorporating aspects of Gurdjieff's, and have written about them. John Bennett is perhaps the best known of these. Rudolph Byrd and Robert B. Jones have done the most to promote Toomer's own psychophilosophical thought.

edge? The three might agree that the question is dilatory, for as both Orage and Gurdjieff insisted, you enter the work to suffer in your person, not to display yourself as an example of anticipated results. Toomer, however, delighted in being and displaying what he taught, and delighted in what he called the "downright pleasure" of being, while Orage was carefully and cautiously cerebral even in his pleasures. Nonetheless, it has seemed to me that all three—and I cannot weigh the importance of the observation—by the force of their personalities, attracted more people toward their persons than toward their work, and all three reaped a greater harvest of personal attention than response to their knowledge. Both Toomer and Gurdjieff had a sense of humor that they displayed openly and often. Both could and did laugh at themselves with gusto. I was exhilarated by Toomer's pride of self, saddened by his disappointments, but unceasingly mystified by Gurdjieff's magical mix of humility of gesture with pride of wisdom. Gurdjieff inspired admiration and sowed rancor. I loved Toomer; I have never achieved the level of consciousness necessary for loving Gurdjieff.[8]

Gurdjieff, I suspect, would not care what people thought of him as long as his work survived. Toomer wanted personal respect and affection as a value-marker of his teaching. He has suffered unjustly, it seems to me, from extant biographical accounts of him which demean his public and domestic postures as sage, husband, and father. I loved Toomer as a boy and love him now, even though between then and now I have been reminded again and again of the myth about a Toomer who wrote a great book of black experience called *Cane,* but who refused to advertise the bond between the blood within him and the particularity of the life he wrote into that book. This myth implies a Toomer who cultivated a public image to hide a private knowledge of self. Books that discuss the life of Jean Toomer contribute in very different ways to that myth of the man as an evader of his essential self. Byrd's sympathetic study, *Jean Toomer's Years with Gurdjieff* (1990), counters the myth, but like my own memoir draws attention to it. The systematic biographical research of Kerman and Eldridge compiles information and opinion from many informants who knew Jean in what Gudjieffians call "The Work," and others who knew him in Mechanicsville after Toomer had left Gurdjieff and had started a new life with Marjorie Content. With the passing of time, while his novel *Cane* has gained in appreciation, the gap between an appreciation of his art and the image of his character has grown wider.[9] If fame is measured by the quan-

---

[8]   I recall Fritz Peters saying that he "loved" Gurdjieff. Gurdjieff disdained love as a feeling independent of reason.

[9]   For example, Alice Walker, cited by Byrd, *Toomer's Years*, p. 62, says: "Keep *Cane's* beauty but let Toomer go."

tity of people who know *about* you, rather than by the number and quality of those who *know* you, then Toomer is by critical consensus famous as a writer, but by dubious report, infamous as a person.

Toomer's daughter, Margot, and I feel betrayed by much of what has been said and apparently thought of Toomer by people who did not know him personally. It is clear to us that many of the negative views of the man are based on information that has been slanted to fit what some would *like* to think of him for one reason or another. There are some minor facts in current biographies that we can correct, but I think it more significant to the record of Jean Toomer to expose my experience under his care as a father and teacher, two functions for which he has been charged particularly with failure, if not with gross and willful mismanagement.

A disharmony of being is a current critical charge against the man that I cannot remove, but I would soften the terms of that charge by recalling a Jean Toomer whose private life was marked by concern, generosity, and love for those about him.[10] Though Jean Toomer himself would have looked disapprovingly at writing that serves only to expose one's own narrow view of things, he saw profit in reshaping circumstances in a quest for an "objective truth" that serves self by serving others. "Let your doing be an exercise," Toomer said, "not an exhibition."[11] A reader of an earlier draft of my recollections of Toomer asked, if I loved him so, why did I have so little to do with him after 1955. The answer is simply that he encouraged me to leave old relationships aside in the pursuit of new. He knew that I had a life to shape on my own and that each time I came back to him, I would come back better to know and love him.

Well then, what can *I* say finally about the man, Jean Toomer? What was it in him that so profoundly marked my consciousness that I am driven to write about him in these terms? The biographical evidence alone is misleading. The testimony of those who knew him needs to be placed in a context that brings out more of him than his circumstances. Even my own recollected "facts" are liable to be deceptive. For example, I cannot document the gifts Jean gave me, or the parlor games we might have played.

---

[10] In the preface to *The Lives of Jean Toomer*, p. xiv, Kerman and Eldridge make a list of contradictions in Toomer: "He claimed to be an archetypal American, yet all his adult life he used an assumed French name. He was egalitarian but aristocratic, could be tender and callous to the same person, wanted to lay out his whole self before the world but was a highly secretive marriage partner. He declared a mystical attachment to the soil, yet seldom got his fingers into it. He was black and white and abdicated from both groups. . . ." I can't reconcile all of these, but "Jean" was short for "Eugene" and never reflected for him or others the French form of "John," and he certainly got his fingers into the soil in the days I was with him on the farm.

[11] Jean Toomer, *Essentials* (Chicago: Lakeside Press, 1931), p. ix.

Besides Disney's *Snow White*, I can't remember films, plays, carnivals, or fairs he took us to. He probably did take us to many, but if I forget those events, it is undoubtedly because my presence with *him* overwhelms the recollection of my presence at events *with* him. I can't recall any specific occasion when he offered me a kiss, a hand to hold in a crowd, but I am sure he did so. I can't even remember asking him for these things, but I certainly never felt that any mark of affection was denied me. In other words, I never missed his affection or yearned for it, because bonds of affection were so sure between us. I have never known anyone so genuinely generous with his love, and so confident in the love of others for himself. What seems complex in long retrospect of this shared affection is simply the lack of images of it. When precisely did he ever take me on his knee to embrace and comfort me? The times I did run to him for help were always rewarded with a firm hug and, best of all, an extraordinary expressive and enfolding look from his eyes.

He was equally generous with his inexhaustible stock of humor. He cavorted, gamboled, danced, and played. He exploited any occasion to "horse around." He was an example for me of what it is to love life deeply, reverently, and joyfully. He could make a sip of ale an ecstatic moment. Even watching baseball on television was more than an entertainment to pass the time; it was an exercise in observation and commentary. He found things of interest and fun everywhere about him; and he was able to speak these things into psychological significance for others. Even at the age of six or seven, I felt this commitment of spirit to everything he did, and I have tried to emulate it. I was not alone in this aura of Toomer's humanity. Argie and I were privileged heirs to it, but the whole community about him shared it. Neither she nor I ever questioned the individual or collective fathering he gave us. Neither of us remember a hand lifted in anger, let alone a hand striking. His word was chastizement enough, but it never belittled or berated either of us. Oh yes, he cajoled, threatened deprivations and restraints, taunted and teased, but never without an indication that he was acting on behalf of our better interests. We were not boy and girl under his heavy wing, but two beings in his watchful care.

Only now do I find myself reconsidering these things at length critically, and not only because of public impugning of Jean's role as a father,[12] but in order to measure more meaningfully the influence of that role on my own life. His daughter and I, for the short time we spent together in

---

[12]   Kerman and Eldridge, *The Lives of Jean Toomer*, pp. 362–365 suggest Toomer's parental mismanagment of his daughter. She has never spoken a word against her father to me, nor I to her. We have always collaborated in our love for him.

Mill House, received the same treatment, though we may have been shaped differently by it. If Jean waited for others to initiate intellectual exchanges with him, he could expect me to make the move more easily than Argie.[13] She was characteristically reticent to display her mind before her father, particularly in public. She was stronger willed than I, and saw no good reason to do so simply as an exercise to please her father. On the other hand, I looked forward to such exchanges. They made me feel special in his eyes, and I had, at the time, no other eyes to shine on me. In his eyes and words lay the charm that was his deep fund of love. Argie did not have to earn her father's love. He adored her simply for her being, and she adored him. He put no price on love, and set no tasks for us to merit it or conditions for expressing it. He refused no one who came to him for affection.

While some have considered that Jean's view of himself as a teacher compromised his role as a father, it has always seemed to me that he combined the two roles successfully. He was loving and understanding to my mother, Fred Leighton, Gorham Munson, Georgia O'Keefe, and indeed to everyone with whom he entered into close relationships, despite the occasional hardships those relations brought him. Even those in the Gurdjieff circle like Louise Welch, Nick Putnam, Daly King, Sherman Manchester, Stanley Spiegelberg, Stanley Nott, Philip Lasell, and Payson Loomis, who questioned his association with Orage and Gurdjieff, or perhaps were envious of it, never uttered in my hearing any negative judgment of his character. Like Gurdjieff, but to a different extent, he expected people to extend themselves to his terms of communication. Unlike Gurdjieff however, who maintained an enigmatic distance from most, those who made the effort with Jean were rewarded with his gift of affection. The fact that few men and women who had known Jean well ever lost their admiration and affection for him after they parted company is evidence of the appreciation of those with whom he shared intimacy. Who did not like Jean? And why not? No one I have talked with who knew him well—even Mabel Dodge Luhan, Waldo Frank, and Gorham Munson, who may have felt let down by him—denied an affection for him to the end. He was admired by Steiglitz and Georgia O'Keefe, even though his appeal for Georgia was a potential threat to Alfred. He was an enormous influence and friend to his stepson, Jimmy, and to those who worked with him at the Mill House, particularly to Lin and Don Davenport and their families , and to those associated with him in Chicago, even to Fritz Peters

---

[13] I knew her by the family names "Argie" and "Arge" when I lived with her. She later preferred the name Margie, and in the fities or sixties asked to be called Margot. Contexts of reference suggest to me which name to use.

who slighted Toomer in his books, but who turned to him in need as a friend and counselor.[14]

I think so many loved Jean even in difficult circumstances because of the undeniable commitment he demonstrated for the well-being of others. I once tried to discuss a philosophic point I had presumed to be in Dostoievski's writings, and he said very directly and seriously: "Do not confuse philosophy with objective thought. The philosopher forces his fears and doubts into a system in order to control them. The good teacher is a psychologist at work to liberate thought from systems so it can join with spirit. The person means more than an idea. Ideas not organically part of the life of a person have no value for me."

As this declaration illustrates, Jean's style of serious speech was aphoristic. He spoke habitually in aphorisms—not as a social posture or stance, but simply as an art, his own method of inviting an audience to look at ordinary things in extraordinary ways. Aphorisms were intellectual bridges to allow his interlocutor to meet him in the middle of a thought. I grew used to his aphorisms from such a young age that they seemed the natural style of the man I loved, and the aphoristic style has become part of my own verbal behavior, much to the occasional dismay of my family and friends, who hear more silliness than sense in them. Had I met Jean Toomer much later in my life, I might have been set aback by his language. Perhaps it has seemed to many others as part of a pose as a sage, but his verbal style was an expression of a deep care for those with whom he exchanged ideas, and of his care for their affection in return. These cares were not distinct considerations, because he conceived of the feelings of others for him as an extension of his feelings for them. Conversation was a *jeu parti* in which aphorisms served as chess pieces on a board of ideas.

It is undeniably true that Jean Toomer displayed himself often as a divided man, wayward and seeking. He expressed himself in ways that suggested that there were many Jean Toomers living many lives, often in conflict, but I think this only *seems* so because the oneness of the man is so elusive. I never sensed disappointment in self in Jean. He seemed always to be enjoying his life. Lifon's and Eldridge's biographical summary of

---

[14] It has always bothered me that Fritz Peters, whom I knew well between 1939 and 1949, felt free between 1931 and 1934 to ask Jean for advice about his love life and his own writing, and after an automobile accident he turned first to Jean to ask for money, which Jean sent immediately (Toomer Collection, Box 6); but, although this was their last personal contact, Peters savagely criticized Jean's teaching in *Gurdjieff Remembered* (London: Victor Gollancz, 1969), pp. 16–29. Luba Gurdjieff told me that Fritz had called her to ask what she thought of his two books. She said that she simply laughed and said they were clever lies. He hung up in anger and never talked to her again.

Marjorie Content's life notes that, in his letters to Marjorie, he "relates everything to himself" (p. 28). I would not deny it one instant, because he saw himself as a magnetic center that must absorb all in order to radiate all. His almost obsessive quest for admiration was balanced by his almost obsessive yearning to admire others. He sought intimacy with everyone, and everyone I knew in his company felt his sensitivity to their thoughts and needs and profited by it. He did not have to reach out to those who needed him, because they came to him. Indeed, playfully with me, perhaps more seriously with others, he would scrutinize, criticize, and even mock the terms in which those needs might be expressed, but he never withheld himself from them. He showed himself before his daughter and myself as a man not only confident in his wholeness, but exultant in it. He knew and relished his magnetic power.

Jean Toomer, like Gurdjieff, was a trickster. He was canny as a fox, leaving false trails everywhere and laughing at the hunters who would catch him and stuff him into their own taxonomic categories. There was a riddling challenge in almost everything he said. He tested people continuously, but with a design charged with affection and fun. Those with whom he could not have fun did not count heavily on his scales of humanity. Even in his most serious moments with me—at least those moments *I* took seriously—he poked fun at my unquestioned assumptions. He looked for play in return, and it was not often enough that I could return him measure for measure.[15]

In reciting these things in order to explain why I loved this man, I am grasping at straws. I did not love him because of his relations with the life of the world, but because of his commitment to mine. I cannot easily rationalize the presence of Jean Toomer in my life, accurately measure its effects, or even understand why he gave so much of himself to me, when I could give so little back to him. I do not know the "truth" of Jean Toomer, but I am sure that his bond of love with his daughter, and no less his bond with me, was none the weaker or firmer because of an assumed concep-

---

[15] In perusing his papers long after these lines were written, I realized how much anguish Toomer held within him during these years about his physical health. From the early 50s he kept a journal recording his physical condition, particularly the pains in his abdomen that terrified him. He also regretted what he thought was a misjudgment of his writing, which suggests to me that he had had hopes of being "rediscovered" and reappreciated. It is sad that, soon after he died, *Cane* was, indeed, rediscovered by the critics and became a touchstone in the growth of Afro-American literature. I haven't noticed in his journal entries, however, anything suggesting insecurity in his domestic life. Marjorie was extraordinarily attentive to his needs during this time, even though she may have disapproved of his return to Gurdjieffian teaching.

tion of himself as a teacher-father. Perhaps he did see in us an occasion to "experiment," but one cannot with much chance of success fake affection and concern to children. Argie has told me many times and in many ways that her father never failed her in her need.

For me, his conception of himself as a teacher never got into the way of his role as a father, and he did not play alternate roles with Argie and myself. If Jean had a program for us, he never advertised it. He improvised with us, leapt into our activities and thoughts when he saw an opening, but never scheduled or planned activities along any ideological lines. His parental genius lay in seizing the moment, making a remark, improvising an aphorism, a criticism to fit the specific instant. He "read" us well, even if—though I was never conscious of it—he lay in wait for, and even incited occasions in order to speak to us about things that concerned him.

Yet, though he treated us as full beings in possession of reason, we were but children, and his easy flow in and out of our activities might not have worked as well later in my life, though it seems to have continued to work its magic in Argie's. It is apparent in the writings of others that his "taking in charge" the psychological development of those already grown up did not always achieve the results he desired, and his attempts to transform those with whom he had sexual relations were probably ill-advised. Nonetheless, for all the time I knew him, he was indefatigably optimistic, and if others abandoned places in his circle of attention, they did so without expressed rancor. This seems to be borne out by the biographical research of Kerman and Eldridge, where the affair between Jean and Waldo Frank's wife seemed to Waldo to be a greater threat to his friendship with Jean than to his marriage with Margaret.

Argie's and my collaboration with Poppy was both physical and verbal, but it was never mere "entertainment." We played croquet regularly, took walks, played basketball. Every conversation was a contest in the sense that she and I knew that whatever we said was listened to, and whatever he said was an invitation to learn. Jean's attention to others was extraordinary. He did not interrupt, look past us into the distance, or display any sign of boredom when we spoke to him. The sense that whatever we said "counted," and that we were being treated not as children, but as responsible persons, gave me a sure sense of trust. It took me several years to learn to be suspicious of others who would only pretend such intense confidence.

In those years, he doted on his daughter, his face beamed whenever she was in his sight, and Argie's love for her father was never shadowed in my presence by expressions of hurt or slight. It is true that Jean enjoyed a particular position as a parent, for his wife Marjorie commanded almost all domestic operations, including discipline of the children.[16] Besides occasional eruptions of anger for being disturbed during his nap, Jean never scolded or punished us, and his rare expressions of disapproval were so gentle that one might feel he would not for a moment cause us grief. In my own case, looking back from afar, I have never for a moment imagined there might be reasons to criticize Jean's behavior with me, though it was easy as I grew older to find fault in my own role with him and in my mother's role as a parent to me. Perhaps this is because I was at an "ideal" age to profit from Jean, before the years when my own artificial sense and pride of self would question his wisdom and rebel against his confident authority. Perhaps imperceptibly, I have built in my mind my own myth of the man over the years. Looking back from here and now, during all those years from 1937 to 1959, the image of Jean Toomer never lost its sure lines.

Then again, what did he, finally, teach me? It was not the aphorisms, the wise counsel I heard him pronounce to Lin Davenport, Jimmy Loeb, and others. What he taught me was the surety and joy of conscious love. He did this by his person, his smile, his eyes, his voice, carriage, and firm stride over the landscape. While I was with Jean, I felt the affection between us, and he never at any moment ever made me feel less loved than another. Jealousy was a foreign concept in his presence. He spoke to me seriously, as if I were a special person, and his language was distinctly private, *only* for me. I felt then, as in memory I feel now, the personal value he infused into such relationships.

It is easier to suppose error than measure success and how can I be sure in my scale of measure what his presence has meant to my life? During a period of some five years after leaving Mill House, I was more or less unable to adapt myself socially to my new surroundings, and I found myself soon disliking the image I saw of myself. This situation lasted for some years. I could hardly blame the situation, however, on Jean's prior teaching. I had failed completely to maintain a balance between my various selves without surrendering what I wanted to think of as my "deepest" self. In giving me the means to understand myself, Jean had, inadvertently, given me the means to misconstrue the world outside of Mill House. I had left a Utopia for another state of being, and then had built an imaginary world around me as a buttress against that reality. Had I been able to ex-

---

[16] Marjorie's voice was even more self-controlled in her chastizing, and I never knew her to strike either of us. The brief biographical summary of Marjorie's life, based on papers in Susan Sandberg's possession in Doylestown, reveals more tension between her and Jean than I or Argie felt. Nevertheless, Marjorie, who had divorced two husbands earlier, remained married to Toomer for the last thirty-three years of his life.

plain these things to Jean then, he would have smiled and said: "But Boy, what I have said to you time and time again was precisely to show you how you can thrive in *any* world, not be passive to circumstances, but seize upon them and shape them for your own good."

More than with the sense of his words, Jean taught with the quality of his voice and its conviction of the truth it spoke. He expressed such confidence in the force of his ideas that it was impossible for me not to share that confidence. I felt in him an extraordinary wealth of spirit. If Gurdjieff had it as well, it was tantalizingly difficult for me to recognize it under the shifting guises of his gestures and speech. Then there were Jean's eyes. To see his eyes while listening to his voice was to be transported into the world of his spirit. It was a hypnotic experience for me ever since that first evening in New York City when he offered me a roof to dance upon. It is an experience that is relived in thoughts and dreams.

So it is Jean Toomer, the man, who holds fast in my memory. Jean Toomer, the teacher, is an abstract conception I had to confront later in life. Looking with as slight a bias as possible at the public record of his teaching, I would have to say that he certainly wasn't the teacher he hoped to be. From his Harlem and Chicago beginnings as a leader of Gurdjieff groups to his Mill House talks in the 1930s and 1940s, his teachings had no sustained success. In my own case, perhaps, the force of the man overwhelmed the sentence of his wisdom. I realize now that, as a boy, I never had to try to grasp his message. I listened admiringly to him. I recall words, but until I grew up, his wisdom was something both obvious and inscrutable. Perhaps his teaching worked on me like a medical aperient, entering my tissues surely but imperceptibly. He imbued me with a power to love life; or, perhaps it is truer to say that he taught me how to find that power within myself. He gave me an example of how to touch others deeply.

The man, in the long run, overwhelms the lesson. Perhaps Gurdjieff was a more sucessful teacher because he refused to allow a single "genuine" personality to exhibit itself in his teaching. He was everything— clown, rug merchant, dance master, storyteller, cook, musician, alarmclock, even demon—but never a plurality of things at once, or the same thing for long. Jean sought to *be* always everything he taught. As a child, I could not help but admire and love him for this commitment, and that love may even have saved me from other instructions that would have harmed me. In the long run, then, I can see myself as not worthy to be a pupil of Jean's, spellbound as I was by his manner and myopic to his matter.

By the 1950s, if he hadn't done so earlier, Jean must have realized the grim truth of his limited success as a teacher outside of his household.

Why else would he return to Gurdjieff's teachings in the mid-50s? The vitality of the groups after Gurdjieff's death must have made Jean aware of the necessity of detaching his own teaching from the life of the teacher. Perhaps it was the same with his writing, for the fullness sought in the writings of the 30s and 40s was never achieved, though he never lost his expectations for his art. He had lost, however, the marvelous and marveling eye of the narrator of *Cane*, because he was looking at a different and despiritualized world. I cannot judge if he belonged less in the white world of Paris, Chicago, New York, and Bucks County days than in the dark and marvelous world of Georgia nights. It is simply that his inside eye, observing himself, could not sustain the interest of others. *Essentials*, despite its occasional beauty and frequent sharpness of observation, lapses too often into a self-celebration that irks the reader who does not hear the voice and see the countenance of the writer. Nonetheless, *Essentials,* the single work which has drawn the admiration of many Gurdjieffians who have never read his fiction or poetry, reveals the most Gurdjieffian side of Toomer's thinking. Michel de Salzmann, the current director of the Gurdjieff foundations and the leading teacher of Gurdjieff's system since his mother's death, wrote some fifteen years ago that the writers in whose works "the tree [of Gurdjieff's works] has borne fruit" are Orage, P. L. Travers, René Daumal, Maurice Nicoll and Jean Toomer.[17] More than one follower of Gurdjieff has told me that *Essentials* carries to the general public the force of Gurdjieff's aphorisms in "Arousing of Thought" (which opens *Beelzebub's Tales to his Grandson)* and in the Prologue to *Life is Real.*

Toomer loved himself with the exuberance he would have others share with him in that love. That love, he felt, included everyone within his circle of regard, and indeed Jean was a beautiful man, much loved and admired; but the world of his intimate circle failed him, for the struggle to understand what those close to Toomer knew as a surety led many to withdraw from the hermeneutic challenge with a glib judgment that he was a poseur. He was no fake,[18] but he was naïvely optimistic about his capacities to communicate and transmit to others the extraordinary belief he had in both himself and them. He believed he could change the world, and saw his own role as an agency of the Creator. He knew himself, but tended to overvalue others. I felt, during many sad years of struggling to adapt to and integrate myself into the society of my peers, that he had overrated me, and I could not help but feel for a long time that I had not lived up to his

---

[17] "Footnote to the Gurdjieff Literature," *Parabola* 5 (1980), p. 98.
[18] Kerman and Eldrige, *The Lives of Jean Toomer,* p. 381, cite Marjorie Content's accusation of Toomer as a fake early in their life at Mill House.

expectations for me. Curiously, I did begin to adapt in just the way he suspected that I would, through physical efforts in sports, but he never pushed me toward career goals. When I told him in 1957 that I wanted to become a teacher, he just nodded his head. I didn't realize it then, and it took Marjorie years later to make me aware that, as far as he was concerned, I had justified his teachings. His hopes were even higher for his daughter, and she grew up with the weight of their burden, and she, too, pleased him.

I've tried to understand and express something of Toomer's qualities that surpass his limited role in my own life. If I am forcing the account here to the positive side of the moral ledger, it is because I cannot find fault in a man who so loved the world that he could not accept the fact that the world found less to love in him. He wanted others to love life with the enthusiasm he brought to loving life and them, and not all did. Jean Toomer was a deeply spiritual man, spiritual in his attachment to a harmony between man and everything that touches his life. He refused to separate into spirit and thought his own deep commitment to harmonious engagement with things and people, but held them together as one force. That was the way he immersed himself in Gurdjieff's teaching, in traditional Christianity, as well as in the Society of Friends and in Dianetics, and that is why he felt that God was a real presence within us that could be addressed as a friend. So he did himself, evoking the cosmos to

> Send thy power to the stones
> That they may grind, that we may live,
> And do it excellently.[19]

---

[19] Jean Toomer, "The Blue Meridian," in *The Collected Poems*, Robert Jones and Margot Toomer, eds. (Chapel Hill, NC: University of North Carolina Press, 1988), p. 68.

Bibliography

All and Everything. Proceedings of the International Humanities Conference. H. J. Sharp and Seymour B. Ginsburg, *et al, eds*. Bognor Regis: Privately published, 1996, 1997, 1998.

Anderson, Margaret. *The Fiery Fountains*. London: Rider & Co., 1953.

———. *The Unknowable Gurdjieff*. London: Routledge & Kegan Paul, 1962.

Baldwin, James. *The Fire Next Time*. London: Michael Joseph, 1963.

Bennett, Elizabeth and John G. *Des Idiots à Paris*. Genève: Georg, 1991; York Beach, ME: Samuel Weiser, 1991.

Bennett, John G. *Gurdjieff: A Very Great Enigma*. York Beach, ME: Samuel Weiser, 1984.

Buzzell, Keith. "Kundabuffer." In *All and Everything '97*.

Byrd, Rudolph. *Toomer's Years With Gurdjieff*. Athens: University of Georgia Press, 1989.

Davis, Charles T. "Jean Toomer and the South: Region and Race as Elements Within a Literary Imagination." *Studies in the Literary Imagination* 7 (1974), 23-37.

Dinnage, Rosemary. "The Great Mystifier," Review of James Webb, *The Harmonious Circle: The Lives and Works of G. I. Gurdjieff, P. D. Ouspensky and Their Followers*, in *The New York Review of Books*, October 23, 1980, 20–24.

Driscoll, J. Walter. *Gurdjieff: An Annotated Bibliography*. Introduction by Michel de Salzmann. Garland Reference Llibrary 225. New York: Garland, 1985.

Field, Andrew. *Djuna*. New York: G. P. Putnam, 1983.

Fitzgerald, F. Scott. *The Great Gatsby*. London: Penguin, 1963.

Fremantle, Anne. "Travels with a Searcher," Review of *Meetings with Remarkable Men* in *The New York Times Book Review*, September 8, 1963.

Gates, Henry Louis, Jr. Introduction: "Tell me, Sir, . . . What is 'Black Literature?'" *PMLA* 105 (1990), 11–22.

———. "White Like Me," *The New Yorker*. June 17, 1996, 66–68.

Gurdjieff, G. I. *All and Everything*. London: Routledge & Kegan Paul, 1950.

———. *The Herald of Coming Good*. Edmonds, WA: Sure Fire Press, 1988 (reprint of 1933 Paris edition).

———. *Life is Real Only Then, When "I Am."* New York: Dutton for Triangle Editions, 1975.

———. *Meetings with Remarkable Men*. A. R. Orage, trans. London: Penguin, 1963.

Gurdjieff, Luba [Everitt] with Marina C. Bear. *Luba Gurdjieff: A Memoir With Recipes*. Berkeley, CA: Ten Speed Press, 1993.

Hartmann, Thomas de. *Musique pour les mouvements de G. I. Gurdjieff*. Paris: Janus, 1950.

———. *Our Life With Gurdjieff*. London: Penguin, 1972; French version, *Notre vie avec Gurdjieff*. Paris: Planète, 1968.

Hughes, Langston. *The Big Sea: An Autobiography*. New York: Hill and Wang, 1963.

Ichazo, Oscar. "Letter to the Transpersonal Community," *The Arican*, 1991, 87–117.

Jones, Robert and Margot Latimer Toomer. *The Collected Poems of Jean Toomer*. Chapel Hill: University of North Carolina Press, 1986.

Kerman, Cynthia Earl and Richard Eldridge, *The Lives of Jean Toomer*. Baton Rouge, LA: Louisiana State University Press, 1987.

King, C. Daly. *The Oragean Version*. New York: Privately published. 1951.

Kirstein, Lincoln. *Mosaic*. New York: Farrar, Straus & Giroux, 1994.

Landau, Rom. *God is My Adventure*. London: Ivor Nicolson and Watson, 1935.

Larson, Charles R. *Invincible Darkness: Jean Toomer and Nella Larsen*. Iowa City: University of Iowa Press, 1993.

LeGoff, Jacques. *La naissance de purgatoire*. Paris: Gallimard, 1981.

Lifon, Ben and Richard Eldridge. "Marjorie Content," in Quasha, 12–38.

Loeb, Harold. *The Way it Was*. New York: Criterion Books, 1959.

Macrobius: Commentary on the Dream of Scipio. William Harris Stahl, trans. New York: Columbia University Press, 1952.

Macrobius opera. Franz Eyssenhardt, ed. Leipzig: Teubner, 1893.

Mairet, Philip. *A. R. Orage: A Memoir*. Hyde Park, NY: University Press, 1966.

[March, Louise]. *The Gurdjieff Years 1929–1949: Recollections of Louise [Goepfert] March*. Beth McCorkle, ed. Walworth, NY: The Work Study Association, 1990.

Milton, John. *Paradise Lost*, Merritt Y. Hughes, ed. New York: The Odyssey Press, 1957.

Moore, James. *Gurdjieff: The Anatomy of a Myth*. Rockport, MA: Element, 1991.

———. *Gurdjieff and Mansfield*. London: Routledge & Kegan Paul, 1980.

Mouravieff, Boris. *Ouspensky, Gurdjieff et les fragments d'un enseignement inconnu*. Bruxelles: Synthèse, 1957.

Murry, John Middleton, ed. *Journal of Katherine Mansfield*. New York: Alfred A. Knopf, 1927.

Nott, C. S. *Journey Through this World*. London: Routledge & Kegan Paul, 1969.

———. *Teachings of Gurdjieff: Journal of a Pupil*. London: Routledge & Kegan Paul, 1961.

Orage, A. R. *On Love: With Some Aphorisms and Other Essays*. York Beach, ME: Samuel Weiser, 1969; reissued 1998.

———. *Psychological Exercises and Essays*. New York: Farrar and Rinehart, 1930; York Beach, ME: Samuel Weiser, 1998.

Ouspensky, P. D. *The Fourth Way*. London: Routledge & Kegan Paul, 1957.

———. *A New Model of the Universe*. London: Routledge & Kegan Paul, 1938.

———. *In Search of the Miraculous*. New York: Harcourt Brace and World, 1949.

———. *The Strange Life of Ivan Osokin*. London: Penguin, 1960.

Panafieu, Bruno de, ed. *Les dossiers H.: Georges Ivanovitch Gurdjieff*. Paris: L'Age d'homme, 1992.

Patterson, William Patrick. "The Kanari Papers," I & II, *Telos* 2 & 3 (1996, 1997).

———. *Struggle of the Magicians*. Fairfax, CA: Arete Communications, 1996.

Peters, Fritz. *Boyhood with Gurdjieff*. London: Victor Gollancz, 1964.

———. *Gurdjieff Remembered*. London: Victor Gollancz, 1969.

Plato: The Collected Dialogues. Edith Hamilton and Huntington Cairns, eds. NY: Pantheon, 1961.

Plato: Timaeus. R. G. Bury, ed. and trans. London: William Heinemann, 1981.

Quasha, Jill. *Marjorie Content: Photographs*. New York: W. W. Norton, 1994.

Rampersad, Arnold. "His Own Best Disciple," *New York Times Book Review*, Aug. 30, 1987, 7–9.

Robinson, Roxanne. *Georgia O'Keefe: A Life*. New York: HarperCollins, 1989.

Rudnick, Lois Palken. *Mabel Dodge Luhan: New Woman, New Worlds*. Albuquerque: University of New Mexico Press, 1984.

Salzmann, Michel de. "Gurdjieff," *Encyclopedia of Religion*. Mircea Eliade, ed. New York: Macmillan, 1987.

Saurat, Denis. "Visite à Gurdjieff," *Nouvelle Revue Française*, Nov. 1, 1933, 686–298.

Selman, Robyn. "Of Human Bondage." *Voice*, May 15, 1990.

Smith, Russell. *Cosmic Secrets*. Sanger, TX: Privately published, 1993.

Smoley, Richard. "Why the Enneagram: An Interview With Helen Palmer." *Gnosis* 30 (Summer, 1994), 18–24.

Storr, Anthony. *Feet of Clay: Saints, Sinners, and Madmen*. New York: The Free Press, 1996.

Toomer, Nathan Jean. *Cane*. New York: Boni and Liveright, 1922.

———. *The Collected Poems of Jean Toomer*, Robert B. Jones and Margery Latimer Toomer, eds. Chapel Hill: University of North Carolina Press, 1988.

———. *Essentials*. Chicago: Lakeside Press, 1931. Reprinted, with introduction by Rudolf Byrd. Athens: University of Georgia Press, 1993.

———. *A Fiction and Some Facts*. Doylestown: Privately published, n.d.

———. *The Wayward and the Seeking*, Darwin T. Turner, ed. Washington, DC: Howard University Press, 1980.

Val, Nicholas de [Nikolai de Stjernvall]. *Daddy Gurdjieff*. Genève: Georg, 1997.

Walker. Kenneth. *The Making of Man*. London: Routledge & Kegan Paul, 1963.

Washington, Peter. *Madame Blavatsky's Monkey*. London: Secker and Warburg, 1995.

Webb, James. *The Harmonious Circle: The Lives and Works of G. I. Gurdjieff, P. D. Ouspensky and Their Followers*. London: Thames and Hudson, 1980.

Welch, Louise. *Orage with Gurdjieff in America*. London: Routledge & Kegan Paul, 1982.

Wilson, Colin. *The War Against Sleep: The Philosophy of Gurdjieff*. Wellingborough, England: Aquarian Press, 1980.

Zigrosser, Carl. "Gurdjieff," *The New Republic*, June 5, 1929, 66–69.

Index

Paul Beekman Taylor was born in London, lived at the Prieuré with Gurdjieff, and studied with him from 1948-1949. He earned a Bachelor of Arts from Brown University in 1954, a Master of Arts from Wesleyan University in 1958, and received his Ph.D. from Brown University in 1961. He was a Fulbright Scholar and then a Fulbright Lecturer before becoming a Professor of Medieval English Languages and Literatures at the University of Geneva. He is also a member of the Planning Committee and Advisory Board of the Bognor *All and Everything* Conference. Of *Shadows of Heaven* he writes, "I am what in French would be called an *insérend:* witness, narrator and occasional participant in their stories."